普通高等教育“十一五”国家级规划教

全国高等医药院校药学类实验双语教材

中药分析实验与指导

Experiment and Guide for Analysis of Chinese Meteria Medica

主　编　王　强

副主编　刘丽芳　俞祥生　夏玉凤

编　委　侯　莉　张　勤　黄　芸

　　　　汪　红　陈丽红　王吓长

　　　　张　莉　薛多清

中国医药科技出版社

内 容 提 要

《中药分析实验与指导》系全国高等院校药学类系列双语实验教材之一，与《中药分析》、《中药制剂分析》等课程的课堂教学配套使用。本书具有内容丰富，涵盖面广，强调含量测定，强调现代分析方法的应用，强调对学生动手能力培养的特点。作为新世纪的实验教材，本书力图能够跟上新世纪高等教育发展的步伐，符合教学改革的要求；在所编写实验的内容和方法上有更新，在质量上有提高，对学生更具指导性。本书亦可作为相关专业人员参考用书。

图书在版编目（CIP）数据

中药分析实验与指导/王强主编 .—北京：中国医药科技出版社，2003.5

普通高等教育“十一五”国家级规划教材. 全国高等医药院校药学类实验双语教材.

ISBN 978-7-5067-2727-3

Ⅰ.中… Ⅱ.王… Ⅲ.中草药-药物分析-实验-医学院校-教材 Ⅳ.R917

中国版本图书馆 CIP 数据核字（2003）第 039412 号

出版 中国医药科技出版社
地址 北京市海淀区文慧园北路甲 22 号
邮编 100082
电话 发行：010-62227427 邮购：010-62236938
网址 www.cmstp.com
规格 787×1092mm 1/16
印张 11 ½
字数 252 千字
初版 2003 年 8 月第 1 版
印次 2013 年 1 月第 3 次印刷
印刷 北京季蜂印刷有限公司
经销 全国各地新华书店
书号 ISBN 978-7-5067-2727-3
定价 19.00 元

全国高等医药院校药学类规划教材常务编委会

出 版 说 明

全国高等医药院校药学类专业规划教材是目前国内体系最完整、专业覆盖最全面、作者队伍最权威的药学类教材。随着我国药学教育事业的快速发展，药学及相关专业办学规模和水平的不断扩大和提高，课程设置的不断更新，对药学类教材的质量提出了更高的要求。

全国高等医药院校药学类规划教材编写委员会在调查和总结上轮药学类规划教材质量和使用情况的基础上，经过审议和规划，组织中国药科大学、沈阳药科大学、广东药学院、北京大学药学院、复旦大学药学院、四川大学华西药学院、北京中医药大学、西安交通大学医学院、华中科技大学同济药学院、山东大学药学院、山西医科大学药学院、第二军医大学药学院、山东中医药大学、上海中医药大学和江西中医学院等数十所院校的教师共同进行药学类第三轮规划教材的编写修订工作。

药学类第三轮规划教材的编写修订，坚持紧扣药学类专业本科教育培养目标，参考执业药师资格准入标准，强调药学特色鲜明，体现现代医药科技水平，进一步提高教材水平和质量。同时，针对学生自学、复习、考试等需要，紧扣主干教材内容，新编了相应的学习指导与习题集等配套教材。

本套教材由中国医药科技出版社出版，供全国高等医药院校药学类及相关专业使用。其中包括理论课教材82种，实验课教材38种，配套教材10种，其中有45种入选普通高等教育“十一五”国家级规划教材。

全国高等医药院校药学类规划教材

编写委员会

2009年8月1日

序

实验教学是高等药学院校最基本的教学形式之一，对培养学生科学的思维与方法、创新意识与能力，全面推进素质教育有着重要的作用。飞速发展的科学技术，已成为主导社会进步的重要因素。高等药学院校必须不断更新教学内容，以学科发展的前沿知识充实实验课程内容。

近年来，中国药科大学坚持以研究促教改，通过承担教育部“世行贷款——21世纪初高等教育教学改革项目”及立项校内教改课题等多种方式，调动了广大教师投身教学改革的积极性，将转变教师的教育思想观念与教学内容、教学方法的改革紧密结合起来，取得了实效。此次推出的国家“十一五”规划教材——药学专业双语实验教学系列，是广大教师长期钻研实验课程教学体系，改革教学内容，实现教育创新的重要成果。他们站在21世纪教育、科技和社会发展趋势的高度，对药学专业实验课程的教学内容进行了“精选”、“整合”和“创新”，强调对学生的动手能力、创新思维、科学素养等综合素质的全面培养。这套教材具有以下的特点：

1. 教材将各学科的实验内容进行了广泛的“精选”，既体现了高等药学教育“面向世界、面向未来、面向现代化”，也考虑到我国药学教育的现状与实际；既体现了各门实验课程自身的独立性、系统性和科学性，又充分考虑到各门实验课程之间的联系与衔接，有助于学生在教学大纲规定的实验教学学时内掌握基本操作技术，提高动手能力，养成严谨、求实、创新的科学态度。

2. 教材中新增的综合性、设计性实验有利于学生全面了解和综合掌握本门实验课程的教学内容。这一举措既满足了学生个性发展的需要，更注重培养学生分析问题、解决问题的能力和创新意识。

3. 教材中适当安排一些反映药学学科发展前沿的实验，有利于学生在掌握实验基本技术的同时，对药学学科的新进展、新技术有所了解，激发他们学习药学知识与相关学科的兴趣。

4. 教材以实践教学为突破口，采用双语体系编写，为实验课程改革构建数字化、信息化和外语教学的平台，有利于提高学生的科技英语水平。通过我校多年的药学系列实验课程双语教学实践，证明学生完全能够接受此套教材的教学。

国家十一五规划教材——药学专业双语实验教学系列教材的陆续出版，必将对推动我国高等药学教育的健康发展，产生积极而深远的影响。由于采用双语体系编写药学教学实验丛书尚属首次，缺乏经验，在内容选择及编写方法上的不妥之处，在所难免。欢迎从事药学教育的同行们批评赐教。

吴晓明

（中国药科大学校长、博士、教授、博士生导师）

Preface

Experimental teaching is one of the most fundamental teaching means in pharmaceutical colleges, playing an important role in training scientific thoughts and methods, creative consciousness and ability of the students as well as in promoting quality-oriented education in all-round way. Fast-advancing science and technology has come to be an important factor in dominating social progress. Teaching materials must be updated continually in pharmaceutical colleges, especially enriching the materials of experimental courses with the most advanced knowledge in the subject.

In recent years, China Pharmaceutical University have been stressing the promotion of teaching reform on the basis of research, succeeding in stimulating teachers' enthusiasm for teaching reform by various means such as undertaking the project of teaching reform in higher education at the beginning of 21st century sponsored financially by World Bank and entrusted by the Ministry of Education as well as approving and ratifying internal programs on teaching reform. Meanwhile, it yields fruits to integrate the transforming of teachers' educational ideology into the reform of teaching materials and methods. This series of textbook of national "the Eleventh Five-Year Plan" bilingual pharmaceutical experimental teaching series, is an important achievement made through studying ueaching system of experimental courses for long, reforming teaching materials and carrying out educational innovation of all the teachers concerned.

Meeting the new demands for education, science and technology and social growth, they select, integrate and innovate the teaching materials of pharmaceutical experimental courses, stressing the overall cultivation of comprehensive qualities, including experimental ability, creative thought and scientific attainments. This set of textbook possesses the following features:

1. These textbooks make an extensive "selection" of the experimental materials of each subject, reflecting the goal of facing the world, facing the future and facing the modernization in higher pharmaceutical education, and taking into account the status quota and reality of our pharmaceutical education; meanwhile embodying the individuality, systematicness and scientificalness of each experimental courses, which helps the students to grasp basic techniques of operation within the class hours of experimental teaching pre-

scribed by teaching syllabus and to improve their experimental ability and finally to cultivate a scientific approach of precision, practicality and creation.

2. The comprehensive designing experiments newly supplemented in the textbooks help the students to learn totally and grasp comprehensively the teaching materials of the experimental courses, which not only meets the students' needs for individual development but also trains their ability to analyze and solve problems and cultivates their creative consciousness.

3. Some experiments representing the latest development in pharmacy are properly included in the textbooks, which helps the students to learn about new advance and technology in pharmacy and to further arouse their interests in studying pharmacy and relevant subjects while grasping some basic techniques of experiment.

4. The textbooks take experimental teaching as starting point and are compiled in a system of bilingualism and aim to set up a platform of digitalization, information and foreign language teaching for the purpose of reforming experimental courses, which serves to enhance the students' level of technological English. It has been proved that the students have no difficulty being adapted to the teaching of this set of textbook through many years of bilingual teaching practice carried out in a series of pharmaceutical experimental courses of our university.

The successive publishing of the series of textbooks used for bilingual pharmaceutical experimental teaching-the national "the Eleventh Five-Year Plan" textbooks, will surely produce good and far-reaching influence in promoting the sound development of higher pharmaceutical education of our country. Since it is the first time that we have compiled this series of textbook of pharmaceutical teaching experiment in a bilingual system, we lack experience and thus some defects in choice of materials and way of compilation are inevitable. Experts engaged in pharmaceutical education are welcome to give any criticisms and advice.

Wu Xiaoming

Ph. D, prof., and supervisor of doctoral candidates
President of China Pharmaceutical University

前　言

《中药分析实验与指导》系中国药科大学系列双语实验教材之一，与《中药分析》、《中药制剂分析》等课程的课堂教学配套使用。作为新世纪的实验教材，本书力图能够跟上新世纪高等教育发展的步伐，符合教学改革的要求；在所编写实验的内容和方法上有更新，在质量上有提高，对学生更具指导性。

本书共分七章，分别为含生物碱类中药分析、含黄酮类中药分析、含皂苷类中药分析、含醌类中药分析、含其它类成分中药分析、中药制剂分析和附录。本书有以下特点：

1. 内容丰富，含盖面广。包括了植物药各主要化学类型、动物药及中药制剂质量控制多方面的实验，共有实验28个，各校可根据具体条件和实际需要选择有关实验内容。

2. 强调含量测定。每个实验都是以定量分析为重点，兼顾定性鉴别、检查等内容。

3. 强调现代分析方法的应用。本书所收载的实验分析方法主要为高效液相色谱、薄层色谱及薄层扫描、气相色谱、紫外－可见分光光度法。

4. 强调对学生动手能力的培养。每个实验后都要作实验小结，并有相关思考题。为了便于学生参考和查阅，特加入附录一章，所介绍内容包括常用中药质量分析方法、中药成分分析常用溶液和试剂、玻璃仪器的洗涤及各种洗液的配制法、常用溶剂性质、色谱法预试中药化学成分和常用色谱显色剂及使用。

限于时间和水平，定有不妥和错误，敬请使用本书的广大师生指正。

王　强

2002年12月

Preface

Experiment and Guide for Analysis of Chinese Materia Medica is one section of the bilingual experimental textbook series and to be used together with such classroom teaching textbook as *Analysis of Chinese Materia Medica* and *Analysis of Chinese Medicine Preparation*. As a textbook of new century, this book aimed at keeping up with the development of higher education in new century and meeting the need of teaching – reform. This book achieved a great progress in both content and quality and it will prove more valuable as a reference to students.

The book is divided into 7 chapters, including analysis of alkaloids, flavonoids, saponins, quinones, other chemical constituents, Chinese Medicine Preparations and appendix. The characteristics of the book are as follows:

1. It has an abundant content and covers a wide range of aspects, involving the principal chemical components of plant medica, animal drugs and quality control of Chinese Medicine Preparations, totally 28 experiments, providing a selection for different colleges considering their practical need and equipment available.

2. Stressing quantitative analysis. Each test underlines quantitative analysis, also giving consideration to identification and examination.

3. Stressing the application of up – to – date analytical methods. Analytical methods recorded in the book are mainly high – performance liquid chromatography, thin layer chromatography, thin layer chromatography scan, gas chromatography and ultraviolet – visible chromatography.

4. Putting emphasis on fostering the students' ability of operation. A brief summary is required at the end of each test, and also relative questions to be answered. Especially an appendix was conceived to provide a reference easy to consult for students. It ranges from quantitative analytical methods of commonly used traditional Chinese medicine (TCM), commonly used solutions and reagents in content analysis of TCM, washing of glass apparatus, properties of frequently used solvents, chromatography for previous testing of content of TCM, to the usage of frequently used colorant in chromatography.

Limited by time and level, there must be mistakes in the book and criticism and constructive suggestions are welcome.

Editor in chief

Wang Qiang

Dec. 2002

目　录

第一章　含生物碱类中药的质量分析

实验一　薄层色谱－紫外分光光度法分析测定黄柏与二妙丸中小檗碱

【目的要求】

1. 熟悉薄层色谱－紫外分光光度法在分析测定生物碱类药物中的应用。

2. 掌握薄层色谱－紫外分光光度法实际应用中的关键技术和主要注意事项。

【定性分析实验】

1．样品

(1) 黄柏：川黄柏或关黄柏，粉碎成粗粉。

(2) 二妙丸：黄柏 50%，苍术 50%。

2．条件

索氏提取器、圆底烧瓶、毛细管、硅胶薄层板、UV 分光光度计、电吹风；

环已烷、苯、醋酸乙酯、5%对二甲氨基苯甲醛的 10%硫酸液、乙醚、氯仿、甲醇、正丁醇、醋酸、水。

3．二妙丸定性分析

(1) 样品溶液的制备

将本品研成细粉，取 3g，精密称定，置于索氏提取器中，加入石油醚约 25ml，回流 1 小时，回收石油醚至干，加 1.0ml 氯仿溶解，成为 A 液，备用。将残渣挥干后，加甲醇 25ml，回流至提取液为微黄色至无色，回收甲醇至干，精密吸取甲醇 5ml，置瓶中，振摇至残渣完全溶解，过滤，成为 B 液。

(2) 鉴别反应

苍术检查：取样品液 A，以苍术对照药材或苍术醇、苍术酮对照。薄层条件为吸附剂：硅胶 G－0.8%CMCNa（1:3w/v），展开系统：环已烷－苯－醋酸乙酯（7:15:1.5），展距：10cm，显色：5%对二甲氨基苯甲醛的 10%硫酸液，110℃加热。

黄柏检查：取样品液 B，以盐酸小檗碱为对照品。薄层条件中吸附剂同苍术，展开系统：正丁醇－醋酸－水（7:1:2），展距：10cm，显色：在紫外灯下观察荧光。

4．黄柏药材的定性分析

取药材粗粉 0.2g，加 90%乙醇 3ml 振摇提取 30 分钟，提取液适当浓缩，点样，其余按黄柏检查项下进行。

【小檗碱的含量测定】

1．原理

黄柏中含有小檗碱，用甲醇提取，经薄层色谱分离后，采用适当的溶剂将小檗碱洗脱，根据小檗碱在 270、331、420nm 处有最大吸收，可用分光光度法测定小檗碱的含量。

2．条件

紫外分光光度计，紫外灯，索氏提取器，吸量管，微量注射器，展开缸，层析板，容量瓶，小漏斗，滤纸，盐酸小檗碱对照品，正丁醇，醋酸，蒸馏水，1% HCl－甲醇液。

3．薄层条件

硅胶 G－0.4% CMCNa（1∶3w/v），展开系统：正丁醇－醋酸－水（7∶1∶2），展距：10cm，紫外灯下检测。

4．标准曲线制备

取盐酸小檗碱对照品 1mg，置于 1.0ml 容量瓶中，用甲醇稀释至刻度，备用。

精密吸取对照品溶液 10.0，20.0，30.0，40.0，50.0μl 分别置于 5ml 刻度试管中，挥尽甲醇，分别精密加入 1% HCl－甲醇试液 50ml，摇匀；以 1% HCl－甲醇试液作为空白对照，于波长 341nm 处测定吸收度，以吸收度为纵坐标，盐酸小檗碱浓度为横坐标作图。并计算回归方程和相对误差。

5．丸药的测定

取定性分析样品溶液 B 20.0～50.0μl（视含量高低而定）两份及对照品溶液 10.0μl，分别画线点样于 3 块薄层板上，置于同一层析缸中，按上述条件展开，定位，刮取小檗碱谱带，压碎，转入小漏斗中，用 45℃的 1% HCl－甲醇试液洗脱，洗脱液置于 10ml 容量瓶中，洗至刻度为止。另取同样量的硅胶，用同法洗脱，作为空白对照。于 341nm 处测定吸收度，用对比法计算样品溶液中小檗碱的含量，并换算出丸药中小檗碱的含量。

丸药中小檗碱的百分含量 $= A_{样}/A_{对} \times C_{对} \times 1/w_{样} \times D \times 100$

其中：$A_{样}$ = 样品的吸收度

$A_{对}$ = 对照品的吸收度

$C_{对}$ = 对照品的浓度

$w_{样}$ = 样品的重量

D = 稀释倍数

6．黄柏药材中小檗碱的含量测定

精密称取药材粉末 1.5g，加甲醇 25ml，回流提取至提取液至微黄色，回收甲醇至干，精密加入甲醇 5.0ml，超声波振荡至完全溶解，制成样品液，精密吸取 20.0μl，按丸药测定项下操作，并计算药材中小檗碱的含量。

【实验记录】

1．简述操作过程，记录实验现象与问题。

2．绘制定性层析图谱，算出主要斑点的 R_f 值。

3．绘制标准曲线，求出回归方程与相关系数。

4．计算二妙丸与黄柏药材中小檗碱的含量。

【思考题】

1．根据前述主要分析方法，说明各分析方法在分析本品中小檗碱含量的优缺点。

2．以二妙丸为待测药品，再设计一分析小檗碱的实验。

3．若不用 HCl－甲醇而用甲醇洗脱如何？改为热水洗脱又怎样？

【相关资料】

1．黄柏的化学成分

黄柏为芸香科植物黄檗 *Phellodendro amurense* Rupr．和黄皮树 *P*． *chinensis* Schnicid 的树皮。前者习称“关黄柏”，后者习称“川黄柏”。黄檗树皮含小檗碱（berberine)，并含少量黄柏碱（phellodendrine)、木兰碱（magnoflorine)、药根碱（jatrorrhizine）、掌叶防己碱（palmatine)、白栝楼碱（candicine)、蝙蝠葛任碱（menisperne)；另含黄柏内酯（obakulactone)、黄柏酮（obacunone）等。黄皮树树皮中含小檗碱等多种生物碱。

据报道，关黄柏总生物碱含量为 0.95%～2.95%，其中小檗碱含量占 33%～63%；川黄柏总生物碱含量为 3.99%～6.09%，其中小檗碱含量占 72%～87.80%。

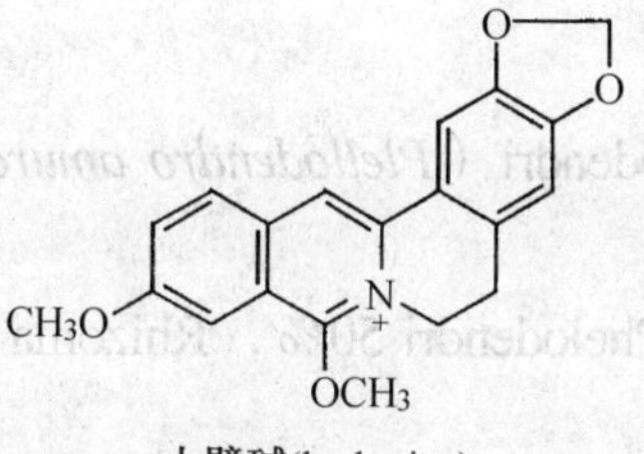

小檗碱(berberine)

2．小檗碱的理化性质

小檗碱：分子量为 336.37，羟基化合物为黄色针状结晶（乙醚），熔点 145℃。游离碱微溶于冷水（1:20），易溶于沸水，几乎不溶于冷乙醇、氯仿和乙醚。碘化物熔点 263～265℃（分解)。$UV\lambda_{Mzx}^{EtOH}$nm（lgε)：225（4.69），270（4.02），331（3.88）。

小檗碱盐酸盐熔点 205℃，微溶于冷水，较易溶于沸水。其硝酸盐及氢碘酸盐极难溶于水。小檗碱的中性硫酸盐、磷酸盐、醋酸盐在水中溶解度大。

1 Determination of Berberine in Cortex Phellodendri And Ermiao Wan by TLC – UV Spectrophotometry

Purpose

1. To be acquainted with the application of TLC – UV spectrophotometry in analysis of alkaloid.

2. To master the chief techniques and principle precautions in the use of TLC – UV Spectrophotometry.

Qualitative analysis

1. Sample

(1) Drugs: Cortex Phellodendri (*Plellodendro amurense* and *P. chinense*), pulverize to coarse powder.

(2) Ingredients: Cortex Phelodendri 50%, Rhizoma Atractylodis 50%.

2. Condition

Soxhlet's extractor, round – bottom flask, capillaries, TLC plate, UV spectrophotometer, hair dryer.

Cyclohexane, benzene, ethyl acetate, 5% solution of *p* – dimethyl aminobenzaldehyde in ethanol containing 10% sulfuric acid, ether, chloroform, methanol, *n* – butanol, acetic acid, water.

3. Qualitative analysis of Ermiao Wan

(1) Preparation of test solution

Weigh accurately 3g of the power to a Soxhlet's extractor, add about 25ml of petroleum ether, heat under reflux on a warm bath for 1 hour, concentrate the extract to dryness. Dissolve the residue in 1ml chloroform as test solution A. After evaporating the chloroform of the residue, add 25ml of methanol, heat the extract under reflux until pale yellow or colorless. Recover methanol from the extract to dryness. Measure accurately 5ml of methanol to a conical flask, shake until the residue completely dissolves, filter, and use the filtrate as test solution B.

(2) Identification reactions

Identification of rhizoma Atractylodis: To test solution A, use rhizoma Actractylodis as reference drug or Hinesol, Atractylon as reference substance. Using silica gel G – 0.8%

CMCNa (1∶3 w/v) as the coating substance and cyclohexane – benzene – ethyl acetate (7∶15∶1.5) as the mobile phase, develop 10 cm, and spray with 5% solution of *p* – dimethyl aminobenzaldehyde in ethanol containing 10% sulfuric acid, heat at 110℃.

Identification of cortex Phellodendri: To test solution B, use berberine hydrochloride as CRS. The coating substance is the same as the identification of rhizoma Atractylodis, using *n* – butanol – acetic acid – water (7∶1∶2) as the mobile phase, develop 10 cm, and examine the fluorescent spots under ultra – violet light.

4. Qualitative analysis of cortex phellodendri

To 0.2g of the coarse power, extract with 3ml of 90% alcohol for 30 minutes, concentrate the extractor, apply it to the plate, and carry out the method for identification of cortex Phellodendri.

Assay

1. Principle

Cortex Phellodendri contains berberine, extract with methanol, after separated by TLC, elute with appropriate solution. For berberine exhibits the absorption maximum at 270nm, 331nm, 420 nm, and use spectrophotometry to examine the content of berberine.

2. Conditions

UV spectrophotometer, ultra – violet lamp, soxhlet's extractor, pipette, micro syringe, developing chamber, TLC plate, volumetric flask, little funnel, filter paper, berberine CRS, *n* – butanol, acetic acid, water, 1% HCl in methanol.

3. Conditions for TLC

Coating substance: silica gel G – 0.4% CMC – Na (1∶3w/v);

Mobile phase: *n* – butanol – acetic acid – water (7∶1∶2);

Development distance: 10 cm;

Detector: UV light.

4. Preparation of standard curve

Weigh accurately 1mg of berberine hydrochloride CRS to a 1.0ml volumetric flask, dilute it with methanol to volume.

Transfer accurately 10.0, 20.0, 30.0, 40.0, 50.0μl of the reference solution to 5ml tubes, respectively, evaporate the methanol, add accurately 5ml of 1% HCl – methanol TS respectively, and mix well; Using 1% HCl – methanol TS as the blank, measure the absorbency at 341 nm, and prepare the standard curve with the absorbance as ordinate and the concentration of berberine hydrochloride as abscissa, and calculate regression equation and relative error.

5. Determination of pills

To three plate, two of 20.0μl ~ 50.0μl of solution B (considering of content) and

10.0μl of the reference solution are applied separately, place in the same development tank, after develop on the previous condition, locate it, scrape off the strip of berberine, packed it to a little funnel, elute with 1% HCl – methanol (45℃), collect the elute to a 10ml volumetric flask, until to volume. Take the equal weight of silica gel; carry out the method as described above, as a blank. Measure the absorbance of the resulting solution at 341 nm, calculate the percentage of berberine in the sample solution with reference to reference substance comparison method, and converse the percentage in pills. The percentage of berberine in pills = $A_x/A_r \cdot C_r \cdot 1/W_x \cdot D \cdot 100$

Where A_x is the absorbance of the test solution; A_r is the absorbance of the reference solution; C_r is the concentration of the test preparation; w_x is the weight of sample; D is diluting times

6. Determination of berberine in cortex phellodendri

Apply 1.5g of the power, weighed accurately, add 25ml of methanol, heat under reflux till the extract to pale yellow, recover the methanol of the residue, add accurately 5.0ml of methanol, ultrasonic disposal until completely dissolved, use as the sample solution. Transfer accurately 20.0μl, carry out the method for determination of pills, and calculate the content of berberine in the drugs.

Experiment record

1. Describe the process of this experiment briefly, and record the test phenomena and problems.

2. Draw the qualitative thin layer chromatogram, and calculate the R_f value of major spots.

3. Plot the standard curve and calculate the regression equation and correlation coefficient.

4. Calculate respectively the content of berberine in Ermiao Wan and Cortex Phellodendri.

Question

1. According to the previous major analytical methods, describe the advantages and disadvantages of them in determination of the content of berberine in sample.

2. Take Ermiao Wan as test drug, please design another experiment of assay of berberine.

3. If not elute with HCl – methanol, how about methanol, or hot water?

实验二　双相滴定法测定延胡索中总生物碱的含量

【目的要求】

1．熟悉双相滴定测定总碱的原理和方法。

2．掌握样品制备方法和生物碱的通性。

【原理】

双相滴定是在水及与水不相溶的有机溶剂（氯仿、苯）中进行的，待测物质先溶于水或有机相中；用已知浓度的水溶液滴定，边滴定边振摇，使滴定产物边产生边溶于有机溶剂中，当滴定剂过量时，所加入的指示剂即在水相或有机相中产生颜色变化或滴定剂本身产生颜色变化，来指示终点。

本实验用双相滴定法测定延胡索中总生物碱的含量，首先从延胡索药材中提取总生物碱使溶于有机溶剂中，加入pH5的缓冲液，摇振后，形成双相溶液，生物碱溶于水相中，再以溴麝香草酚蓝对照品溶液滴定，染料与生物碱盐形成离子时，此产物边产生边溶于有机溶剂，待水相中的生物碱盐全部转为离子对后，过量的滴定剂立即使水相产生颜色变化（黄色），以指示终点，根据所耗滴定剂的含量，计算总生物碱的含量。

【定性分析】

1．沉淀反应　取总碱测定项下残渣 A，加 0.25mol/L 硫酸溶液 20ml，振摇，过滤，取滤液 2ml，加 1％铁氰化甲溶液 0.4ml－1％三氯化铁溶液 0.3ml 的混合液即显深绿色，渐变深蓝色，放置后，底部有较多蓝色沉淀；另取滤液 2ml，加 7.5％重铬酸甲试剂 1 滴即发生黄色沉淀。

2．薄层层析　取总碱项下残渣 A，加 $CHCl_3$ 1.0ml，点样，以四氢巴马亭纯品为对照品。

薄层条件：吸附剂为硅胶 G－0.8％ CMCNa（1∶3），展开系统为正己烷－氯仿－甲醇－二乙胺（5∶3∶0.5∶1d），展距为 1cm。显色在碘蒸气熏后，紫外灯下观察荧光。

【含量测定条件】

0.001M 溴麝香草酚蓝对照品溶液（称取本品 0.327g，溶于 5mol/L NaOH 加水稀释 500ml，必要时过滤）。

乙醚－氯仿－甲醇（25∶8∶2.5）混合溶媒。

pH5.0 缓冲液（0.2M 邻苯二甲酸氢钾溶液 2ml，加入 0.2M NaOH 溶液 11.83ml，混合均匀，酸度计调整）。

容量瓶（10ml，50ml）各一只。

刻度试管（20ml）10 只。

吸量管（1ml，2ml）各一只。

滴定管。

对照品溶液的标化：精密称取阿托品 5.15mg，置 10ml 容量瓶中，以氯仿溶解，并加氯仿至刻度，再用吸量管取阿托品溶液 0.5ml，置具塞刻度试管中，加氯仿至 10ml，再加 pH5.0 缓冲液 2.0ml，以溴麝香草酚蓝溶液滴定，至水层微显黄色为止，按下式计算：

$$MV = G/0.2894$$

其中：

V——所耗对照品溶液体积（ml）；

G——阿托品重量（g）；

0.2894——阿托品毫克分子量。

从上式计算标准液（溴麝香草酚蓝）的克分子浓度（M）

【总生物碱测定】

精密称定延胡索粉末 2g，置 50ml 具塞三角瓶内，加氨水湿润，密塞 15 分钟，准确加入混合溶媒 25ml，冷浸 24～48 小时，吸取 20ml，蒸去溶媒至干，得到残渣“A”，加 $CHCl_3$，溶解成 10.0ml，成为待测样品液。吸取样品液 1.0ml，置具塞刻度试管中，加 2.0ml $CHCl_3$ 和 15ml 缓冲液，以溴麝香草酚蓝滴定，根据消耗的量计算含量（总碱按延胡索乙素计算，$C_{12}H_{25}O_4N$ 毫克分子量为 0.3554），根据四次平均值计算含量：

$$含量\% = MV.0.3554/药材重量(g) \times 100$$

【实验记录】

1. 简要记录实验过程和出现问题。
2. 计算含量、平均值、相对标准偏差（RSD，%）

【思考题】

1. 含量计算为什么按延胡索乙素（$C_{21}H_{25}O_4N$）计算而不按其盐酸盐（$C_{21}H_{25}O_4N \cdot HCl$）计算。
2. 列出本次实验含量计算化简公式。

【相关资料】

1. 延胡索的化学成分

延胡索为罂粟科植物延胡索 *Corydalis yanhusuo* W. R. Wang 的块茎，含生物碱类成分，其中有叔胺类、季胺类生物碱。主要生物碱有延胡索甲素（延胡索碱，*d*－corydaline）、乙素（*dl*－四氢掌叶防己碱、四氢巴马亭，*dl*－tetrahydropaimatine）、丙素（原阿片碱，protopine）丁素（1－四氢黄连碱，l－tetrahydro coptisine）、黄连碱（coptisine）、延胡索胺碱（corydalmine）等。

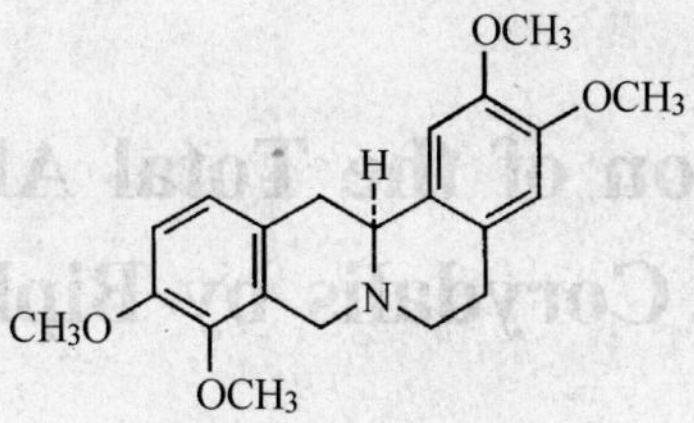

四氢巴马亭(延胡索乙素)

2. 延胡索乙素的理化性质

结晶（稀甲醇），熔点 147℃。盐酸盐，针晶（甲醇），熔点 215 ~ 216℃。UVλ_{Max}^{EeOH} nm（logε）：282（3.82），230（肩，3.35），273（3.06）。游离碱不溶于水，能溶于热乙醇（在冷乙醇中溶解度较小），易溶于氯仿、苯、乙醚中。酸性硫酸盐为无色针状结晶，熔点 245 ~ 246℃，在冷水中溶解度较小，在热水中较大；其中性硫酸盐为长柱结晶，熔点 220℃，在水中溶解度较酸性硫酸盐溶解度为大，其盐酸盐难溶于水。

2 Determination of the Total Alkaloids Content in Rhizoma Corydalis by Biphase Titrimetry

Purpose

1. To be familiar with the principle and method of determining the total alkaloids by biphase titrimetry.

2. To master the method of preparation of the sample and the general character of alkaloids.

Principal

Biphase titrations refer to the titration operating in the aqueous solvent and organic solvent. Organic solvent, such as chloroform or benzene, can not be solved in water. After dissolve test substance in aqueous solvent or organic solvent, titrate it with aqueous solution whose concentration is already known. Shake it while titrating, so the titration products can solve in the organic solvent. When titrant is superfluous, the color of indicator will be changed in solvent (aqueous or organic) or titrant itself produce color change, which indicate the end point of the titration.

In this experiment, we determine the content of general alkaloids in Rhizoma Corydalis by biphase titrimetry. Extract the total alkaloids from crude drugs of Corydalis yanhusuo and solve it into organic solvent, add BS in, shake it to form a biphase solvent. The alkaloids are solved in the aqueous solvent. Titrate it with bromothymol blue as reference solution. The ion – pairs that dyestuff and the alkaloid salt formed will solve in the organic solvent when they produced. After the alkaloid salt in aqueous are all turned into ion – pairs, the superfluous titrant make the aqueous solvent change the color to yellow simultaneously, which indicate the end point of the titration. Calculate the concentration of total alkaloids according to the consumption of the titrant.

Qualitative analysis

1. Precipitation

To residue A in the item of determination of total alkaloids in 20ml of sulfuric acid solution (0.25mol/L), shake and filter. Add 2ml of the filtrate into a mixture of 0.4ml of 1% potassium hexacyanoferrate solution and 0.3ml of 1% iron sesquichloride solution, a deep green color is produced which gradually turns to deep blue, then a deep blue precipitate is produced while standing. Add 1 drop of 7.5% potassium dichromate reagent to another 2ml of the filtrate, a yellow precipitate will be produced.

2. TLC

To residue A in the item of determination of total alkaloids into 1.0ml of chloroform, then apply the sample and use tetrohydropalmatine as CRS.

Conditions of TLC: Using silica gel G – 0.8% CMCNa (1:3) as the coating substance and *n* – hexane – chloroform – methanol – diethylamine (5:3:0.5:1d) as mobile phase. After developing 10cm, exposing the plate to iodine vapor, examine the fluorescence spot under ultra – violet light.

Conditions of the concentration determination: 0.001M bromothymol blue reference solution (to 0.327g of the CRS to 5mol/L sodium hydroxid solution, add water to 500ml, filter it when necessary.); Ethyl ether – chloroform – methanol (25:8:2.5) mixed solvent; pH5 BS (add 11.83ml of 0.2M sodium hydroxid solution to 2ml of 0.2M potassium hydrogen phthalate solution, mixed well, adjust PH with acidometer); volumetric flask (10ml × 1, 50ml × 1); graduated test tube (20ml × 10); pipette (1ml × 1, 2ml × 1); buret.

Standardization of reference solution: weigh accurately 5.15mg of atropine in a 10ml volumetric flask, dissolve it in chloroform, add chloroform to volume. Transfer accurately 0.5ml of the atropine solution to a graduated test tube, add chloroform to 10ml, add pH 5.0 BS 2.0ml, titrate with bromothymol blue till a little yellow is produced in the water phase. Calculate the concentration according to the following formula: $MV = G/0.2894$

In this formula, V is the volume of reference solution consumed (ml); G is the weight of atropine (g); 0.2894 is the milligram molecular weight of atropine. So we can calculate the molarity (M) of standard solution (bromothymol blue).

Determination of total alkaloids

Weigh accurately 2g of the power of Rhizoma Corydalis in a 50ml stoppered triangle flask, macerate with ammonia water, allow to stand for 15 min. Add accurately 25ml of the mixed solvent into it, soak coldly for 24 ~ 48h. Make 20ml of it to evaporate to dryness, take the residue as "A". Dissolve it with chloroform and add chloroform to10ml, take it as the test solution. Transfer 1.0ml of the solution to a stoppered test tube, add 2.0ml of chloroform and 15ml of the BS in, then titrate with bromothymol blue. According the consumption of titrant, we can calculate the concentration (consider total alkaloids as tetrahydropalmatine, the milligram molecular weight of $C_{21}H_{24}O_4N$), and get the concentration from the average value of 4 datum.

$$C\% = MV \times 0.3554/W_d \times 100$$

Experiment record

1. Make a brief record of the process of the experiment and the problems.

2. Calculate the concentration, average value and the coefficient of variation.

Question

1. Why do we consider total alkaloids as tetrahydropalmatine ($C_{21}H_{25}O_4N$) but not as the chlorhydride of tetrahydropalmatine ($C_{21}H_{25}O_4N \cdot HCl$)?

2. List the simplified formula in this experiment to calculate the concentration.

实验三　薄层扫描法测定延胡索乙素的含量

【目的要求】

1．熟悉 TLC－光密度测定原理和技术。

2．学习叔胺类生物碱 TLC－光密度测定方法。

【原理】

在薄层上直接测量被分离成分的斑点对于一定波长光的吸收或反射的强度，可以测定斑点所含成分的量。测量所用的光可分为可见光、紫外光和荧光三种，所选择的波长应为该物质的最大吸收波长。延胡索乙素在 280nm 处有最大吸收，故可选为样品波长，另选一被测化合物无吸收或很少吸收的参比波长，进行双波长薄层扫描。

【条件】

仪器：CS－930 型或 CS－9000 型双波长薄层扫描仪，微量注射器，1ml 容量瓶。

薄层条件：硅胶 G 薄层板（室温下干燥过夜）

展开系统：正己烷－氯仿－甲醇（5:3:0.5），展距约 15cm（上行），碘蒸气熏后，紫外光灯下定位。

扫描条件：$\lambda_S = 280nm$，$\lambda_R = 400nm$，狭缝 1.25×1.25mm，锯齿形扫描。

【含量测定】

标准曲线图：精密称取延胡索乙素对照品 2mg 于 1ml 容量瓶中，用乙醇溶解至刻度。

用微量注射器精确吸取对照品溶液 1.0，2.0，3.0，4.0，5.0μl，点于薄层板上（条状），用上述展开剂展开约 1 小时，挥尽溶媒，碘蒸气熏后，紫外灯光下定位，于扫描仪上按上述条件测定积分值，并以积分值为纵坐标，纯品量为横坐标绘图。

样品测定：精密称取延胡索细粉 0.5g，置具塞三角瓶中，加入少量氨水，润湿后密塞 15 分钟，加苯 10.0ml（移液管加入）冷浸 24 小时，精密吸取上清液 1ml 于小三角瓶中，室温挥去溶媒，于残渣中加入苯 100μl 溶解后密塞备用。

用微量注射器吸取样品液 5～20μl（视含量高低而定），点于薄层板上（条状），并同时点对照品溶液 2μl，按上述方法展开，定位，经扫描测量积分值，用对比法计算延胡索乙素的量，并换算出药材中的百分含量。

【实验记录】

1．简述操作过程，记录出现问题。

2．绘制标准曲线，层析图谱，求待测斑点 R_f 值。

3．计算药材中延胡索乙素的百分含量，CV 值。

【思考题】

1. 列出延胡索乙素百分含量的计算公式［令：测得积分值在标准曲线上的读数为(mg/ml)，*w* 为药材重量（克），D 为稀释倍数］。

2. 重新设计该实验提取精制方案。

3 Determination of The *dl* – Tetrahydropalmatine by Thin Layer Chromatography Scan (TLCS)

Purpose

1. To study the mechanism of the assay by TLC – densitometry
2. To learn the assay of trialkylamine alkaloids

Principle

The isolated spot is measured directly on the TLC plate. At a particular wavelength, it has maximum absorption, which is directly proportional to its concentration. *dl* – tetrahydropalmatine is determined by DBTLC at a wavelength of 250nm.

Apparatus

A double – wavelength TLC scanner CS930 or CS – 9000 micro – syringe, volumetric flask (1ml), silica gel G – TLC plate (dried at room temperature over a night).

Reagent

n – hexane – chloroform – carbonol (5:3:0.5) as the mobile phase, Iodine vapor as the spray reagent.

Assay

1. Preparation of the reference solution

Weigh accurately 2mg of tctevahydropalmatine CRS into 1ml volumetric flask, add ethanol to dissolve and fill to the mark.

2. Preparation of the standard curve

Pipette 1.0, 2.0, 3.0, 4.0, 5.0μl solutions of the reference solution with a micro syringe and spot them on the TLC plate. Using the above mobile phase, develop the plate for an hour, dry and spray the plate with iodine vapor. Locate the isolated spots under UV at 280nm. Measure the integral value according the mentioned scanning – condition and plot a graph of integral value against purity.

3. Preparation of test solution

Weigh accurately 0.5g fine powder of Rhizoma Corydalis into a conical flask with ground stopper. Add a little ammonia solution to wet the sample. Cover and leave to stand for 15minutes. Add benzene by a suction pipette and macerate for 24 hours. Pipette 1ml supernatant into a small conical flask and volatilize the solvent completely at room temperature. To the residue add 100μl benzene and pipette 5 ~ 10μl of the test solution by a micro – syringe and spot it on the TLC plate. Develop, locate and measure the integral value in the same way as above. Using the correlation method, find out the amount of *dl* – tetrahydropalmatine in the test solution. Calculate the percentage concentration of *dl* – tetrahydropalmatine in the medicinal material.

Experiment record

1. Briefly describe the experiment procedure and state the difficulties encountered.
2. Draw the standard curve, and calculate the R_f value of the sample
3. calculate the CV (%) and the content (%) of *dl* – tetrahydropalmatine in the material

Question

1. What is the formula of calculating the percentage concentration of *dl* – tetrahydropalmatine? Taking *w* (g) as the weight of the material, D as the dilution factor and the integral reading on the standard curve in mg/ml.
2. Redesign the experimental scheme of refining and extraction.

实验四　酸性染料比色法测定延胡索中总生物碱的含量

【目的要求】

1．熟悉酸性染料比色的原理及测定总碱的方法。

2．掌握样品液与空白对照液的制备方法。

【原理】

本实验采用酸性染料比色法测定延胡索中总生物碱的含量，首先从延胡索药材中提取总生物碱，溶于有机溶剂中，加入一定量以 pH4.5 的缓冲溶液溶解的溴甲酚绿溶液，使生物碱盐与染料形成离子对，该产物能被氯仿定量提取，并产生颜色变化（黄色），可以比色法测定该有色溶液的吸收度，从而计算延胡索中总生物碱的含量。

【条件】

1．试剂

（1）0.04%溴甲酚绿（40mg 本品，加 100ml pH4.5 的缓冲液，略加热使溶解，过滤即得。（2）pH4.5 缓冲溶液：0.2M 邻苯二甲酸氢钾（pH4），用 0.1M 氢氧化钾调 pH4.5（可在 pH25 型酸度计上调节）。

2．仪器

721 型或 7520 型可见－紫外分光光度计，25 型酸度计，分液漏斗，25ml 容量瓶，吸量管。

【实验步骤】

1．标准曲线制作

精密称取 4.0mg 延胡索乙素对照品，置 25ml 容量瓶中，用氯仿溶解后，加氯仿至刻度。

分别吸取延胡索乙素对照品溶液 0.20，0.40，0.60，0.80，1.00ml 置分液漏斗中准确加入氯仿至 10.00ml，再加 pH4.5 溴甲酚绿缓冲液 5.0ml，振摇 3 分钟后，放置 1 小时，空白对照液除不加对照品溶液外，其余操作同上，于波长 410nm 处测吸收度，以吸收度为纵坐标，以浓度（μg/ml）为横坐标，绘制标准曲线。

2．含量测定

精密称取延胡索粉 2.0g，置具塞三角瓶中，加少量氨水湿润后，密塞放置 15 分钟，加乙醚:氯仿:甲醇（25:8:2.5）混合溶剂 25ml，轻轻摇匀，随即称重，冷浸一周，称重补充挥失的混合溶剂量，精密吸取 10.0ml 于 25ml 磨口圆底烧瓶中，挥去溶剂至干，准确加入氯仿，使完全溶解，即得待测样品液。

精密吸取待测样品液 0.2ml，置分液漏斗中，加氯仿至 10.0ml，再加入 pH4.5 溴甲酚绿缓冲液 5.0ml，振摇 3 分钟后，放置 1 小时。

空白对照液的制备：取氯仿 15ml，置分液漏斗中，加 pH4.5 溴甲酚绿缓冲液 5.0ml，振摇 3 分钟后，放置 1 小时，精密吸取该氯仿液 10.0ml 置分液漏斗中，精密加入供试液 0.2ml，振摇 3 分钟，放置 1 小时，作空白用。

于波长 410nm 处测得吸收度，从标准曲线上查出其含量，换算样品中总生物碱的含量。

【实验记录】

1．简述操作过程，记录出现问题。

2．绘制标准曲线。

3．计算延胡索中总生物碱含量。

【思考题】

1．说明空白样品制备的每一步骤消除了何种因素的干扰。还存在什么问题。

2．酸性染料比色法测定生物碱最关键的因素有哪些，为什么？

4 Determination of the Total Alkaloids Content in Rhizoma Corydalis by Acid – dye Colorimetry

Purpose

1. Be familiar with the principle of acid dye colorimetry and the method of the determination of total alkaloid.

2. Master the method of preparation of sample solution and blank control solution

Principle

This experiment uses the acid dye colorimetry to determinate of the quantity of total alkaloid in corydalis tuber. Firstly, abstract the total alkaloid from crude drugs and dissolve it in organic solvent. Add buffer solution of bromocresol green (pH4.5) to certain capacity, so the ion – pair can be formed by the alkaloid salt and acid dyes. This product can be abstracted by chloroform quantitatively. With the color changed to yellow and the solution's absorbance determinated, the quantity of total alkaloid in rhizoma corydalis can be calculated.

Condition

1. Reagent

(1) 0.04% solution of bromocresol green (obtained by weighting 40mg this sample, add 100ml pH4.5 BS, heated slightly to dissolve then filtrate)

(2) pH4.5 BS: 0.2M pH4.5 potassium acid phthalate, adjusting pH to 4.5 by 0.1M potassium hydroxide.

2. Apparatus

721 – type or 7520 – type UV – VIS spectrophotometer, 25 – type pH meter, separating funnel, 25ml volumetric flask, pipette.

Operation procedure

1. Preparation of calibration curve

Weight accurately 4.0mg of tetrahydropalmatine CRS dissolve and dilute with chloroform to volume in a 25ml volumetric flask and mix well.

Transfer accurately 0.20, 0.40, 0.60, 0.80, 1.00ml of the resulting solution to separating funnels separately, and add chloroform to 10.00ml then pH4.5 bromocresol green BS 5.0ml. Shaking vigorously for 3min, allow to stand for 1h, except adding the CRS, the preparation of the blank control solution is just the same as what has been mentioned above.

Measure the absorbance at 410nm, and plot a standard curve with absorption degree as ordinate and concentration (μg/ml) as abscissa.

2. Assay

Weight accurately 2.0g of the powder in a stoppered three – necked flask, and moisten it with little aqua ammonia. After lay it aside with stopper for 15min, add 25ml of mixture reagents of aether – chloroform – methanol (25:8:2.5), and shake it gently and weight it presently. Macerate coldly for 1 week and weight it again, and make up the loss in weight with the mixture reagents. Draw accurately 10.0ml of the solution, add to 25ml ground round bottom flask, evaporate the solution to dryness. Dissolve the residue in chloroform to certain capacity as the test solution.

Draw accurately 0.2ml of the test solution to separating funnel, add chloroform to 10.0ml, then 5.0ml of buffer solution of bromocresol green (pH4.5), shake for 3min, and allow to stand for 1h at room temperature.

The preparation of blank control solution: Draw 15ml of chloroform to a separating funnel, add pH4.5 bromocresol green BS 5.0ml, shake for 3min, allow to stand for 1h at room temperature. Transfer accurately 10ml of the chloroform solution to a separating funnel, add the test solution 0.2ml accurately, shake for 3min, allow to stand for 1h, and use it as blank solution. Detect the absorbance at 410nm, read out the total content in the test solution from the standard curve, and calculate the quantity of total alkaloid in sample.

Experiment record

1. Describe the procedure of the operation, and take a brief note of the problem occurred in the experiment.
2. Plot the standard curve.
3. Calculate the content of total alkaloid in Rhizoma Corydalis.

Question

1. Explain what interfere factor each step of preparation for the blank solution. What another problems still have?
2. What is the key element in the determination of the quantity of total alkaloid by acid dye colorimetry? And why?

实验五 高效液相色谱法测定延胡索中叔胺类生物碱的含量

【目的要求】

1. 通过对延胡索中叔胺类生物碱的 HPLC 分析，学习 HPLC 的一般操作步骤和使用方法

2. 熟悉高效色谱柱的使用，保养方法。

3. 掌握色谱保留数据如保留时间（t），容量因子（K′），理论塔板数，分离度的测定方法。

4. 掌握样品的精制方法和原则。

【原理】

高效液相色谱法（High Performance Liquid Chromatography）系指用液体作为流动相，根据组分在固定相上吸附或分配不同使之分离的一种高效能色谱方法或高速液相色谱法。

影响色谱分离效率有两大主要因素，其一为热力学因素如不同组分容量因子（k′），其二是动力学因素如色谱峰的展宽。反映这些物理过程的指标是保留时间和理论塔板数（n）。

其中 $k' = \frac{t_R - t_0}{t_0}$； $n = 16\left(\frac{t_R}{W_b}\right)^2$

密切注视和努力解决这两个因素引起的矛盾，组分间的分离就成功了，分离的表现指标是分离度 R。

$$R = \frac{2(t_2 - t_1)}{W_{b1} + W_{b2}}$$

本实验采用岛津高效色谱柱，用甲醇－水－10%醋酸（65:35:2）（用 10% 氢氧化铵调至 pH 至 6.0）作为流动相，延胡索乙素等叔胺类生物碱 k′值差别显著，峰扩散小即理论塔板数多，分离数达到定量要求，因该叔胺类生物碱在 280nm 有强吸收，故选用 280nm 为检测波长进行测定，分析效果较为满意。

【条件】

岛津高效色谱仪－10A，紫外检测器，ODS 柱、甲醇、水、10% 醋酸、10%氢氧化铵、延胡索药材或含延胡索的中成药。

【实验步骤】

1. 色谱条件：流动相甲醇－水－10%醋酸（65:35:2）（用 10% 氢氧化铵调 pH6.0），流速 0.5ml/min，柱温室温。

2．仪器参数：UV280nm；灵敏度 0.04AuFS，纸速 2mm/min；衰减 2 。

3．样品液制备：取药材粉末 1.0g，用 14%氨水湿润，20 分钟后用 20ml 苯冷浸 24 小时，取 10ml 苯提取液，减压蒸干，加 1%醋酸溶解并定容至 10ml 容量瓶中，摇匀后，用 0.45μm 微孔滤膜过滤，滤液即为样品液。

4．样品测定：取样品液数 μl（响应在线性范围内）进样，根据打印峰面积代入如下回归方程计算相对含量，再换算成样品的百分含量。

延胡索乙素的回归方程 $y = 4.32 \times 10^5 x - 0.0147 \times 10^5$（0.05 ~ 0.2665μg）

紫堇碱的回归方程 $y = 381 \times 10^5 x - 0.00207 \times 10^5$（0.048 – 0.209μg/μl）。

其中：

x 为浓度（μg/μl）：y 为峰面积。

【实验记录】

1．简述实验过程，记录实验中出现的问题。

2．计算延胡索乙素，紫堇碱的容量因子 K′，理论塔板数 H（数/米），及两者的分离度。

【思考题】

1．正相色谱和反相色谱在样品精制方面应注意什么问题。

2．根据反相色谱对样品精制的要求，试设计一提取精制方案来测定季胺类生物碱。

5 Determination of Tetiary Amine Alkaloid in Rhizoma Corydalis by High – Performance Liquid Chromatography

Purpose

1. To learn the ordinary operational method of HPLC.
2. To be familiar with the use and maintenance of high – performance chromatographic column.
3. To learn how to interpret chromatographic data.
4. To learn the extraction method.

Principle

High – performance liquid chromatography is a high efficiency or high – speed liquid chromatography and uses a liquid as the mobile phase. Sample components can be separated due to their differences in adsorption or partition on the stationary phase.

The two important factors responsible for chromatographic separation efficiency are: thermodynamic factor such as capacity factor (k') of different components and the dynamic factor, the broadening width of the peak. The indexes to reflect these physical processes are retention time (t_R) and number of theoretical plates of column (n). The value of k' and n are calculated as follows:

$$k' = \frac{t_R - t_0}{t_0}; \quad n = 16 \left(\frac{t_R}{W_b}\right)^2$$

Where, t_0 is the retention time of the unretained solute

W_b is the width of the peak

The resolution factor (R) is often used as an Index to express the separation efficiency and its value is calculated as follows:

$$R = \frac{2\,(t_2 - t_1)}{W_{b1} + W_{b2}}$$

The resolution factor is the ratio of the distance between the two peak maxima i. e. the distance between the two retention times and the arithmetic mean of the two – peak width. A wavelength of 289nm is used because at that wavelength the trialkylamine alkaloids have strong absorption.

Apparatus

Agillent1100 series HPLC (U. S. A) with Ultraviolet detector. ODS column.

Reagents

Methanol, water, 10% acetic acid, 10% ammoniun – hydroxide; crude drugs of Rhizoma Corydalis or preparation containing of Rhizoma Corydalis.

Procedure

1. Chromatographic system and system suitability

Use octadecylsilane bonded silica gel as the stationary phase, methanol – water – 10% acetic acid (65:35:2) (adjusted to pH6.0 with 10% ammonium – hydroxide) as the mobile phase, flow rate: 0.5ml/min, Detector wavelength 280nm and room temperature as the column temperature. The number of the theoretical plates of the column is not less than 3000.

2. Preparation of test solution

Moist the powder with 14% ammonia for 20 minutes. Macerate in benzene for 24hrs and evaporate the extract to dryness. Dissolve the residue in 10% acetic acid and centrifuge. Filter with a filter membrane (particle size 0.45μm). Dilute with 10% acetic acid.

Assay

Inject an appropriate quantity of test solution and calculate the relative content according to the following regression parameters. Convert to percentage content of the sample.

Regression parameters of tetrahydropalmatine is:

$$Y = 4.32 \times 10^5 x - 0.014 \times 10^5 \quad (0.05 \sim 0.2665 \mu g/\mu l)$$

Regression parameters of corydaline is:

$$Y = 381 \times 10^5 x - 0.00207 \times 10^5 \quad (0.048 \sim 0.209 \mu g/\mu l)$$

Where X – concentration μg/μl

Y – peak area

Experiment record

1. Briefly describe the experiment procedure and state the difficulties encountered.
2. Calculate capacity factor (k′), Height of the theoretical plates (H) of tetrahydropalmatine and corydaline. What is the resolution factor?

Question

1. In the respect of refining sample in normal – and reversed – phase chromatography,

what should attention be paid to?

2. According to the requirements of sample refining for reversed – phase chromatography, design an extracting and refining plan to determine quaternary amine alkaloids.

实验六 酸性染料比色法测定洋金花中莨菪碱和东莨菪碱的含量

【目的要求】

1．掌握酸性染料分光光度法测定总碱的方法和原理。

2．学习根据生物碱的酸碱性强弱用酸性染料进行分离测定方法。

【原理】

酸性染料比色法在一定 pH 条件下，生物碱（B）与氢离子（H^+）结合成阳离子（BH^+）（即生物碱盐），而此时某些酸性染料 HIn 则成为阴离子 In^-，这两种离子能结合成有色复合物 BHIn，并能定量被有机溶剂提取，然后直接用分光光度法测定该复合物的颜色，也可以将复合物碱化使染料释出，测染料颜色。

本实验根据上述原理，使莨菪碱与溴甲酚紫在 pH6.6 缓冲溶液中选择性地结合并被氯仿提取而不被东良菪碱干扰，在 420nm 处按分光光度法测定莨菪碱的含量，然后改用溴甲酚绿在 pH5.6 缓冲液中使二者均与该染料结合并被氯仿提取，而后碱化氯仿提取液，按分光光度法在 620nm 处测定释出的溴甲酚绿的颜色的吸收值，即为两者总量，用总生物碱量减去莨菪碱的含量即为东莨菪碱的含量。

【条件】

仪器：751 型可见－紫外分光光度计，25 型 pH 计，三角烧瓶（50ml），移液管，刻度吸管，容量瓶（25ml），分液漏斗。

试液：pH5.6 溴甲酚绿缓冲液（溴甲酚绿 80mg 溶于 pH5.6 的邻苯二甲酸氢钾缓冲液 200ml 中），pH6.6 溴甲酚紫缓冲液（溴甲酚紫 80mg 溶于 pH6.6 邻苯二甲酸氢钾缓冲液 200ml 中），氯仿。

【操作步骤】

1．标准曲线制作

（1）标准曲线 A：精密吸取阿托品盐对照品适量，溶于适量水中，使其浓度为相当于莨菪碱（游离）200mg/ml，分别吸取 0，0.5，1.0，3.0，5.0ml 于 50ml（玻璃）锥形瓶中，再分别加入 6.0，5.5，5.0，3.0，1.0ml 蒸馏水使总体积各为 6.0ml 。然后，在五只锥形瓶中各加入 0.4% 溴甲酚绿 pH5.6 的缓冲溶液 2.0ml 及 10.0ml 氯仿，密塞依次剧烈振摇 2 分钟，移入 20ml 分液漏斗中放置 1.5 小时，待氯仿层完全分清后，分取 6.0ml 氯仿液置于 10ml 带塞刻度试管中，再加入 1.0ml 0.01mol/L 氢氧化钾无水乙醇溶液，摇匀，以加入 0ml 样品液的为空白，在 620nm 处测得此蓝色溶液的吸收值，然后，以吸收值为纵坐标，浓度（μg/ml）为横坐标作图。

（2）标准曲线 B：按标准曲线 A 项下同法操作至“……使总体积各为 6.0ml”。然后在五只锥形瓶中各加入 2.0ml 0.4% 溴甲酚紫 pH6.6 的缓冲液及 10.0ml 氯仿，密塞依次剧烈振摇 2 分钟，移入 20ml 分液漏斗中放置 1 小时，待氯仿完全分清，分取氯仿液在 420nm 处测定复合物（黄色）的吸收值，空白，作图方式同“标准曲线 A”。

2．样品制备和测定

（1）样品液的制备：取生药粉末 2g，精密称定，加氨水湿润，密塞 15 分钟，加氯仿 30.0ml，称重，冷浸一周，然后，称重补足到原重量，为“A”液。

（2）莨菪碱的测定：精密吸取 A 液 3～5ml，蒸干，加 6.0ml 蒸馏水，按“标准曲线 B”项下自“各加入 2.0ml 0.4% 溴甲酚紫 pH6.6 的……”开始同法操作、测得吸收值即可由标准曲线 B 上读出相应的莨菪碱的 μg/ml 数，然后换算出样品中所含莨菪碱的百分含量。[标准曲线斜率为 2.57（吸收度/mg）]。

（3）总碱的测定：精密吸取 A 液 3～5ml，蒸干，加 6.0ml 蒸馏水，按“标准曲线 A”项下自“各加入 2.0ml 0.4%溴甲酚绿缓冲液……”开始同法操作，测得吸收值即可由标准曲线 B 上读取相当于总碱的 μg/ml 数，然后换算出总碱的含量，最后用总碱含量减去莨菪碱含量即为东莨菪碱的含量。

$$含量\% = R.\ D/w \times 100\%$$

其中：R—从标准曲线上读取的碱的浓度；

D—稀释倍数；

w—样品重量。

【实验记录】

1．简述实验过程，记录所出现的问题。
2．R 单位取（μg/ml），w 单位为（g），列出莨菪碱和总碱计算简式。
3．计算莨菪碱、东莨菪碱、总碱含量。
4．绘定性薄层图谱及莨菪碱和东莨菪碱的 R_f 值。

【思考题】

1．若氯仿与水分不清（即分层不完全），此时测出含量偏高还是偏低，为什么？
2．测总碱时，为什么要测定量释出的染料颜色？测复合物颜色如何？

【相关资料】

1．洋金花的化学成分

洋金花为茄科植物白花曼陀罗 *Datura metel*. L 的干燥花。含总生物碱 0.37%（盛花期）～0.75 %（凋谢期），主要成分为东莨菪碱（scopolamine），少量为莨菪碱（hyoscoamine）。莨菪碱的消旋体是阿托品（atropine）。

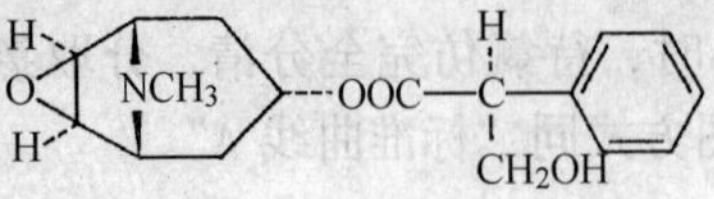

东莨菪碱

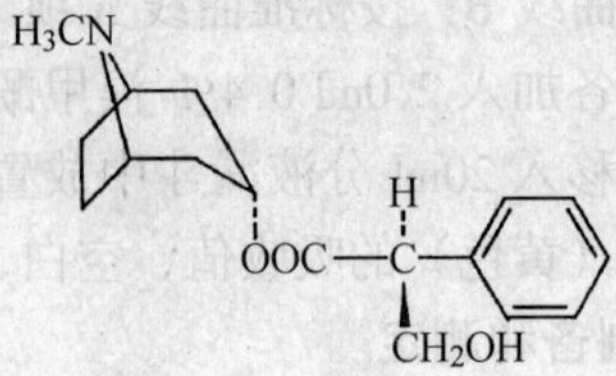

莨菪碱

2．莨菪碱和东莨菪碱的理化性质

莨菪碱为四方细针状结晶（乙醇），分子量为354.30，熔点108.5℃，$[\alpha]_D^{20}-21°$（乙醇），溶于乙醇、氯仿和苯，稍溶于水和乙醚，本品在提取过程中很容易消旋化成为atropine，易被碱水解成莨菪醇（tropine）和消旋莨菪酸（tropine acid）。

东莨菪碱为粘性液体，分子量为303.35，$[\alpha]_D^{20}-28°$（C=2.7），溶于95份水，形成水合物结晶体，熔点59 ℃，易熔于热水、乙醇、乙醚、氯仿和丙酮，微溶于苯和乙醚，易被酸水解，溴氢酸盐熔点195 ℃，$[\alpha]_D^{25}-24\sim-26°$（C=5）。

6 Acid Dyed Colorimetry Assaying the Content of Hyoscyamine and Hyoscine in Flos Daturae

Purpose

1. To master the principle and the method of acid – dye Colorimetry assaying the content of total alkaloids.

2. To study the method to separate and assay with acid dyes on the basis of pH of alkaloids.

Principle

Acid – dye colorimetry: In a certain pH value the alkaloid (B) and the hydrion (H^+) combine into the cation (BH^+), which is the alkaloids salt. Meanwhile, some acid dyes HIn turn into the anion In^-. These two kinds of ions can combine into the colored compound BHIn that can be extracted by organic solvent quantitatively. Then assay the color of the compound using the spectrophotometry directly or alkalized the compound to release the dyes then assay the color of the dye.

In this experiment on the basis of the principle mentioned above, hyoscyamine combine with bromocresol purple selectively in BS of pH6.6 and can be extracted by chloroform while hyoscine can't be influenced. Detect the content of the hyoscyamine at 420nm, according to the method of spectrophotometry then change bromocresol purple into bromocresol green in the BS of pH5.6, all of the hyosyamine could combine with the dye and can be extracted by chloroform, then alkalized the chloroform extract. Carry out the method of spectrophotometry, measure the absorbance of the color of the bromocresol green that has been released. It is the content of the two alkaloids. Then make the content of the total alkaloids minus that of hyoscyamine. We can get the content of hyoscine.

Condition

Instrument: 751 UV – VIS spectrophotometer, 25 pH meter, triangular flask (50ml), transfer pipette, angaved pipette, volumetric flask (25ml), separating funnel

Test solution: pH5.6 bromocresol green BS (dissolve 80mg of bromocresol green to 200ml of pH5.6 protassium acid phthalate BS), pH6.6 bromocresol purple BS (dissolve 80mg of bromocresol purple to 200ml of pH6.6 potassium acid phthalate BS), chloroform.

Procedure

1. Preparation of standard curve

(1) Standard curve A: Accurately place an appropriate quantity of atropine salt CRS, dissolve in an appropirate quantity of water, make the concentration to 200mg/ml corresponding to hyoscyamine (free state), transfer separately 0.00, 0.5, 1.0, 3.0, 5.0ml to 50ml glass conical flasks, add 6.0, 5.5, 5.0, 3.0, 1.0ml of distilled water respectively, make the total volume of to 6.0ml each, then add 2.0ml of pH5.6 0.4% bromocresol green BS and 10.0ml chloroform, stopper tightly, shake violently for two minutes in turn, transfer to a 20ml separating funnel, allow to stand for 1.5 hours. After making the chloroform layer demix fully, transfer 6.0ml of the chloroform solution to stoppered tubes respectively, add 1.0ml of 0.01mol/L potassium hydroxide in absolute alcohol. Shake thoroughly, taking the one which add 0.00ml of the sample solution as the blank solution, measure the absorbance of the blue solution at 490 nm, plot the standard curve with the absorbance as ordinate and concentration (μg/ml) as abscissa.

(2) Standard curve B: Proceed as described under "preparation of standard curve A", ending in the words "the total volume of each 6.0ml", then add 2.0ml of pH6.6 0.4% bromocresol purple and 10.0ml of chloroform, to those 5 triangular flasks respectively, stopper tightly, shake violently for two minutes in turn, transfer 20ml to separating funnel, stand for 1 hour, after the chloroform layer is completely mixed, take out the chloroform solution respectively, measure the absorbance of the yellow solution at 420nm, take the flank, plot the standard curve in the same method as 'the preparation of standard curve A'.

2. Preparation and assay of the sample solution:

(1) Sample solution preparation: Weigh accurately 2g of the powder, moisten with aqua ammonia, stopper for 15 min, and add 30.0ml of chloroform, weigh, macerate cold for a week, weigh again and make up the loss. Take it as solution A.

(2) Assay of hyoscyamine: Apply accurately 3 ~ 5ml of the solution A, evaporate to dryness, proceed as what has been described under "preparation of standard curve B", beginning with the words "add 2.0ml of 0.4% bromocresol green pH 6.6 BS", measure the absorbance, read out the corresponding content (μg/ml) in the standard curve B [the slope of the standard curve is 2.57 (absorbance/mg)], then convert it to the quality percent in the sample.

(3) Assay of the total alkaloids: Apply 3 ~ 5ml of solution A accurately, evaporate to dryness, add 6.0ml of distilled water, proceed as described under 'preparation of standard curve A', beginning with the words 'add respectively 2.0ml of 0.4% bromocresol green BC', measure the absorbance, then read out the value (μg/ml) of the content of the total alkaloids, change to the content of the total alkaloids, then minus from the content of

hyoscyamine, we can get the content of hyoscine.

$$\text{Content}\% = R \cdot D/w \cdot 100\%$$

where: R – the consistency of the alkaloid read out from the standard curve

D – the diluting times

w – the weight of sample

Experiment record

1. Outline the procedure of the experiment and note the problems that appears.

2. The unit of R takes μg/ml, w takes g, set out the calculating simple formula of hyoscyamine and total alkaloids.

3. Calculate the content of hyoscyamine, hyoscine and total alkaloids.

4. Draw the thin layer chromatogram of identification and calculate R_f value of hyoscyamine and hyoscine.

Question

1. Will the content determined be higher or lower then, if the chloroform layer and water layer can't mix fully? Why?

2. Why do we determine the color of the dye that has been released in assay the total alkaloids? And what about to determine the color of the complex?

第二章 含黄酮类中药的质量分析

实验七 紫外分光光度法测定槐米中芦丁的含量

【实验原理】

本实验选用紫外分光光度法，即样品通过聚酰胺柱后，先水洗，然后用甲醇洗脱，在360nm或276nm处测定吸收度，这是鉴于黄酮类化合物常有较明显的紫外吸收，可用紫外分光光度法进行测定。

【定性实验方法】

1．颜色反应

取样品粉末0.1g加乙醇10ml，置水浴上加热5分钟，过滤，取滤液1ml，加盐酸2~3滴，再加镁粉少许，即显樱红色。

2．点滴反应

在滤纸上点一滴样品溶液，加一滴试剂（含有1%盐酸的0.5%对二甲氨基苯甲醛乙醇溶液，斑点直径为3mm，置于100℃烤箱1分钟，芦丁即显黄色。

3．薄层层析

槐花样品的甲醇提取液点于0.8% CMCNa－硅胶G薄层板上，用乙酸乙酯－甲酸－水（10:2:3）展开15cm后，喷0.1M三氯化铝甲醇溶液，芦丁的 R_f 值约为0.60，在紫外光下观察荧光。

【含量测定】

1．条件

(1) 仪器：751型或7520型紫外分光光度计、恒温水浴、三用紫外分析仪、索氏提取器、小层析柱、圆底烧瓶、容量瓶、漏斗、吸量管。

(2) 试剂：芦丁对照品，层析用聚酰胺粉（40~80目）、甲醇、石油醚、蒸馏水。

(3) 用品：滤纸，脱脂棉。

2．标准曲线的制备 精密称取芦丁（120℃干燥至恒重）5.00mg，至于100ml容量瓶中，加甲醇定容，摇匀，精密吸取1.0，2.0，3.0，4.0，5.0ml分别置于10ml容量瓶中，加甲醇稀释至刻度，摇匀，以甲醇为空白对照，于360nm处测定吸收度，并绘出标准曲线。

3．样品测定 将槐米干燥粉碎，称取药材细粉1.2~1.4g，置于索氏提取器中，加石油醚60ml，回流至无色，放冷，弃去醚液；取出脱脂药粉，置蒸发皿上，挥去溶剂至干，精密称取该药粉1g，置带塞三角瓶中，精密加入甲醇50ml，称重；冷浸24小时，用甲醇补足原重，过滤，取续滤液2.0ml置50ml容量瓶中，用甲醇稀释至刻度，再吸取该稀释液1.0ml置10ml容量瓶中，加甲醇至刻度，以甲醇为空白对照，于751型分光光度计上，进行紫外分光测定，测定波长360nm，由标准曲线计算出含量。

计算公式：

$$生药中芦丁的含量\% = A/w \times 100\%$$

其中：A——由标准曲线中查得的样品相当于芦丁的微克数；

w——样品液中相当于生药的微克数。

【实验记录】

1. 定性实验记录，绘制薄层层析图谱。
2. 绘制芦丁的标准曲线图。
3. 计算槐米中芦丁的含量。

【思考题】

1. 为什么要取续滤液作为测定溶液？否则对测定结果有何影响？
2. 样品测定项下加石油醚回流的目的是什么？

【相关资料】

1. 槐（花）米的化学成分

槐（花）米为豆科（Leguminosae）植物槐 *Sophora japonica* L. 的干燥花及花蕾。主含芦丁（芸香苷、rutin，quercetin-3-O-rutinonile），约占28%，其苷元为槲皮素（quercetin）；并含有桦皮醇（betulin）、槐二醇（sophoradiol）、槐花米甲~丙素（sophorin A，B，C）等。

中国药典规定本品含芦丁，槐花不得少于8.0%，槐米不得少于20.0%（用高效液相色谱法）；另规定醇浸出物（30%甲醇）槐花不得少于37%，槐米不得少于43%。

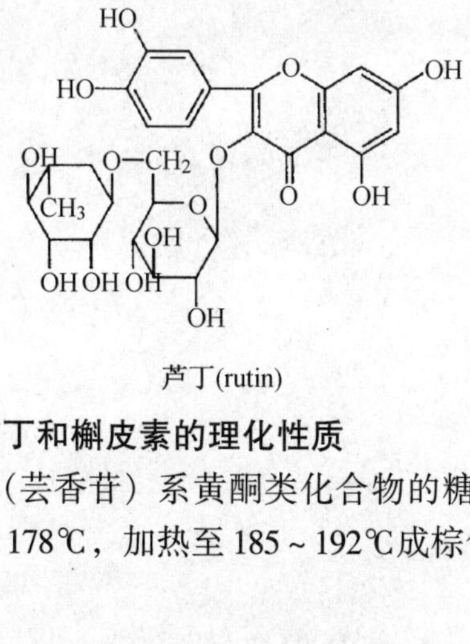

芦丁(rutin)

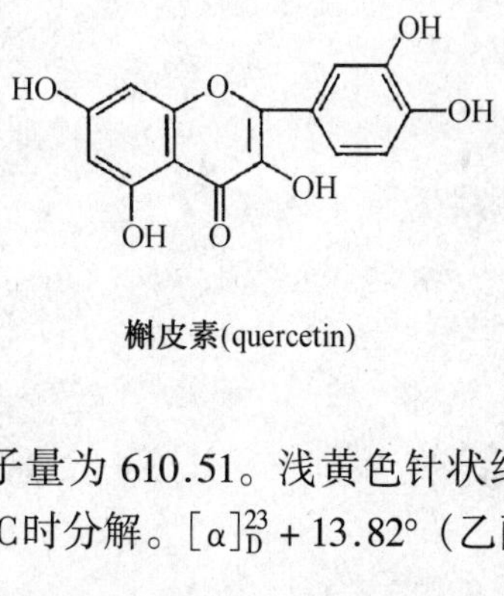

槲皮素(quercetin)

2. 芦丁和槲皮素的理化性质

芦丁（芸香苷）系黄酮类化合物的糖苷，分子量为610.51。浅黄色针状结晶（水），熔点176~178℃，加热至185~192℃成棕色，215℃时分解。$[\alpha]_D^{23}+13.82°$（乙醇）。1g溶于 7ml 甲醇、8000ml 水、200ml 沸水。UVλ_{Max}^{MeOH}nm（lgε）：258，361。在 2%稀酸下水解得苷元槲皮素。

槲皮素分子量为 302.23。二水合物为黄色针状结晶（稀乙醇），在 95 ~ 97℃成为无水物，熔点 314℃（分解）。1g 溶于 290ml 无水乙醇、23ml 沸乙醇，溶于冰醋酸，碱性水溶液呈黄色，几乎不溶于水。UVλ_{Max}^{MeOH}nm（lgε）：258（2.75），375（2.75）。

7 Determination of Rutin in Flos Sophorate Immaturus By Ultraviolet Spectrophotometry

Principle

This experiment uses the method of ultraviolet spectrophotometry. After the sample is passed through the column of polyamide and elute first with water and then with methanol. The absorbance is measured at 360nm or 276nm at these wavelengths flavones have a strong ultraviolet absorption.

Qualitative analysis (Identification)

1. Color reaction

To 0.1g of the powder add 10ml of ethanol, heat for 5 minutes on a water bath and filter. To 1ml of the filtrate, add 2 ~ 3 drops of hydrochloric acid followed by a small quantity of magnesium powder, the solution takes on a cherry red color.

2. Drop reaction

Drip a drop of the test solution on a piece filter paper, add a drop of the reagent (0.5% solution of *p* – dimethylaminobenzaldehyde in ethanol containing 1% solution of hydrochloric acid). Place the paper in an oven (100℃) for 1 minute, a yellow color is produced.

3. Thin layer chromatography

Carry out the thin layer chromatography, using silica gel G containing 0.8% of CMC – Na as the coating substance and acetate – formic acid – water (10:2:3) as the mobile phase. Apply separately the test solution and the reference solution and develop up to 15 cm. Dry the plate in air and spray with 0.1 M aluminium chloride in methanol. The R_f value of rutin is about 0.6. Examine under ultra – violet light (365nm), the fluorescent spot in the chromatogram obtained with the test solution corresponds in position and color to the spot in the chromatogram obtained with the reference solution.

Procedure

1. Apparatus: ultraviolet spectrophotometer (9100), three – purpose ultraviolet analyzer, constant temperature bath, Soxhlet's extractor, a small chromatographic column, round – bottom flask, volumetric flask, funnel, measuring pipette, evaporating dish.

2. Reagents: Rutin CRS, chromatographic grade polyamide powder (40 ~ 80 mesh), methanol, petroleum ether, distilled water, filter paper, absorbent cotton.

3. Preparation of standard curve

Weigh accurately 5.00mg of rutin (previously dried in vacuum to constant weight at 120℃) into a 100ml volumetric flask, add methanol to the mark. Mix well. Measure accurately 1.0, 2.0, 3.0, 4.0, 5.0ml of the solution into 10ml volumetric flasks separately, dilute with methanol to the mark and mix well Using methanol as the blank, measure the absorbance at 360nm and plot the standard curve.

4. Assay

Weigh 1.2 ~ 1.4g of the sample powder into a Soxhlet's extractor, add 60ml ether and heat under reflux until the extract is colorless. Allow it to cool and discard the ether solvent. Place the defatted powder on an evaporating dish and dry it in air. Weigh accurately 1 g of the powder into a stopper conical flask; carefully add 50ml of methanol and weigh. Macerate for 24 hours; replenish the lost of the solvent with methanol and filter. Dilute 2.0ml of the successive filtrate to 50ml with methanol. Transfer accurately 1.0ml of the above solution to a 10ml volumetric flask, add methanol to the mark. Using methanol as the blank solution, measure the absorbance at 360nm by spectrophotometer (751) and calculate the percentage content of $C_{27}H_{30}O_{16}$ from the standard curve.

The following equation can be used to calculate the percentage content of rutin in Flos Sophorate immaturus

The percentage content of rutin in crude drug = A/W × 100%

A – weight (μg) of rutin in the test solution from the standard curve

w – weight (μg) of crude drug in the test solution

Experiment record

1. Record the qualitative tests and draw the TLC chromatogram.
2. Plot the standard curve of rutin
3. Calculate the percentage content of rutin in Flos Sophorate immaturus

Question

1. Why do we use successive filtrate as the test solution? What the results would be if not?
2. What is the purpose of refluxing with petroleum ether?

实验八　薄层扫描法测定槐米中芦丁及槲皮素的含量

【实验原理】

本实验选用双波长薄层扫描法，将对照品与样品通过薄层展开后，紫外灯下斑点定位，再扫描测定含量。

【含量测定】

1．条件

(1) 仪器：双波长扫描仪（岛津 CS－930 或 CS－9000 型）；容量瓶；索氏提取器；微量进样器；紫外灯；展开缸。

(2) 试剂：芦丁及槲皮素对照品；硅胶 GF254；甲醇；乙酸乙酯；甲酸；苯；蒸馏水；

2．薄板制备　取硅胶 GF254 加水调匀，铺成 20×20cm 薄板，晾干后置于烘箱 105～110℃活化 30 分钟，贮于干燥器中备用。

3．展开系统　芦丁用乙酸乙酯－甲酸－水（5∶1∶2 上层）；槲皮素用乙酸乙酯：甲酸－水－苯（7∶1∶1∶7 上层）。

4．对照品溶液配制　取芦丁和槲皮素对照品各约 10mg，在 60℃恒重 2 小时后，精密称定，用甲醇定容于 10ml 容量瓶中。

5．样品溶液的制备　称取槐米粗粉约 1g，精密称定。加甲醇适量，冷浸过夜。用索氏提取器回流至无色，回收甲醇，将浓缩液用甲醇定容于 25ml 容量瓶中。

6．扫描条件　芦丁 $\lambda_s = 370nm$，$\lambda_R = 450nm$；槲皮素 $\lambda_s = 380nm$，$\lambda_R = 500nm$，扫描方式为反射法、锯齿扫描，扫描速度 20mm/min，光束狭缝 1.25×1.25mm，灵敏度×1，纸速 20mm/min，线性 CH_1，散射参数 Sx = 7。

7．定量法　用微量进样器取一定量样品和对照品溶液，并列点于薄层板上，用展开剂展开 10cm，取出挥去溶剂，紫外灯下定位后进行薄层扫描，分别计算样品中芦丁和槲皮素含量。

【实验记录】

1．简述实验过程。

2．绘制芦丁及槲皮素的薄层层析图谱。

3．绘制芦丁及槲皮素的标准曲线图，并计算回归方程。

4．计算槐米中芦丁及槲皮素的含量。

【思考题】

1．进行薄层扫描测定时，透射法和反射法的优缺点各有哪些？

2．薄层法含量测定中，对点样量有何要求？为什么？

8 Determination of the Contents of Rutin and Quercetin in Flos Sophorae immaturus by TLCS

Principle

Dual wavelength thin layer chromatogram scanning is used. First, develop the reference sample and test sample by TLC, then locate the spots in thin layer plate under UV light, last determine the content by scanning.

Procedure

1. Requirement

(1) Apparatus: Dual – wavelength TLC scanning (shimadzuCS – 930 or CS – 9000); volumetric flask; Soxhlet's extractor; microsyringe; ultraviolet light; developing tank.

(2) Reagents: rutin and quercetin CRS; silica gel GF254; methanol; ethyl acetate; formic acid; benzene; distilled water.

2. Preparation of thin layer plate

To silica gel GF254, add some distilled water and mix well, pour the mixture on some 20 × 20cm thin layer plates and spread it. Allow the plate to dry at room temperature, then heat at 105 ~ 110℃ for 30 minutes in oven, store them desiccator for use.

3. Developing system

Ethyl acetate – formic acid – aqua (5:1:2 upper layer) for rutin;

Ethyl acetate – formic acid – aqua – benzene (7:1:1:7 upper layer) for quercetin.

4. Preparation of reference solution

Weigh about 10mg rutin and quercetin CRS, respectively, dry to constant under 60℃ for 2 hours, then weigh accurately, dissolve in methanol and transfer into a 10ml volumetric flask, add methanol to volume.

5. Preparation of test solution

Take 1g Flos Sophorae immaturus powder, weigh accurately, add some methanol and macerate overnight. Reflux in Soxhlet's extractor until colorless, reclaim methanol. Transfer the concentrated liquid to a 25ml volumetric flask, add methanol to volume.

6. Scanning requirement

Rutin λ_s = 370nm, λ_R = 450nm; quercetin λ_s = 380nm, λ_R = 500nm; Reflective and zigzag scanning is used as scanning patterns.

Scanning speed 20mm/min; light – beam slit1.25 × 1.25mm; sensitivity × 1;

Paper speed 20mm/min; linear CH_1; scattering parameter Sx = 7.

7. Quantitative analysis

Apply some test solution and reference solution by microsyringe to thin layer plate, develop to 10cm with mobile phase. Remove the plate and volatilize the solvent, thin layer scanning is processed after locating the spots under UV light, calculate the contents of rutin and quercetin respectively.

Experiment record

1. Describe the process of this experiment briefly.
2. Draw thin layer chromatogram of rutin and quercetin.
3. Plot standard curve of rutin and quercetin and calculate the regression equations.
4. Calculate the content of rutin and quercetin respectively.

Question

1. What are the advantages and disadvantages of transmission and reflection, respectively, in using thin layer chromatography scanning?

2. What is the requirement to applying sample volume in quantification by thin layer method? Why?

实验九　高效液相色谱法测定槐米中槲皮素的含量

【实验原理】

本实验选用高效液相色谱法，以槲皮素对照品进样，作标准曲线，在与对照品相同保留时间处确定样品中槲皮素的峰位置，并测定其峰面积，计算含量。

【条件】

（1）仪器：高效液相色谱仪；超声仪；反相柱；容量瓶；微量进样器；具塞试管；离心机；漏斗；吸量管。

（2）试剂：甲醇；冰乙酸；95%乙醇；槲皮素对照品；槐米。

（3）用品：滤纸。

（4）色谱条件：YWG C_{18}反相柱（4.6mm×150mm），粒径 10μm，流动相为甲醇－水－冰乙酸（45:46:9），流速 1.0ml/min，检测器灵敏度 0.05AUFS，柱温 30℃，纸速 5min/cm。进样量 10μl。

【含量测定】

1．标准曲线的制备　精密称取槲皮素对照品约 2mg，置 10ml 容量瓶中，加入 95%乙醇溶液并稀释至刻度（贮备液）。分别吸取贮备液 100，200，400，600，800μl 置 1ml 容量瓶中，加入 95%乙醇稀释至刻度，摇匀，分别进样 10μl。取 3 次峰面积的平均值，对峰面积和对照品浓度关系用最小二乘法作线性回归，得回归方程。并计算相关系数和线性范围。

2．样品测定　精密称取槐米粉末约 0.10g，平行 2 份，置 10ml 具塞试管中，精密加入 95%乙醇 5ml，用超声波提取法提取 30min，离心 20min（3500r/min），过滤，准确吸取滤液 10μl 进样。将槐米在 4.95min 左右的色谱峰与对照品色谱峰相对照，确认为槲皮素。并记录样品峰中槲皮素峰面积值，由回归方程计算样品中槲皮素的含量。

【实验记录】

1．简述实验过程。

2．绘制槲皮素的标准曲线图，并计算回归方程。

3．计算槐米中槲皮素的含量。

【思考题】

1．在本实验中，用超声波提取法提取槲皮素，与其他提取方法相比，本法有哪些优点？

2．试根据有关文献，选择适用于槲皮素和芦丁的流动相。

9 Determination of Content of Quercetin in Flos Sophorae immaturus by HPLC

Principle

The method of HPLC is used in this experiment, inject the quercetin reference sample and make a standard curve, locate the peak of quercetin test sample at the point with the retain time of sample, assay the peak area and calculate the content.

Requirement

1. Apparatus: high - performance liquid chromatogram; ultrasonic wave instrument; reversed - phase column; volumetric flask; microsyringe; stopper tube; centrifuger; funnel; measuring pipet.

2. Reagents: methanol; glacial acetic acid; 95% ethanol; quercetin CRS.

Material: filter paper

3. Chromatographic system:

YWG C_{18} reversed - phase column (4.6mm × 150mm), particle size 10μm, mobile phase is methanol - aqua - glacial acetic acid (45:46:9), flow rate 1.0ml/min, sensitivity of detector is 0.05AUFS, column temperature 30℃, injection volume 10μl.

Prcedure

1. Preperation of standard curve

Weigh 2g of quercetin CRS accurately, into a 10ml volumetric flask, add some 95% ethanol to volume (store up solution). Mcasure accurately 100, 200, 400, 600, 800μL of the store solution respectively to 1ml volumetric flask, add 95% ethanol to volume, mix well, inject 10μl into chromatograph, respectively, make 3 times peak area average value. Make linear regression to the peak area and concentration of reference sample by the method of minimum squares and get regression equation, calculate correlation coefficient and linear range.

2. Assay

Weigh the powdered Flos Sophorae 0.10g accurately, the same process with another share, to a 10ml stopper tube, add 95% ethanol 5ml accurately, ultrasonic distill for 30 minutes, centrifuge for 20 minutes (3500r/min), filter, measure filtrate 10μl accurately and inject. Contract the peak at 4.95min of Flos Sophorae powder has a peak at 4.95min correspond with quercetin CRS, and ensure it is quercetin, record the peak area value of quercetin in the sample peaks, calculate the content of quercetin in the sample with regression equation.

Experiment record

1. Describe the process of this experiment briefly.

2. Plot standard curve of quercetin, and calculate the regression equation.

3. Calculate the content of quercetin in Flos Sophorae.

Question

1. In this experiment, ultrasonication is used to extract quercetin, compared to other extraction method, what is the advantage of ultrasonication?

2. Select mobile phase applicable for quercetin and rutin according to documents.

实验十　高效液相色谱法测定银杏中黄酮类成分的含量

【实验原理】

银杏黄酮主要是以黄酮苷的形式存在，经酸水解后生成黄酮醇类化合物，其主要是槲皮素、山柰素、异鼠李素三种组分，本实验用高效液相色谱法测定其含量，再换算成总黄酮醇苷的含量。

【含量测定】

1．条件

（1）仪器：高效液相色谱仪、泵、紫外检测器、微量进样器、索氏提取器。

（2）试药：槲皮素对照品 、山柰酚对照品、异鼠李素对照品、银杏叶粉末。

（3）试剂：甲醇－0.4%磷酸溶液（50:50）、甲醇、氯仿、甲醇－25%盐酸溶液（4:1）。

（4）实验条件与系统适应性试验：用十八烷基硅烷键合硅胶为填充剂；甲醇－0.4%磷酸溶液（50:50）为流动相；检测波长为360nm，理论板数按槲皮素峰计算应不低于2500。

2．实验方法

（1）对照品溶液的制备：分别精密称取经五氧化二磷干燥过夜的槲皮素、山柰酚、异鼠李素对照品，各加甲醇制成每1ml分别含0.03mg、0.03mg、0.02mg的溶液，作为对照品溶液。

（2）供试品溶液的制备：取本品粗粉约1g，精密标定，置索氏提取器中，加氯仿回流，提取2小时，弃取氯仿，药渣挥干，加甲醇回流4小时，提取液蒸干，残渣加甲醇－25%盐酸溶液（4:1）混合液25ml，回流30分钟，放冷，转移至50ml量瓶中，并加甲醇至刻度，摇匀，即得。

（3）测定法：分别精密吸取上述三种对照品溶液与供试品溶液各10μl，注入液相色谱仪测定，分别计算三种黄酮甙元的含量，以下式换算成总黄酮的含量。

总黄酮甙含量＝（槲皮素含量＋山柰酚含量＋异鼠李素含量）×2.51

【实验记录】

1．简述实验过程。

2．绘制标准曲线图，并计算回归方程。

3．计算银杏中总黄酮苷的含量。

4．小结与讨论

【思考题】

1．换算因子2.51的含义是什么？

2．本实验中为什么使用酸性溶液作为流动相？

【相关资料】

1．银杏叶的化学成分

银杏叶为银杏科植物银杏 *Ginkgo biloba* L. 的干燥叶。含黄酮和内酯类成分，黄酮成分主要为双黄酮，如银杏双黄酮（ginkgetin）、异银杏双黄酮、去甲基银杏双黄酮及芸香苷等，苷元有槲皮素（quercetin）、山柰酚（kaempferol）、异鼠李素（isorhamnetin）。内酯类成分有银杏内酯（ginkgolide）A、B、C、E 等。

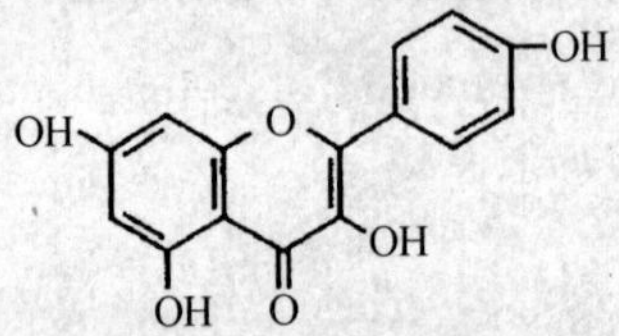

山柰酚(kaempferol)

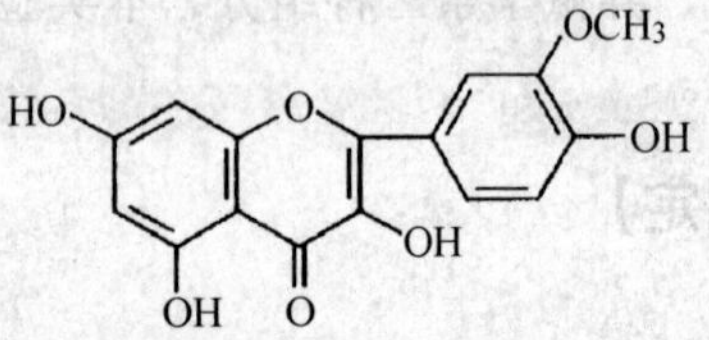

异鼠李素(isorhamnetin)

2．银杏黄酮类成分的理化性质

槲皮素见实验 7。

山柰酚分子量为 286.23。黄色针状结晶，熔点 276～278℃。微溶于水，溶于热乙醇、乙醚或碱。UV$\lambda_{max}^{CH_3OH}$nm（logε）：368（4.38），266（4.35）。二水合物为黄色针状结晶（稀乙醇），在 95～97 ℃成为无水物，熔点 314℃（分解）。1g 溶于 290ml 无水乙醇、23ml 沸乙醇，溶于冰醋酸，碱性水溶液呈黄色，几乎不溶于水。UVλ_{Max}^{EtOH}nm（lgε）：258（2.75），375（2.75）。

异鼠李素：分子量为 316.27。黄色针晶（稀甲醇），熔点 312℃（分解）。UVλ_{max}^{MeOH}nm：257，370。

10 Determination of Flavonoids In Folium Ginkgo by HPLC

Purpose

1. To master the principle and operation of HPLC through this experiment.

2. To be familiar with the use of HPLC in determination of components in traditional Chinese medicine.

Principle

The chemical substances contained in Folium Ginkgo were reported as flavone glycosides, which can produce flavonols by acid hydrolysis, such as quercetin, kaempferol and isorhamnetin. In this experiment, we determine the contents of these three substances by HPLC and convert to the content of total amount of flavonol glycosides.

Procedure

1. Apparatus and reagents

Agilentl100 HPLC (U. S. A) with Ultraviolet detector. Column: Zorbax C_{18}, Soxhlet's extractor, crude drug of Folium Ginkgo, quercetin, kaempferol and isorhamnetin CRS, methanol, phosphoric acid, hydrochloric acid, water.

2. Chromatographic system and system suitability

Use octadecylsilane bonded silica gel as the stationary phase and methanol – 0.4% phosphoric acid solution (50:50) as the mobile phase; flow rate: 1.0ml/min; detector wavelength: 360nm; column temperature is set at room tempcrature.

3. Preparation of reference solution

Weigh accurately quercetin CRS, kaempferol CRS and isorhamnetin CRS, previously dried overnight over phosphorious pentoxide, add methanol to produce three solutions containing 0.03mg, 0.03mg, 0.02mg per ml respectively as the reference solutions.

4. Preparation of test solution

Weigh accurately 1g of the coarse powder in a Soxhlet's extractor, add chloroform and heat under reflux for 2 hours. Discard the chloroform, evaporate the residue to dryness, add a quantity of methanol, heat under reflux for 4 hours, and evaporate the extract to dryness. Dissolve the residue in 25ml of a mixture of methanol – 25% hydrochloric acid (4:1), heat under reflux for 30 minutes, cool, transfer accurately to a 50ml volumetric flask. Add methanol to volume, mix well, filter it with filter membrane (particle size 0.45μm), and use the successive filtrate as the test solution.

5. Assay

Inject accurately 10μl each of the above three reference solutions and the test solution into chromatograph separately, and determine the contents of three flavonoids respectively. Calculate the content of total amount of flavonol glycosides using the following equation.

The content of total amount of flavone glycosides = (the content of quercetin + the content of kaempferol + the content of isorhamnetin) × 2.51.

Experiment record

1. Describe the processes of this experiment briefly.
2. Calculate the content of total amount of flavone glycosides in Folium Ginkgo.

Question

1. What is the meaning of the conversion factor 2.51?
2. Why do we use acid mobile phase in this experiment?

第三章　含皂苷类中药的质量分析

实验十一　薄层层析－比色法测定人参中总皂苷含量

【定量方法原理】

本实验采用薄层层析－比色法，测定人参总皂苷的含量，即选择适当的薄层条件，将人参总皂苷适当集中，并与糖加以分离，然后将总皂苷斑点刮下，加入香草醛－冰醋酸与高氯酸，使之显色。

【含量测定】

1．条件

（1）仪器：9100 型分光光度计、索氏提取器、恒温水浴、层析用玻璃板、具塞磨口试管、碘缸、微量注射器、小漏斗。

（2）试剂：层析用硅胶、羧甲基纤维素钠、甲醇、石油醚、氯仿、香草醛、冰醋酸、高氯酸、蒸馏水、人参二醇对照品。

（3）用品：小刀、滤纸、脱脂棉、硫酸纸（样品纸）。

2．标准曲线的绘制　取人参二醇约 5mg，精密称定，置于 2ml 容量瓶中，加甲醇溶解并稀释至刻度，精密吸取 5、10、20、25μl，置于磨口具塞试管中，用加热风吹去溶剂（勿使过热），加入 5% 香草醛－冰醋酸溶液（新配制）0.2ml、高氯酸溶液 0.8ml，置恒温水浴中，60℃加热 15 分钟后，冷却，加冰醋酸 5ml 摇匀，于波长 560nm 处进行比色测定，绘制出对照品吸收度的标准曲线。

3．样品测定

（1）样品制备：将干燥人参根粉碎（过 40 目筛），精密称取药粉 1g，于索氏提取器中，先加石油醚 30ml 脱脂，挥干石油醚，加入 40ml 甲醇，回流提取 4 小时，回收甲醇至干，将提取物残渣仔细转移至 1ml 容量瓶中，容器用少量甲醇洗涤，洗液合并，精密稀释至刻度。

（2）总皂苷的测定：用微量注射器吸取上述样品溶液 10～20μl，在硅胶薄层板上点成条状，用氯仿－甲醇－水（70∶55∶10）展开 5cm，取出板挥尽溶剂，置碘缸中数秒，待色点刚显出，立即取出，划出斑点位置，用冷风将碘吹尽，刮取斑点，置于 10ml 具塞磨口试管中，精密加入 5% 香草醛－冰醋酸溶液 0.2ml 与高氯酸 0.8ml 混匀，密塞置 60℃水浴中加热 15 分钟，冷却，精密加入冰醋酸 5ml，摇匀、离心，取上清液于 560nm 处测定，同时取与色斑同样大小的空白硅胶，以上法显色，作为空白对照。测得的吸收度自标准曲线查得相当于人参二醇（A）微克数。

计算公式：

$$生药中总皂苷\% = A \times 2.5 \times 100/w$$

其中：w——点样量相当于生药的微克数；

2.5——R_b组皂苷平均分子量与人参二醇分子量之比。

【实验记录】

1. 记录定性试验结果，绘制薄层层析图谱。
2. 绘制定量层析图谱。
3. 绘制人参二醇的标准曲线图。
4. 计算人参中人参总皂苷的含量。

【思考题】

1. (2) 和 (3) 项下，最后加冰醋酸 5ml 的目的是什么？
2. 用薄层层析－比色法测定人参中总皂苷的含量的优缺点？

【相关资料】

1. 人参的化学成分

人参系五加科植物人参 *Panax ginsenge* A. Mey 的干燥根。含有多种人参皂苷，系三萜皂苷，多数为达玛烷型皂苷，其中有人参皂苷（ginsennosides）R_{b1}、R_{b2}、R_e、R_{g1}、R_{g2}等；少数为齐墩果酸型（C 型）皂苷，如人参皂苷 R_o。由于苷元不同，达玛烷型皂苷又分为 20S－原人参二醇类皂苷（A 型）和 20S－原人参三醇类皂苷（B 型）。其中 A 型和 B 型皂苷水解后，分别得到人参二醇（panaxadiol）和人参三醇（panaxatriol）。另外还有挥发油，人参多糖，氨基酸等化合物。

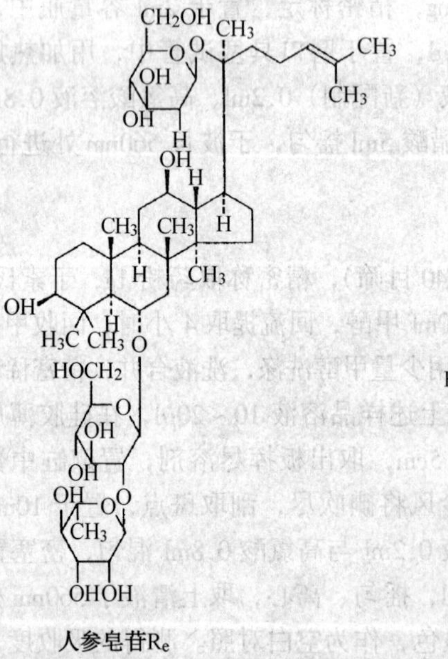

人参皂苷R_e

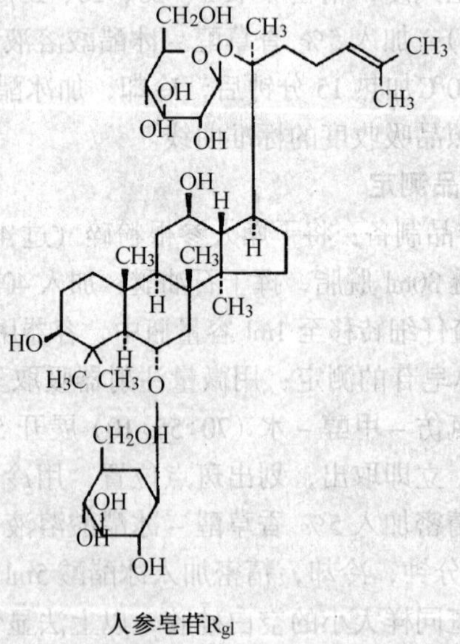

人参皂苷R_{g1}

中华人民共和国药典（2000 年版）规定本品含人参皂苷 R_{g1}和人参皂苷 R_e 的总量不得少于 0.25%（用高效液相色谱法）。

2. 人参皂苷的理化性质

大多为白色无定形粉末或无色针晶，味微甘苦，易溶于水、甲醇、乙醇，可溶于正丁醇、醋酸乙酯、不溶于乙醚、苯。仅在紫外光区的末端有吸收（C 型皂苷除外）。

人参皂苷 R_{g1}分子量为 830.03。无色半结晶物（正丁醇 – 甲基乙基酮），熔点 194 ~ 196.5℃，$[\alpha]_D^{19.5}+32°$（吡啶）。溶于甲醇、吡啶及热丙酮，稍溶于醋酸乙酯、氯仿。

人参皂苷 R_e 分子量为 947.12。无色针状结晶（50%乙醇），熔点 201 ~ 203℃，$[\alpha]_D^{30}0$ 至 – 1.00°（C = 1.00，甲醇）。

11 Determination of Total Ginsenosides in Radix Ginseng By TLC – UV Spectrophotometry

Principle

In this experiment, we determine the content of total ginsenoside in Radix ginseng by thin – layer chromatogram and UV spectrophotometry. We select the suitable conditions of thin – layer chromatogram, concentrate total ginsenoside and separate saccharides from it, scrape the spot of total ginsenoside, add vanillin – glacial acetic acid and perchloric acid to it, colorize it.

Requirement

1. **Apparatus** 9100 spectrophotometer, Soxhlet's extractor, water bath, chromatographic glass plate, stopper tube, Iodine bottle, filter

2. **Reagents** silica gel for chromatography, CMC – Na, methanol, petroleum ether, chloroform, vanillin, glacial acetic acid, perchloric acid, distilled water, panaxadiol CRS

3. **Materials** knife, filter paper, absorbent cotton, cellophane paper

Procedure

1. Preparation of standard curve

Weigh accurately 5mg of panaxadiol to 20ml volumetric flask, add methanol to dissolve it and dilute to volume, transfer accurately 5, 10, 20, 25 μl of reference solution to stopper tubes respectively. Evaporate solvent by warm air (not too hot), add 0.2ml of 5% vanillin – glacial acetic acid and 0.8ml of perchloric acid, and mix well. Warm on a water bath at 60°C for 15 minutes, take out and cool it, add 5ml of glacial acetic acid, mix well. Measure the absorbance at 560 nm, and plot the standard curve of.

2. Preparation of test solution

Weigh accurately 1g of powdered dried Radix ginseng 40 mesh to a Soxhlet's extractor. Add 30ml of petroleum ether for degreasing. Evaporate petroleum ether, add 40ml of methanol and heat under reflux on a water bath for about 4 hours. Reclaim methanol and carefully transfer the residue to 1ml volumetric flask, wash the bottle with a little of methanol and transfer it to flask, dilute to volume.

Using chloroform – methanol – water (70:55:10) as the mobile phase, apply 10 ~ 20μl of test solution in stripe to the silica gel plate, develop to 5 cm and dry it. Put the plate into Iodine vat for several seconds, take it out and mark the spot. Evaporate Iodine with cool air, scrape off the spot and transfer it to a 10ml stopper tube. Accurately add 5% vanillin – glacial acetic acid and 0.8ml of perchloric acid, mix well, centrifugation, take solution at the top of layers, carry out spectrophotometry, measure the absorbance at 560nm. Scrape off equal area of silica gel as a blank, treat it in the same manner too. According to the standard curve, absorbance can be got.

Calculation formula:

$$\text{The content of the total gensenoside (\%)} = A \times 2.5 \times 100/w$$

Where, w——weight of Radix genseng (μg)

2.5——the ratio between the average molecular weight of gensenoxside in R_b group and molecular weight of panaxadiol

Experiment record

1. Record the identification of Radix genseng and draw the thin layer chromatogram.
2. Draw the quantitative chromatogram.
3. Plot the standard curve of total gensenosides.
4. Calculate the content of total ginsenosides in Radix ginseng.

Question

1. In item 2 and 3, why should we add 5ml of glacial acetic acid into solution?
2. What are advantages and disadvantages of determining total ginsenoside in Radix ginseng by thin – layer chromatography and spectrophotometry.

实验十二　高效液相色谱法测定人参中单体皂苷含量

【实验原理】

本实验采用高效液相色谱法，分别以人参皂甙 R_{g1}、人参皂甙 R_e 作为对照品，测定人参中皂甙 R_{g1}、人参皂甙 R_e 的含量。

【含量测定】

1．条件

（1）仪器：Agolent 1100 高效液相色谱仪、泵、紫外检测器、微量进样器、超声仪、索氏提取器

（2）试药：人参皂甙 R_{g1} 对照品、人参皂甙 R_e 对照品、人参药材粉末（过四号筛）

（3）试剂：甲醇、氯仿、正丁醇、乙腈－0.05%磷酸溶液（99:400）

2．色谱条件与系统适应性试验： 用十八烷基硅烷键合硅胶为填充剂；乙腈－0.05%磷酸溶液（99:400）为流动相；检测波长为 203nm，理论塔板数按人参皂甙 R_e 峰计算应不低于 2500。

3．对照品溶液的制备： 精密称取人参皂甙 R_{g1} 对照品 12.5mg、人参皂甙 R_e 对照品 10mg，加甲醇分别制成每 1ml 含人参皂甙 R_{g1}0.5mg、人参皂甙 R_e0.4mg 的溶液即得。

4．供试品溶液的制备： 取本品粉末（过四号筛）1g，精密称定，置索氏提取器中，加氯仿 40ml，加热回流 3 小时，弃取氯仿液，药渣挥去氯仿，连同滤纸筒移入具塞锥形瓶中，精密加入水饱和的正丁醇 50ml，密塞，放置过夜，超声处理（功率 250W，频率 50kHz）30 分钟，滤过，精密量取续滤液 25ml，置蒸发皿中蒸干，残渣加甲醇溶解并转移至 5ml 量瓶中，甲醇至刻度，摇匀，即得。

5．测定法： 分别精密吸取上述两种对照品溶液各 10μl 与供试品溶液 10～20μl，注入液相色谱仪测定，即得。

【实验记录】

1．记录实验结果。

2．分别计算人参中人参皂甙 R_{g1}、人参皂甙 R_e 的含量。

【思考题】

1．本实验应注意什么?

2．流动相中为什么用乙腈，用甲醇可以吗?

12 Determination of Ginsenosides in Radix Ginseng by HPLC

Principle

The content of ginsenoside R_{g1} and ginsenoside R_e in Radix Ginseng are determined by the method of HPLC.

Procedure

1. Apparatus and Reagents

Agilentl100 HPLC (U. S. A) with Ultraviolet detector. Column: Zorbax C_{18}, Soxhlet's extractor, ultrasonic cleaner, crude drug of Radix Ginseng (through No.4 sieve), ginsenoside R_{g1} CRS and ginsenoside R_e CRS, methanol, phosphoric acid, chloroform, acetonitrile, water.

2. Chromatographic system and system suitability

Use octadecylsilane bonded silica gel as the stationary phase and acetonitrile – 0.05% phosphonic acid (99:400) as the mobile phase. The wavelength of the detector is 203nm. The number of theoretical plates of the column is not less than 2500, calculated with the reference to the peak of ginsenosides R_e.

3. Preparation of reference solution

Weigh accurately 12.5mg of ginsenoside R_{g1} CRS and 10mg of ginsenosides R_e CRS respectively, dissolve in methanol to produce two solutions separately containing 0.5mg of ginsenoside R_{g1} per ml and 0.4mg of ginsenosides R_e per ml.

4. Preparation of test solution

Place 1g of the powder (through No. 4 sieve), weigh accurately, into a Soxhlet's extractor, add 40ml of chloroform, heat under reflux on a water bath for 3 hours, discard the chloroform solution, expel the chloroform in the residue. Transfer the residue with the filter paper tube into a stopper conical flask, accurately add 50ml of *n* – butanol saturated with water, tightly stoppered, allow to stood over night, ultrasonic shake for 30 minutes (power 250w, frequency 50kHz) and filter. Measure accurately 25ml of the successive filtrate, evaporate to dryness in an evaporating dish. Dissolve the residue in methanol and transfer to a 5ml volumetric flask, dilute to volume and mix well, filter it with filter membrane (particle size 0.45um), and used the successive filtrate as the test solution.

5. Accurately inject 10μl of each of the two reference solutions and 10 ~ 20μl of the test

solution, into the column separately, determine and calculate the contents.

Experiment record

1. Record the results of this experiment.
2. Calculate the content of ginsenoside R_{g1} and ginsenoside R_e in Radix Ginseng.

Question

1. What should we pay attention to in this experiment?
2. We use acetonitrile – 0.05% phosphonic acid (99:400) as the mobile phase, can we use methanol in behalf of acetonitrile?

实验十三　直接薄层比色–光密度法测定穿山龙中薯蓣皂苷元的含量

【定量方法实验原理】

本实验采用薄层色谱–扫描法，因薯蓣皂苷元系甾体皂苷元，没有明显的紫外吸收，且无颜色，故在薄层层析后，加显色剂（磷钼酸）显色后采用可见光区的波长进行薄层扫描。

【含量测定】

1．条件

（1）仪器：岛津 CS–930 型双波长薄层扫描仪，索氏提取器，恒温水浴、电炉、圆底烧瓶、冷凝管、层析用玻璃，微量注射器、玻璃板。

（2）试剂：薯蓣皂苷元对照品，层析用硅胶，羧甲基纤维素钠、盐酸、石油醚、氯仿、丙酮、磷钼酸、乙醇。

（3）用品：pH 试纸，滤纸、脱脂棉。

2．薄层层析及薄层扫描条件

（1）薄层层析：吸附剂为 0.8% CMCNa–硅胶 G，薄层板 110℃ 活化 1 小时，展开剂为氯仿–丙酮（9:1），展距 15 cm，显色剂为 4% 磷钼酸乙醇液，在 105 ℃ 加热 15 分钟。

（2）薄层扫描：$\lambda_S = 595$nm，$\lambda_R = 480$nm，狭缝 1.25×1.25mm，锯齿形扫描 Sx = 3。

3．标准曲线的制备　精密称取 1mg 薯蓣皂苷元对照品，置于 1ml 容量瓶中，加氯仿溶解，并稀释至刻度，吸取标准液 1.0，2.0，3.0，4.0，5.0ul 点于薄层板上，按上述薄层条件展开 15cm，取出挥尽溶剂，喷洒 4% 磷钼酸溶液，于 105℃加热 15 分钟，显色，在薄层扫描仪上测定，计算对照品的面积值，绘制标准曲线。

4．样品测定　将穿山龙或粉萆薢根茎晒干切碎，精密称取 1g，放入圆底烧瓶中，加入 2M 盐酸 10ml，电炉上加热水解 2 小时，吸滤，用水洗至中性，残渣在 80℃烘干，然后装入滤纸筒中，于索氏提取器中，加石油醚（60～90℃）30ml，回流提取 5 小时，提取液回收石油醚至干，残留物用氯仿溶解并转移至 10ml 容量瓶中，用氯仿定容至刻度，供薄层点样用，吸取样品液 10μl，点于薄层板上，并同时点对照品溶液 6μl。按上述同法展开，4%磷钼酸乙醇显色，经扫描测量积分值，用对比法计算样品液中薯蓣皂苷元的量，并换算出药材中的百分含量。

【实验记录】

1．记录定性试验结果，绘制薄层层析图谱。

2．绘制薯蓣皂苷元的标准曲线图。

3．计算穿山龙中薯蓣皂苷元的含量。

【思考题】

1．薄层扫描法测定中药中化学成分的优势及不足之处？

2．利用本法测定薯蓣皂甙元的含量应在那些步骤中特别注意？

【相关资料】

1．穿山龙的化学成分

穿山龙系薯蓣科植物穿山薯蓣 *Dioscorea nipponica* Makino 的根茎，主要含薯蓣皂苷（dioscin）及其水解产物，水解可得薯蓣皂苷元（diosgenin），另外含有甾醇，尿囊素等。

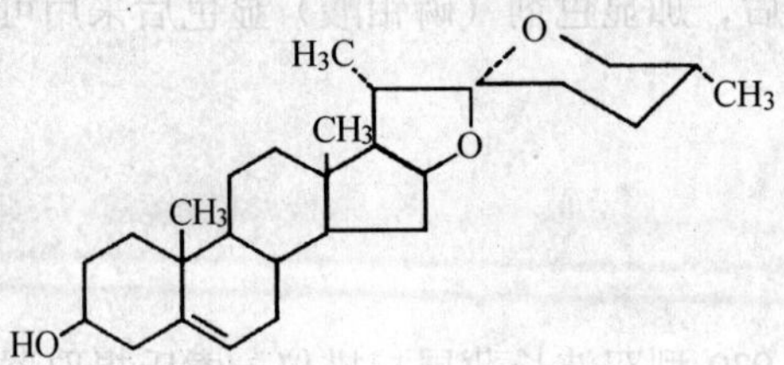

薯蓣皂苷元(diosgenin)

2．薯蓣皂苷和薯蓣皂苷元的理化性质

薯蓣皂苷为白色针状结晶，分子量 869.08，分解点为 275～277℃，$[\alpha]_D^{30}$ –115°（C＝0.373，乙醇）。

薯蓣皂苷元为白色针状结晶，分子量 414.61，熔点 204～207℃，能溶于常用有机溶媒、醋酸。

13 Determination of the Content of Diosgenin in Rhizoma Dioscoreae Nipponicae by Direct TLC. Colorimetry – photic Densitomety

Principle

Being a kind of steroids, Diosgenin has no obvious ultraviolet absorbance and color, so we choose thin – layer chromatography scanning. After TLC and adding colorant (phosphomolybdic acid), it will take on color and can be scan under visible light.

Requirement

1. **Apparatus** ShimadzuCS – 930 type dual wave length scanner, Soxhlet extractor, constant – temperature water bath, electric cooker, round – bottom flask, condensing tube, chromatographic glass, microsyringe, glass plate.

2. **Reagents** DiosgeninCRS, chromatographic silica gel, carboxymethyl – cellulose sodium, petroleum – ether, chloroform, acetone, phosphomolybdic acid, alcohol.

3. **Materias** pH test paper, filter paper, absorbent cotton.

4. **TLC and scanning conditions**

TLC: CMC – Na and silica gel, TLC plate should be activated for 1 hour. Mobile phase: chloroform – acetone (9 : 1), developing distance: 15cm, colorant (4% alcohol phosphomolybdic acid), heat at 105℃ for 5 minute.

TLC scanning: $\lambda_S = 595$nm, $\lambda_R = 480$nm, slit1.25 × 1.25mm, serrated scanning Sx = 3

Procedure

1. **Preparation of standard curve**

Dissolve 1g of diosgenin CRS, accurately weighed, with chloroform in a 1ml volumetric flask and dilute to volume. Apply separately 1.0, 2.0, 3.0, 4.0, 5.0ul of the solution, after developing and removal of the olate, dry it in air, spray with 4% phosphomolybdic acid in alcohol, heat it at 105℃for 5 minutes until visualizing clearly, scan it, calculate the area of the reference, and the standard curve is obtained.

2. **Assay**

Cut dried Rhizoma Dioscoreae Nipponicae into pieces, add 1g accurately in a flask containing 10ml of 2N hydrochloride, heat and hydrolysis it for 2 hours in electric stove, filter, wash it with water until pH7, dry the residue at 80℃, put it into a filter paper cylinder in a

Soxhlet extractor add 30ml petroleum ether (60 ~ 90℃), extract it for 5 hours under reflux. Dry the solvent, dissolve the residue with chloroform and transfer the solution to 10ml volumetric flask and dilute it to volume with chloroform. Apply 10ul of solution and 6μl of solution of reference sample. Develop the plate as above, color it, scan and examine the value of integration, the amount of Diosgenin is obtained by calculating under the contrast method, after conversion, you will know contains in the medicina.

Experiment record

1. Record the result of qualitative experiment, and draw the graph of TLC.
2. Prepare the standard curve of Diosgenin
3. Calculate the amount of Diosgenin in rhizoma dioscoreae nipponicae.

Question

1. what are the advantages and disadvantages of TCL scanning used in the component analysis of Chinese traditional medicine?
2. Which procedure should be paid more attention to?

第四章　含醌类成分中药的质量分析

实验十四　比色法测定大黄中有效成分的总量

【目的要求】

掌握羟基蒽醌苷类及游离羟基蒽醌的性质，通过本次实验了解大黄类药材中有效成分的含量测定方法。

【原理】

有色物质的溶液对不同波长的入射光线有不同程度的吸收，这是物质的性质。溶液颜色的深浅往往是溶液浓度高低的标志，而颜色的深浅与对一定波长光的吸收度有关。因此，可以通过比较溶液对被吸收光的吸收度来测定溶液中物质的含量。

【条件】

仪器：分光光度计，移液管，容量瓶，锥形瓶，量筒。

试剂：$NaHCO_3$，10% $FeCl_3$，浓盐酸，氯仿，0.5% 醋酸镁甲醇溶液。

对照品溶液及标准曲线：精密称取 1,8－二羟基蒽醌 2.5mg 于 25ml 容量瓶中，加氯仿溶解并加至刻度，精密吸取对照品溶液 0.5，1，2，3，4ml，分别置于 25ml 容量瓶中，蒸去氯仿，加 0.5%醋酸镁甲醇溶液至刻度，摇匀。以甲醇为空白，在 515nm 处测定，以吸收度为纵坐标，浓度（μg/ml）为横坐标，绘图。

【样品的定性及定量分析】

1．定性分析

取本品粉末 0.1g，加水 50ml，置于水浴上加热 30 分钟，滤过，滤液中加盐酸 2 滴，用乙醚提取 2 次，每次 20ml，除去乙醚层，水层加盐酸 5ml，置水浴中加热 30 分钟。冷后，再用乙醚 20ml 提取，分取乙醚层，加碳酸氢钠试液 10ml，振摇，水层显红色。

2．定量分析

精密称取药材粉 0.1g，置 100ml 烧瓶中，精密加入水 25ml，称定重量。置水浴中回流加热 15 分钟，放冷，称定重量，用水补足至原重量，加碳酸氢钠 50mg，摇匀，静置后用干燥滤纸滤过，弃去初滤液，精密吸取续滤液 10ml，置 100ml 具塞烧瓶中，加 10% $FeCl_3$ 溶液 20ml，水浴回流 20 分钟，加 HCl 1ml，继续回流 30 分钟，放冷，加入氯仿 25ml，盖好瓶盖，用力振摇，转移至 125ml 分液漏斗中，使分层，分取氯仿层，再用 25ml 氯仿

（洗涤烧瓶后）萃取一次，分取氯仿层与上次合并，并用水洗涤二次，每次用水 15ml，将氯仿层用干燥滤纸滤过于 100ml 容量瓶中，用氯仿洗涤滤纸，洗液合并于容量瓶中，用氯仿稀释至刻度，摇匀。精密吸取 10ml 氯仿提取液，置 25ml 具塞烧瓶中，蒸去氯仿，放冷，精密加入 0.5% 醋酸镁甲醇溶液 10ml。摇匀，以甲醇为空白，在 515nm 处测定吸收值，由标准曲线计算含量。

【实验记录】

1．绘标准曲线图。
2．计算大黄中结合蒽醌和游离大黄酸的总含量。

【思考题】

1．加水提取的是何类成分，加入 10% $FeCl_3$ 的目的是什么？
2．加入浓盐酸的目的是什么？
3．用比色法测定蒽醌类成分应注意什么？

【相关资料】

1．大黄的化学成分

大黄为蓼科大黄属植物掌叶大黄 *Rheum palmatum* L.、药用大黄 *R．officinale* Baill 或唐古特大黄 *R．tanguticum* Maxim et Regel 的根茎。含蒽醌（anthraguinone）类化合物，包括游离及结合状态的大黄酚（chrysophanol）、大黄酸（rhein）、芦荟大黄素（aloeemodin）、大黄素（emodin）、大黄素甲醚（physcion）及番泻苷（sennoside）A、B、C、D。

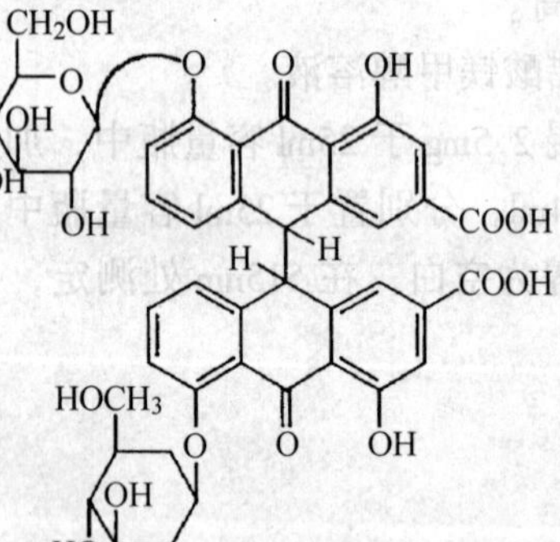

番泻苷(sennoside A)

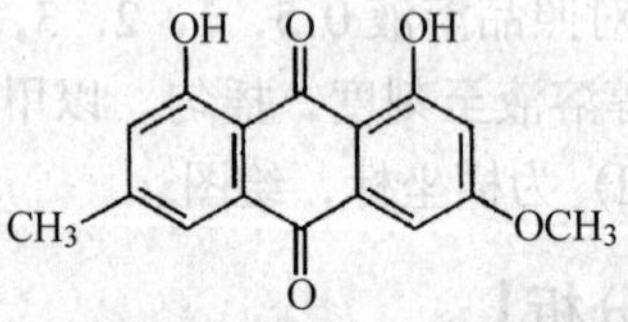

大黄素甲醚(physcion)

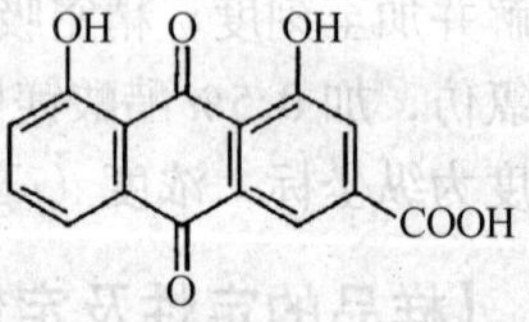

大黄酸(rhein)

2．蒽醌类化合物的理化性质

大黄酸的分子量为 284.21。黄色针状结晶，熔点 321 ~ 322℃。$UV\lambda_{Max}^{MeOH}$nm：229、258、435。几乎不溶于水，溶于碱液，略溶于乙醇、苯、氯仿、乙醚和石油醚。

大黄素甲醚分子量为 284.26。砖红色单斜针状结晶，熔点 203 ~ 207℃。$UV\lambda_{Max}^{MeOH}$nm：266、255、267、288、440。不溶于甲醇、乙醇、乙醚和丙酮，溶于碱液、苯、氯仿、甲苯。

番泻苷 A 的分子量为 862.72。黄色长方形片状结晶（稀丙酮），熔点 200 ~ 240℃（焦化分解）。不溶于苯、乙醚和氯仿，略溶于甲醇、丙酮和二氧六环，溶于碳酸氢钠水溶液。

14 Determination of the Total Content of Effective Components in Radix et Rhizoma Rhei by Colorimetric Method

Purpose

Master the properties of hydroxyanthraquinone glycosides and free hydroxyanthraquinone. Comprehenol the assay method of effective components in Radix et Rhizoma Rhei through the experiment.

Principle

Solution of colored substance can absorb beam of different wavelength in different degree, which is a quality of substance. The solution's color is always the sign of the solution's concentration, while the colour is relevant to the absorbance at a definite wavelength. For the reason, we can determinate the content of substance in solution by the means of comparing the absorbency of the solution.

Condition

1. Apparatus spectrophotometer, pipette, volumetric flask, conical flask, graduated cylinder.

2. Reagent $NaHCO_3$, 10% $FeCl_3$, concentrated hydrochloric acid, chloroform, 0.5% magnesium acetate in methanol.

Procedure

1. Preparation of reference solution and standard curve

Weigh accurately 2.5ml of 1,8 – dihydroxy – anthraquinone to a 25ml volumetric flask, dissolve in chloroform, and dilute to the volume. Transfer accurately 0.5, 1, 2, 3, 4ml of the reference solution to 25ml volumetric flasks respectively, evaporate the chloroform, dilute with 0.5% magnesium acetate in methanol to volume, and mix well. Use methanol as the blank, measure the absorbance at 515nm, and prepare the standard curve with the absorbance as ordinate and the concentration (μg/ml) as abscissa.

2. Qualitative and quantitative analysis of the sample

Qualitative analysis

To 0.1g of the powder, add 50ml of water, heat on a water bath for 30 minutes, and filter. To the filtrate add 2 drops of hydrochloric acid, extract with tow 20ml quantities of ether, discard the ether extracts, add 5ml of hydrochloric acid to the combined water solutions, and heat on a water bath for 30 minutes. Allow to cool, extract with 20ml of ether again, separate the ether layer, add 10ml of sodium bicarbonate TS, shake, a red colour is produced in the water layer.

Quantitative analysis:

Weigh accurately 0.1g of the powder to a 100ml conical flask, accurately add 25ml of water and weigh, heat under reflux on a water bath for 15 minutes, allow to cool, weigh again, replenish the loss of the solvent with water, add 50mg of sodium bicarbonate, mix well, and allow to stand, filter through a piece of dry filter paper, discard the initial filtrate, transfer accurately 10ml of the successive filtrate to a 100ml stopper conical flask, add 20ml 10% ferric chloride solution, heat under reflux on a water bath for 20 minutes, add 1ml of hydrochloric acid, continue to heat under reflux for 30 minutes, allow to cool, add 25ml of chloroform, tightly stopper and shake vigorously, transfer to a 125ml separating funnel, allow to stand, separate the chloroform layer, extract with 25ml of chloroform (wash the flask with it first) again, separate the chloroform layer. Wash the combined chloroform extracts with two 15ml quantities of water. Filter the chloroform solution through a piece of dry filter paper to a 100ml volumetric flask, wash the filter paper with chloroform to the same flask, dilute with chloroform to volume, and mix well. Transfer accurately 10ml of the chloroform solution to a 25ml stopper conical flask, evaporate the chloroform, allow cool, add accurately 10ml of 0.5% solution of magnesium acetate in methanol, and mix well. Using methanol as the blank, measure the absorbance at 515nm. Calculate the content by the standard curve.

Experiment record

1. Plot the standard curve of reference solution.

2. Calculate the total content of combined anthraquinone and free rhein in the Radix et Rhizoma Rhei (Dahuang)

Question

1. What's component extracted by water? What's the purpose of adding 10% $FeCl_3$?

2. What's the purpose of adding concentrated hydrochloric acid?

3. Which procedure should we pay more attention to in determining anthraquinones using colorimetric method?

实验十五　比色法测定紫草中总萘醌的含量

【目的要求】

了解萘醌成分的性质，掌握紫草的定性，定量原理及操作。

【原理】

紫草素类成分为脂溶性色素（为脂类化合物）。在室温下，1% NaOH 溶液可使其分解为紫草素和相应的酸，并显蓝紫色，于 610nm 处有最大吸收，故可用分光光度法测定。

【条件】

仪器：分光光度计，沙氏提取器；容量瓶，移液管；圆底烧瓶，回收装置。

试剂：1% NaOH、苯或石油醚。

对照品溶液及标准曲线：

精密称取紫草素 20mg，置 500ml 容量瓶内，加 1% NaOH 试液溶解，并稀释至刻度。

精密吸取 1.0，2.0，3.0，4.0，5.0ml 分别置 10ml 容量瓶内，加 1% NaOH 试液稀释至刻度，以 1% NaOH 试液为空白对照液，于 610nm 处测吸收度，绘吸收度－浓度的曲线。

【样品的定性及定量分析】

1．定性分析

取紫草粉末约 0.1g，加苯 2ml，振摇后滤过，滤液为鲜红色透明溶液，加入等体积的 95% 乙醇，混匀，加 NaOH 试液 2 滴后，立即变成蓝色溶液。

2．定量分析

精密称取紫草药材粉末 1.00g，于沙氏提取器中，加适量苯或石油醚，浸提至无色为止。提取液回收溶剂至干，残渣用 1% NaOH 试液转溶于 100ml 容量瓶内，并稀释至刻度，混匀，过滤，取续滤液 1.0ml，于 10ml 容量瓶内，以 1% NaOH 试液稀释至刻度，测吸收度，于标准曲线上查得其含量。

【实验记录】

1．绘标准曲线图。

2．计算紫草中紫草素的含量。

【思考题】

1．比色法测定紫草中紫草素类成分的优势是什么？

2．如某一中药制剂中含有紫草，如何排除其他干扰成分对紫草素类成分含量测定的影响？

【相关资料】

1. 紫草的化学成分

紫草为紫草科植物新疆紫草 *Arnebia euchroma*（Royle）Johnst、内蒙紫草 *A. guttata* Bunge 或紫草 *Lithospermum erythrorhizon* Sieb. et Zucc. 的干燥根，前二者称“软紫草”，后者称“硬紫草”。紫草含有的多种萘醌类色素，是其有效成分。紫草素（shikonin）为紫草素类的母体，多结合成酯而存在。硬紫草根中主要成分为乙酰紫草素（acetylshikonin），软紫草根中含量最多的为 β,β′－二甲基丙烯酰紫草素（β,β′－dimethylacrylshikonin）。

中华人民共和国药典（2000 年版）规定本品含羟基萘醌总色素以左旋紫草素计，不得少于 0.80%（用分光光度法）。

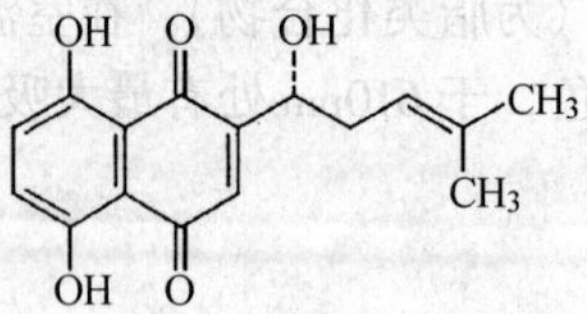

紫草素(shikonin)

2. 紫草素的理化性质

紫草素的分子量为 288.31。紫色片状结晶或结晶粉末，熔点 147～149℃，$[\alpha]_D^{20}+138°$（苯）。不溶于水，溶于醇、有机溶剂和植物油。UV$\lambda_{Max}^{CCl_4}$nm（ε）：560（5012），543（5012），524（7943），488（6310）。

15 Colorimetric Assay of the Total Naphthoquinone Content in Radix Arnebiae (or Radix Lithospermi)

Purpose

To comprehend the properties of naphthoquinone and master the principle and operation of qualitative and quantitative assay of Radix Arnebiae (or Radix Lithospermi).

Principle

The shikonin is lip souble pigment (a kind of lipid). At room temperature, it can be decomposed into shikonin and corresponding acid in 1% NaOH. Since the products appear bluish violet and have the maximum absorbance at 610nm, it can be assayed by spectrophotometry

Conditions

1. Apparatus spectrophotometer, Soxhlet's extractor; volumetric flask, pipette; round bottom flask, reclaimed apparatus.

2. Reagent 1% NaOH, benzene or petroleum ether

3. Reference solution and standard curve

Weight accurately 20mg of the shikonin to 500ml volumetric flask, dissolve with 1% sodium hydroxide solution and dilute to volumes. Measure accurately 1.0, 2.0, 3.0, 4.0, 5.0ml of the solution respectively, separately to 10ml volumetric flasks, dilute with 1% sodium hydroxide to volumes and mix well, use 1% sodium hydroxide solution as blank. Measure the absorbance at 610nm and plot the curve of absorbance to concentration

Assay

1. Qualitative assay

Shake about 0.1g of the Radix Arnebiae (or Radix Lithospermi) powder with 2ml of benzene, stir and filter. The filter is red transparent solution. Add the equal volume of 95% ethanol to the filtrate and mix well, after add 2 drops of sodium hydroxide solution, a blue color is produced immediately.

2. Quantitative assay

Weigh accurately 1.00g of the Radix Arnebiae powder to Soxhlet's extractor, add benzene or petroleum ether properly and extract until the solution appear colorless. Evaporate the extraction to dry. Dissolve the residue with 1% sodium hydroxide solution and transfer to 100ml volumetric flask and dilute to volume, mix well, and filter. Measure 1.0ml of the filtrate to 10ml volumetric flask, dilute with 1% sodium hydroxide solution to volume, measure the absorbance and look up the content in the standard curve.

Experiment record

1. Plot the standard curve.
2. Calculate the content of shikonin in Radix Arnebiae (or Radix Lithospermi).

Question

1. What is the advantage of colormetric assay of shikonin in Radix Arnebiae (or Radix Lithospermi).
2. If one kind of Chinese traditional medicinal preparation contains Radix Arnebiae (or Radix Lithospermi), how to eliminate the influence of interfering components in the quantitative assay of shikonin.

实验十六　紫外分光光度法测定丹参中总丹参酮的含量

【目的要求】

了解菲醌化合物的性质，掌握紫外分光光度法测定中药有效成分的原理及操作。

【原理】

丹参中相对含量最高的丹参酮ⅡA的最大吸收波长与总丹参酮的最大吸收波长一致，在268nm处，因此可以丹参酮ⅡA为对照，测定总丹参酮的含量。

【条件】

仪器：751G型紫外-可见分光光度计；移液管；容量瓶；小层析柱。

试剂：氯仿。

对照品溶液及标准曲线：精密称取丹参酮ⅡA 2mg，置25ml容量瓶中，加氯仿溶解并稀释至刻度，分别吸取0.1，0.2，0.4，0.6，0.8，1.2ml置10ml容量瓶中，加氯仿稀释至刻度，于268nm处测定吸收值，绘制吸收度-浓度标准曲线。

【样品的定性及定量分析】

1. 定性分析

(1) 取样品少许，加浓硫酸2滴，丹参酮Ⅱ显绿色，隐丹参酮显棕色，丹参酮Ⅰ显蓝色。

(2) 取丹参细粉约20mg，加氯仿约5ml浸泡片刻，过滤，吸取滤液约50μl，隐丹参酮和丹参酮ⅡA对照品溶液（1mg/ml）各20μl，并点成带状于硅胶G薄层（盐酸处理的200目青岛海洋化工厂硅胶4.5g加石膏0.5g，加0.5%碳酸钾溶液13ml，混匀，铺板，105℃活化30分钟）上，用苯-甲醇（9:1）展开，薄层上的红黄色带为隐丹参酮，紫红色带为丹参酮ⅡA。

2. 含量测定

精密称取生药粉末（40目）100mg，置小层析柱中，用氯仿洗脱，洗脱液以25ml容量瓶接收，定容，适当稀释后于268nm处测定吸收值，利用标准曲线或回归方程计算含量。

【实验记录】

1. 绘制定性薄层图，计算隐丹参酮及丹参酮ⅡA斑点的 R_f 值。
2. 绘制标准曲线图，计算回归方程。
3. 计算丹参中总丹参酮的含量。

【思考题】

1. 用盐酸处理硅胶的目的是什么？
2. 简述丹参中脂溶性成分与水溶性成分的药理作用及含量测定方法。

【相关资料】

1. 丹参的化学成分

丹参为唇形科鼠尾草属植物丹参 *Salvia miltiorrhiza* Bunge 的干燥根，含酮类和酚类成分，脂溶性酮类成分有丹参酮ⅡA（tanshinone ⅡA）、隐丹参酮（cryptotanshinone）、丹参酮Ⅰ（tanshinone Ⅰ），丹参新酮（miltirone）；水溶性酚类成分有原儿茶醛（protocatechuic aldehyde）、丹参素（danshensu）、丹参酚酸 B（salvianolic acid B）等。

中华人民共和国药典（2000 年版）规定本品含丹参酮ⅡA 不得少于 0.20%（用高效液相色谱法）。

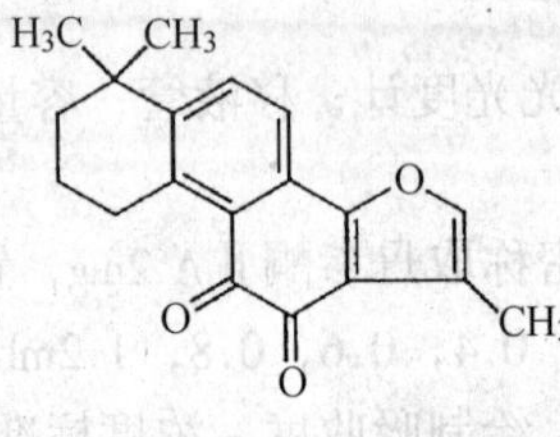

丹参酮ⅡA(tanshinone ⅡA)

2. 丹参酮ⅡA 的理化性质

丹参酮ⅡA 分子量为 294.33。樱红色针状结晶（甲醇），熔点 209～210℃。不溶于水，溶于醇或其他有机溶剂。$UV\lambda_{Max}^{EtOH}$ nm（lgε）：224（4.24），250（4.37），268（4.51），273，352（394），455（3.25）。

16 Ultraviolet Spectrophotometric Assay of Total Tanshinone Content in Radix Salviae Miltiorrhizae

Purpose

Comprehend the quality of phenanthrenequinone, master the principle and operation of the ultraviolet spectrophotometry in the assay of Chinese traditional medical components.

Principle

The maximum absorption wavelength of tanshinone Ⅱ A, the relatively highest content component in Radix Salviae Miltiorrhizae, is the same as the total tanshinone at 268nm. So the total tanshinone content can be assayed with tanshinone Ⅱ A as the reference.

Condition

Apparatus: 751 G ultraviolet spectrophotometer ; pipette; volumetric flask; small chromatographic column.

Reagent: chloroform

Assay

1. Reference solution and standard curve

Weigh accurately 2mg of tanshinone Ⅱ A to 25ml volumetric flask, dissolve with chloroform and dilute to volumes. Measure accurately 0.1, 0.2, 0.4, 0.6, 0.8, 1.2ml of the solution respectively, separately to 10ml volumetric flasks, dilute with chloroform to volumes and mix well. Measure the absorbancy of the solutions at 268nm and portray the curve of absorbance to consistency.

2. Qualitative assay

To the three samples respectively, separately add 2 drops of concentrated sulfuric acid, a green color is produced for tanshinone Ⅱ A, a brown color for cryptotanshinone and a blue color for tanshinone.

To about 20mg of tanshinone powder, add about 5ml of chloroform, immerse for a while and filter. Use silica gel G as the coating substance (4.5g of 200 – mesh silica gel, produced by Qingdao Ocean Chemical Factory and dealt with hydrochloric acid, add 0.5g of plaster and 13ml of 0.5% potash solution, mix well, and spread the slurry on the glass plate, activated under 105℃ for 30minnutes and a mixture of benzene – methanol (9:1) as the mobile phase. Apply separately to the plate 5μl of the filtrate, 20μl of the cryptotanshinone solution and 20μl of the tanshinone Ⅱ A solution (1mg per ml). After developing and removal of the plate, dry it in air. A red – yellow spot in the chromatogram obtained with the test solution corresponds in position and color to the spot in the chromatogram obtained with the cryptotanshinone reference solution. And a violet – red spot in the chromatogram obtained with the test solution corresponds in position and color to the spot in the chromatogram obtained with the cryptotanshinone reference solution.

3. Procedure

Weigh accurately 100mg of the powder to small type chromatographic column, elute with chloroform to 25ml volumetric flask, dilute to volume. After dilute properly, measure the absorbance at 268nm, calculate the content with standard curve or regression equation.

Experiment record

1. Draw the chromatogram of thin layer chromatography, calculate the R_f value of cryptotanshinone and tanshinone Ⅱ A.

2. Plot the standard curve, and calculate regression equation.

3. Calculate the total tanshinone content in Radix Salviae Miltiorrhizae.

Question

1. What is the purpose of dealing with silica gel by hydrochloric acid?

2. Describe precisely about the pharmacological function and method of liposoluble and water – soluble component in Radix Salviae Miltiorrhizae.

第五章　含其他类成分中药的质量分析

实验十七　气相色谱法测定薄荷中薄荷醇的含量

【目的、要求】

了解气相色谱仪的操作，掌握内标法测定样品含量的计算。

【原理】

用二氯甲烷将薄荷醇提取出来，加入一定量内标物质，再用气相色谱法分析。

【仪器、药品】

气相色谱仪：岛津 GC－RIA 型，联岛津 GC Processor RPR－G1 型，色谱柱：5% Carbowax－20M，3mm×2M，微量注射器：1μl，色谱对照品癸醇－1（decanol），含量大于 99%（上海试剂一厂）；二氯甲烷，四氯化碳。

【样品的定性及定量分析】

（一）定性分析

取薄荷粉末 5～10g，置 500ml 蒸馏瓶中，加水 150～200ml，用直火（小火）蒸馏收集馏出液约 100ml，用乙醚 50ml 提取，将乙醚提取液移至蒸发皿中，任乙醚自然挥发，取出薄荷油约 30mg，加氯仿 10ml 溶解，取此液 5～10μl 点于硅胶 G 薄层上，用苯－丙酮（9:1）或正已烷－乙酸乙酯（8:2）展开，喷以 2%香草醛硫酸溶液，然后置于 110℃烤 2 分钟，薄荷醇斑点呈玫瑰红色。

（二）定量分析

实验溶液的配制：精密称取药材粉末 2g，于索氏提取器中，用二氯甲烷在水浴上提取 3 小时，浓缩。定量转移至 10ml 容量瓶中，同时加入内标癸醇 3mg，用四氯化碳稀释至刻度，摇匀。用脱脂棉过滤，得澄清液，供测定用。

气相色谱条件：5% Carbowax－20M，101 白色担体 80－100 目，柱 2M×3mm，氢火焰离子化检测；检测器和气化室温度 150℃，柱温 85℃，氮气 30ml/min，氢气 57ml/min，空气 300ml/min；进样量 1μl 。薄荷醇对照品和内标的重量校正因子 fi/fs＝0.8778

$$\text{薄荷醇含量 } i\% = \frac{Ws \times fi\ Ai}{Wm \times fsAs} \times 100\%$$

Ws、Wm 为内标物和样品重量；As、Ai 为内标物和薄荷醇的峰面积。

【实验记录】

1．画出定性薄层图，计算薄荷醇 R_f 值。

2．详细写出计算公式，计算薄荷醇的含量。

【思考题】

1．气相色谱法测定薄荷醇含量的优缺点？

2．采用内标法计算含量的优点是什么？

【相关资料】

1．薄荷的化学成分

薄荷为唇形科植物薄荷 *Mentha haplocalyx* Briq 的干燥地上部分。含挥发油，油中主要含薄荷醇（menthol）、薄荷酮（menthone），另含胡薄荷酮（pulegone）、乙酸薄荷酯（menthyl acetate）、苯甲酸薄荷酯、乙酸癸酯（decyl acetate）等。

中华人民共和国药典（2000 年版）规定本品含挥发油不得少于 0.80%。

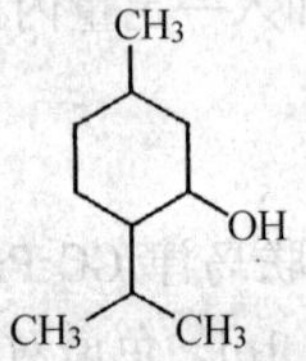

薄荷醇(menthol)

2．薄荷醇的理化性质

薄荷醇的分子量为 156.26。颗粒或结晶，有薄荷气味和味道，溶点 41～43℃，沸点 212℃，d 0.890。略溶于水，溶于乙醇、氯仿、乙醚和石油醚，易溶于冰醋酸。

17 Determination of Menthol in Herba Menthae by GC

Purpose

To comprehend the operation have the gas chromatography and master the calculation of percentage content of the sample by internal standard method.

Principle

Extract the menthol with dichloromethane, add an appropriate quality of internal standard substance, and then determine by gas chromatography.

Apparatus and Reagent

ShimadzuGC – 9A, Detector: FID; chromatogram; column: 5% Carbowax – 29M, 3mm × 2m; 1μl mycrosyringe; decanol – 1 (> 99%), dichloromethane, tetrachloride.

Qualitative and Quantitative analysis

1. Identification

Take 5 ~ 10g of the powder into a 500ml distillation flask, add 150 ~ 200ml waters, heat gently and distil. Collect 100ml distillate; extract with 50ml ether and transfer the extract to the evaporateol – plate. Dry it in air. Take 30mg bergamot oil, and dissolve with 10ml chloroform. Using silica gel G as the coating substance and a mixture of benzene – acetone (9:1) or *n* – Hexane – ethyl acetate (8:2) as the mobile phase. Apply to the plate 5 ~ 10μl of the test solution, after developing and removal of the plate, dry it in air and spray with a mixture of 2% w/v solution of vanillin in sulfuric acid. then heat at 110℃ for 2 minutes, The spot of methanol appears a rose – red color.

2. Assay

Preparation of test solution: Take 2g of the powder. Weigh accurately, to a Soxhlet's extractor, extract with dichloromethane for about 3 hours on a water bath, concentrate. Transfer accurately to a 10ml volumetric flask, add 3mg internal standard and dilute to the volume with the tetrachloride and mix well. Filter with absorbent cotton and use filtrate as the test solution.

GC systems: 5% Carbon – 20M, 101 white carrier 80 – type, 3mm × 2M, FID detector, monitor and gasification room temperature: 150℃, column tempreture: 85℃, Flow rate of nitrogen: 30mm/min, Hydrogen: 5ml/min; volume input: 1μl, menthanol reference and internal standard weight correct factor fi/fs = 0.8778

$$\text{Concentration of menthol (\%)} = \frac{Ws \times fiAi}{Wm \times fsAs} \times 100\%$$

Ws is weight of the internal standard substance;

Wm is weight of the sample;

As: peak area of the internal standard;

Ai: peak area of the sample.

Experiment record

1. Draw the TLC chromatogram and calculate the R_f value of the methanol.

2. Write the calculating formula in detail and calculate the content of methanol.

Question

1. What are the advantages and disadvantages of measuring the content of menthol by gas chromatography?

2. What's the advantage of using internal standard method to calculate the content?

实验十八　HPLC 法测定五味子中五味子醇甲的含量

【实验原理】

本实验以五味子醇甲作为对照品，采用高效液相色谱法测定了药材中五味子醇甲的含量，药典规定五味子中醇甲的含量不得少于0.4%。

【含量测定】

（一）条件

1．仪器：高效液相色谱仪、泵、数据处理机、紫外检测器、微量进样器、超声仪

2．试药：五味子醇甲对照品、五味子粉末（过三号筛）

3．试剂：甲醇－水（13:7）、甲醇

4．实验条件与系统适应性试验：用十八烷基硅烷键合硅胶为填充剂；甲醇－水（13:7）为流动相；检测波长为250nm，理论板数按五味子醇甲计算应不低于2000。

（二）实验方法

1．对照品溶液的制备：取五味子醇甲对照品15mg，精密称定，置50ml量瓶中，用甲醇溶解，并稀释至刻度，摇匀，即得（每ml含五味子醇甲0.3mg）。

2．供试品溶液的制备：取本品粉末（过三号筛）约0.25g，精密称定，置20ml量瓶中，加甲醇约18ml，超声处理（功率250W，频率20kHz）20分钟，取出，加甲醇至刻度，摇匀，滤过，即得。

3．测定法：分别精密吸取对照品溶液与供试品溶液各10ul，注入液相色谱仪测定，即得。

【实验记录】

1．记录实验结果，绘制标准曲线图。

2．计算五味子中醇甲的含量。

【思考题】

木酯素类成分的结构特点是什么？

【相关资料】

1．五味子的化学成分

五味子为木兰科植物五味子 *Schisandra chinensis*（Turcz.）Baill. 的干燥成熟果实。含多种木脂素类成分，其中有五味子醇甲（schizandrin）、五味子乙素（wuweizisu B）、五味子醇（schizandrol）、五味子酯甲和酯乙（schisantherinA，B）等。商品分1～2等。

中国药典规定本品含五味子醇甲不得少于0.40%（用高效液相色谱法）

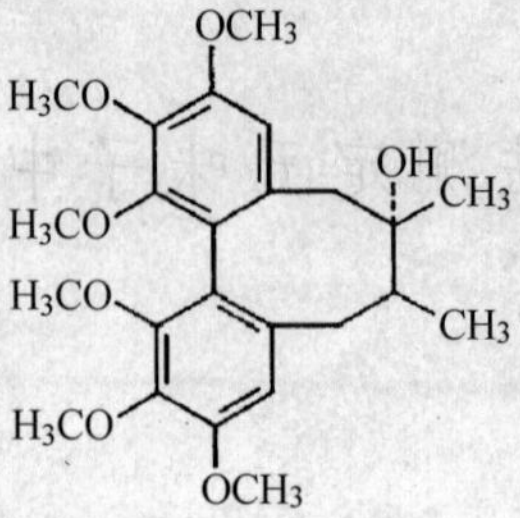

五味子醇甲(schizandrin)

2．五味子醇甲的理化性质

分子量432.50。结晶（乙醚－石油醚），熔点133℃，$[\alpha]_D^{26}$ + 78（C = 1，氯仿）。UVλ_{Max}^{MeOH}nm（lgε）：277（4.72），251（4.26），280（3.63）。

18 Determination of Schizandrol A in Fructus Schisandrae Chinensis by HPLC

Principle

The content of schizandrol A in Fructus Schisandrae Chinensis are determined by the method of HPLC. The Pharmacopoeia of the P. R. C. stipulated that the content of schizandrol A in Fructus Schisandrae Chinensis should be not less than 0.4%.

Apparatus and Reagent

Agilent 1100 HPLC (America) with Ultraviolet detector. Column: Zorbax C_{18}, ultrasonic cleaner, crude drugs of Fructus Schisandrae Chinensis (through No. 3 sieve), schizandrol A CRS, methanol, water.

Assay

1. Chromatographic system and system suitability

Use octadecylsilane bonded silica gel as the stationary phase and a mixture of methanol - water (65:35) as the mobile phase. The wavelength of the detector is 250nm. The number of theoretical plates of the column is not less than 2000, calculated with the reference to the peak of schizandrol A.

2. Preparation of reference solution

Weigh accurately 15mg of schizandrol A CRS in a 50ml volumetric flask, dissolve and dilute with methanol to volume, mix well and use as the reference solution. (Containing 1mg of schizandrol A per ml).

3. Preparation of test solution

Weigh accurately 0.25g of the powder (through No. 3 sieve) in a 20ml volumetric flask, add about 18ml of methanol, ultrasonic disposal for 20 minutes (power 250w, frequency 20kHz), take out, add methanol to volume, mix well and filter with filter membrane (particle size 0.45μm), use the successive filtrate as the test solution.

4. Procedure

Accurately inject 10μl of each of the reference solution and the test solution respectively into the column, determine and calculate the content.

Experiment record

1. Record the results of this experiment.

2. Calculate the content of schizandrol A in Fructus Schisandrae Chinensis.

Question

What is the structure characteristic of lignin?

实验十九　高效液相色谱法测定栀子药材中栀子苷的含量

【目的要求】

1．掌握高效液相色谱法的基本原理及操作步骤；

2．熟悉高效液相色谱法在中草药有效成分测定中的应用。

【实验原理】

高效液相色谱法是用高压输液泵将具不同极性的单一溶剂或不同比例的混合溶剂，缓冲液等流动相泵入装有固定相的色谱柱，经进样阀注入供试品，由流动相带入柱内，在柱内各组分被分离后，依次进入检测器，色谱信号由记录仪或积分仪记录。

所用的仪器为高效液相色谱仪。色谱柱的填充剂和流动相的组分应按待测组分的性质而定，常用的色谱柱填充剂有硅胶和化学键合硅胶，后者以十八烷基键合硅胶最为常用，辛基硅烷键合硅胶次之，氰基或氨基键合硅胶也有使用。除另有规定外，柱温为室温，检测器有紫外检测器，二极管阵列检测器，示差折光检测器等。

影响色谱分离效率有两大主要因素，其一为热力学因素如不同组分容量因子（K′），其二是动力学因素如色谱峰的展宽。反映这些物理过程的指标是保留时间和理论塔板数（n）。

其中　$K' = \frac{t_R - t_O}{t_O}$；$n = 5.54\left(\frac{t_R}{W_{1/2}}\right)^2$

密切注视和努力解决这两个因素引起的矛盾，组分间的分离就成功了，分离的表现指标是分离度（R）。

$$R = \frac{2\ (t_2 - t_1)}{W_{b_1} + W_{b_2}}$$

【仪器与试剂】

Agllent 1100 高效液相色谱仪，超声波清洗器，Zorbax C_{18}柱（4.6×250mm），栀子苷对照品，乙睛，甲醇，水。

【含量测定】

1．色谱条件　色谱柱：Zorbax C_{18}柱（4.6×250mm）；流动相：乙腈－水（15∶85）；检测波长：238nm，流速：1ml/min。

2．对照品溶液的制备和标准曲线的绘制　精密称取栀子苷对照品适量，加甲醇制成每 ml 含 100μg 的溶液，摇匀后，分别取该液 1，2，3，4，5ml，置 10ml 容量瓶中，加甲醇稀释至刻度，摇匀后，分别进样 10μl，按上述色谱条件测定，以峰面积为纵坐标，浓度为横坐标绘制标准曲线，计算回归方程和相关系数。

3．供试品溶液的制备　取本品粉末 0.1g，精密称定，置具塞锥形瓶中，精密加入甲醇 25ml，密塞，称定重量，超声处理 20mins。放冷，再称定重量，用甲醇补足减失的重量，摇匀，滤过。精密量取续滤液 10ml，置 25ml 容量瓶中，加甲醇至刻度，摇匀，过微孔滤膜，取续滤液，作为供试品溶液。

4．测定法　吸取供试品溶液 10μl 注入液相色谱仪，测定。由标准曲线法计算样品中栀子苷的含量（$C_{17}H_{24}O_{10}$）。

【实验记录】

1．扼要说明操作步骤及实验结果；

2．绘制标准曲线图，及回归方程，相关系数；

【思考题】

1．在仪器操作过程中，应重点注意哪些方面。

2．用 HPLC 法测定中药中有效成分的含量的主要优势是什么？

【相关资料】

1．栀子的化学成分

栀子为茜草科植物栀子 *Gardenia jasminoides* Ellis 的干燥成熟果实。含栀子苷（gardenoside）、栀子新苷（shanzhiside）、栀子酮苷（gardoside）、京尼平龙胆二糖苷（genipingentiobioside）、番红花苷（crocin）、熊果酸（ursolic acid）等。

中华人民共和国药典（2000 年版）规定本品含栀子苷不得少于 1.8%（用高效液相色谱法）。

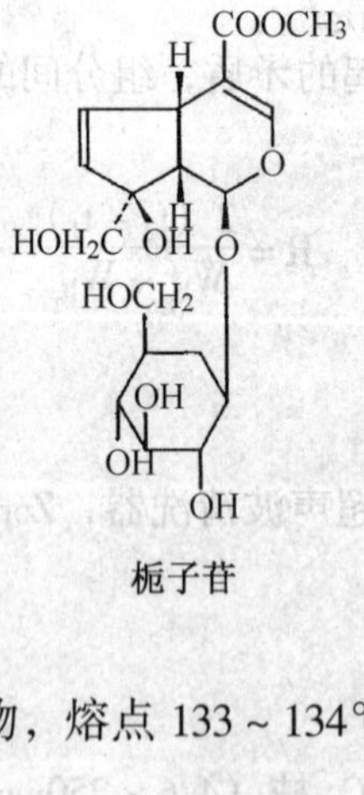

栀子苷

2．栀子苷的理化性质

栀子苷分子量为 404.36。粉状物，熔点 133～134℃。$[\alpha]_D-100.8°$（甲醇）。$UV\lambda_{Max}^{MeOH}$ nm（lgε）：237（4.01）。

19 Determination of Gardenoside in Fructus Gardeniae By HPLC

Purpose

1. Master the principles and operational method of HPLC through this experiment.

2. Be familiar with the use of HPLC in determination of components in traditional Chinese medicine.

Principle

In high performance liquid chromatogram, the mobile phase, a solvent or solvent mixture of suitable polarity (or a buffer solution of suitable ion strength) is pumped through injector. Column contains the stationary phase and detector. While the sample is injected into an injector and carried into the column by the mobile phase, the components are separated on the stationary phase and each components passes through the detector in succession and a chromatogram is thus record.

The stationary phase and the component part of the mobile phase should be in the accordance with the qualities of test sample. Silica gel and chemically bonded silica gel are commonly used as the packing. For chemically bonded silica gel, octadecylsilane type is most useful one, octylsilane type is also used, occationally cyano and amino group bonded silica gel are used. The column is maintained at room temperature, The kinds of detector have UV, DAD, SPDand so on.

There are two important factors responsible for chromatographic separation efficiency. One is thermodynamic factor, such as capacity factor of different components (K′), the other is dynamic factor, such as broadening width of the peak. The indexes to reflect these physical processes are retention time (t_R) and number of theoretical plates of column (n). Calculate the value of K′ and n as follows:

$$K' = \frac{(t_R - t_O)}{t_O}; \quad n = 5.54\left(\frac{t_R}{W_{1/2}}\right)^2$$

To pay close attention to and try to solve the contradictions caused by the above factors, the separation of different components will succeed. The term "resolution factor" is often used as a Index to express separation efficiency. Calculate the value of R as follows:

$$R = \frac{2\ (t_2 - t_1)}{(W_{b_1} + W_{b_2})}$$

Apparatus and Reagent

Agllent 1100 HPLC (America) with Ultraviolet detector. Column: Zorbax C_{18}, ultrasonicate cleaner crude drugs of Fructus gardeniae, gardenoside CRS, acetonitrile, methanol, water.

Assay

1. Chromatographic system

Use octadecylsilane bonded silica gel as the stationary phase and acetonitrile – water (15:85) as the mobile phase; flow rate: 1.0ml/min; The wave length of the detector is 238nm and the column temperature is set in room temperature.

2. Preparation of reference solution

Weigh accurately a quantity of gardenoside CRS, dissolve in methanol to produce a solution containing 100μg/ml, mix well, as the reference solution.

3. Preparation of standard curve

Measure accurately 1.0, 2.0, 3.0, 4.0, 5.0ml of the reference solution to 10ml volumetric flasks separately, dilute with methanol to volume, and mix well. Inject accurately 10μl of these solutions respectively into the column, determine according to the above chromatographic system and plot the standard curve.

4. Preparation of test solution

Weigh accurately 0.1g of the powder in a stopper conical flask, add accurately 25ml of methanol, stopper tightly and weigh, ultrasonic disposal for 20mins, weigh again, add methanol to the weight, filter, transfer accurately 10ml of the successive filtrate to 25ml volumetric flask. Add methanol to the volume mix well, filter it with filter membrane (particle size 0.45um), and use the successive filtrate as the test solution.

5. Procedure

Inject accurately 10μl of test solution into the column, determine and calculate the content of the sample according to the standard curve.

Experiment record

1. Describe briefly the processes of this experiment.
2. Plot the standard curve and calculate the regression equation and relative factor.

Question

1. What should be paid attention to in the operating of the instrument?
2. What are the main advantages of HPLC in determination of the components in the TCM?

实验二十 容量法测定斑蝥中总酸性成分的含量

【目的要求】

1．了解动物药质量分析的特点。

2．熟悉斑蝥素的性质及其含量测定的原理。

【原理】

用氯仿将斑蝥素提取出来，纯化并定容后，加入过量碱液，再用酸液回滴定。根据消耗的碱液摩尔数，计算斑蝥素含量。

【斑蝥素的定性】

取斑蝥粉为0.15g，微量升华得白色升华物，在显微镜下观察为柱形、棱形结晶，升华物用石油醚洗2~3次，加浓硫酸2~3滴，微热溶解后，转入试管内，再继续用小火加热至发生气泡，立即离火，滴加二氨基苯甲醛硫酸溶液1滴，溶液即显樱红色或紫红色。

【含量测定】

1．对照品溶液

（1）氢氧化钠溶液（0.1mol/L）按《中华人民共和国药典》（2000年版，二部），附录130页，氢氧化钠液项下进行配制和标定。

（2）硫酸液（0.05mol/L）按《中华人民共和国药典》（2000年版，二部），附录133页硫酸液项下进行配制和标定。

2．样品测定

取斑蝥粗粉5g，精密称定，置500ml锥形瓶中，加氯仿30ml，HCl 1ml密塞，振摇30分钟，放置24小时，过滤于50ml容量瓶内，药渣用氯仿洗涤4次，第一次10ml，以后每次5ml，每次洗液均过滤，合并于容量瓶内，最后加氯仿至刻度，摇匀，准确吸取20ml溶液，置250ml三角瓶内，在60℃水浴上回收氯仿至干，残留物用石油醚（60~90℃）－无水乙醇（2:1）的混合液洗4次，第一次10ml，以后每次5ml，至洗液无色，得白色结晶，于60℃干燥，取出，放冷，加丙酮10ml，使溶解，准确加入氢氧化钠液（0.1mol/L）20ml，充分振摇于60℃水浴20分钟，取出冷至室温，加酚酞指示液2滴，用硫酸液（0.5mol/L）滴定至无色，按同样方法做空白实验，按下式计算斑蝥素（$C_{10}H_9O_4$分子量196.2）的含量。

$$斑蝥素\% = M_{H_2SO_4} \times [V_{H_2SO_4(空白)} - V_{H_2SO_4(样品)}] \times 196.2/1000/样品重(g) \times 2/5 \times 100\%$$

【实验记录】

1．记录定性实验的现象及结果。

2．计算样品中斑蝥素的含量。

【思考题】

1．酸碱滴定法测定斑蝥中斑蝥素的原理是什么？

2．药典收载斑蝥素的含量测定方法为气相色谱法，对照有关文献，比较不同方法的差异。

【相关资料】

1．斑蝥的化学成分

斑蝥为芫青科（Meloidae）昆虫南方大斑蝥 *Mylabris phalerata* Pallas、黄黑小斑蝥 *Mylabris cichorii* Linnaeus 的干燥虫体。含斑蝥素（cantharidin）、挥发油、甲壳质、甲酸等成分。

中华人民共和国药典（2000 年版）规定本品含斑蝥素不得少于 0.35%（用气相色谱法）。

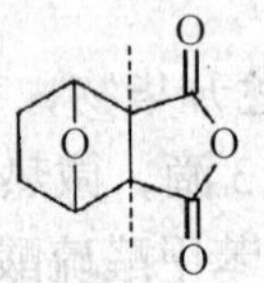

斑蝥素

2．斑蝥素的理化性质　分子量为 196.21。鳞片状结晶，熔点 218℃，易升华。不溶于冷水，微溶于热水，1g 可溶于 40ml 丙酮、65ml 氯仿、500ml 乙醚、150ml 乙酸乙酯。

20 Determination of the Total Acid Content in Mylabris by Volumetric Method

Purpose

1. To comprehend the feature of the qualitative analysis of animal drugs.

2. To be familiar with the properties of cantharidin and the principle of the determination of its content.

Principle

Extract cantharidin with chloroform, purify it and dilute to volume. Then add excessive base solution and carry out back – titration with acid solutions. Calculate the content of cantharidin according the amount of used base solutions.

Identification

Weigh 0.15g of powered cantharidin. Sublimate to get white sublimate, column and rhomboid crystal under microscope. Wash sublimates with petroleum ether for 2 ~ 3 times, add 2 ~ 3 drops of concentrated sulfuric acid. Dissolve with slight heat, transfer to test tube and then continue to heat with slight fire till bubble produced, disperse fire immediately, add 1 drop of sulfuric acid solutions of diamino – benzaldehyde, red or violet red produced.

Procedure

1. Preparation of reference solution

(1) 0.1mol/l sodium hydroxide Preparation and standardization according to pharmacopoeia of the people's Republic of China (2000) volume Ⅱ Appendix.

(2) 0.05mol/l sulfuric acid preparation and standardization according to pharmacopoeia of the people's Republic of China (2000) volume Ⅱ Appendix.

2. Assay

Weigh accurately about 5g of the coarse powder to a 500ml conical flask, add 30ml of chloroform, 1ml of hydrochloric acid, stopper tightly, shake for 30minutes, Allow it to stand for 24 hours, and filter into a 50ml volumetric flask. Wash the residue with Chloroform for 4 times, the first time with 10ml, the others each with 5ml, filter the washings each time, then combine them into a volumetric flask and dilute to volume with chloroform, mix well. Measure accurately 20ml of the solution to a 250ml conical flask, evaporate on a water bath at 60℃ to dryness. Elute the residue with a mixture of petroleum ether (60 ~ 90℃) - anhydrous ethanol (2:1) for 4 times, the first time with10ml and the others with 5ml until the eluent colorless and white crystal is achieved, dry it at 60℃, take out and cool, dissolve it with 10ml of acetone, add accurately 20ml of sodium hydroxide (0.1mol/l), put on water bath at 60℃ and mix well for 20minutes, take out and cool to room temperature, add 2 drops of phenolphthalein indicator, titrate with sulfuric acid (0.5mol/l) until colorless. Take blank experiment in the same manner. Calculate the content of cantharidin ($C_{10}H_9O_4$W196.20) as follows:

$$\text{Cantharidin\%} = M_{H_2SO_4}\left[V_{H_2SO_4(\text{blank})} - V_{H_2SO_4(\text{sample})}\right] \times 196.2/1000/\text{sample} - \text{weight}\ (\text{g}) \times 2/5 \times 100$$

Experiment record

1. Record the phenomena and results of qualitative test.
2. Calculate the content of cantharidin in sample.

Question

1. What is the principle of determination of cantharidin in mylabris using the method of acid - base titration?

2. The method for determination of cantharidin colleted in pharmacopoeia is gas chromatography. Compare the relative articles and find the differences of different methods.

第六章　中药制剂质量分析

实验二十一　牛黄解毒丸中胆酸及去氧胆酸的含量测定

【目的、要求】

了解中成药质量分析的一般方法，熟悉甾体化合物的性质。

【原理】

用有机溶剂将胆酸、去氧胆酸提取出来，薄层分离、显色，再用双波长薄层扫描仪进行测定。

【含量测定】

1．对照品溶液的制备

（1）胆酸对照品溶液：精密称取胆酸对照品 0.9mg，置 1ml 容量瓶中，加无水乙醇溶解后，加至刻度，摇匀，备用。

（2）去氧胆酸对照品溶液：精密称定去氧胆酸对照品 0.7mg，置 1ml 容量瓶中，加无水乙醇溶解后加至刻度，摇匀，备用。

2．样品液的制备

取牛黄解毒丸烘干，粉碎，精密称定，置磨口试管中，精密加入乙酸乙酯－乙醇(10:1) 2.5ml，超声波振荡 30 分钟，放置过夜，备用。

3．分析条件

硅胶 G－0.8％CMC 薄层板；展开剂：异辛烷－乙酸乙酯－甲醇－冰醋酸（7:25:0.8:1.6）；显色剂：3.5％磷钼酸无水乙醇液。

扫描条件：CS－930 型或 CS－9000 型双波长薄层扫描仪，λ_R720nm，λ_s480nm，狭缝 1.25×1.25mm，扫描速度 20mm/min，灵敏度：×2，锯齿扫描，反射法。

4．含量测定

分别精密吸取胆酸和去氧胆酸对照品溶液各 1ul、4ul 和一定量样品液，点在薄层板上行展开 12cm，取出，吹干溶液，快速浸渍显色，稍干后，烘板 15 分钟，取出，放置 30 分钟，冷却至室温。用 CS－930 型或 CS－9000 型薄层扫描仪扫描，测其积分值。

计算公式：

$$y - y_1/y_2 - y_1 = x - x_1/x_2 - x_1$$

$$x = (y - y_1)(x_2 - x_1)/(y_2 - y_1) + x_1$$

$$\% = x/w . V_x/V \times 100\%$$

其中：x_1——对照品液 1μl 中的 μg 数；

x_2——对照品液 4μl 中的 μg 数；

y_1——对照品液 1μl 中的扫描积分值（mm）；

y_2——对照品液 4μl 中的扫描积分值（mm）；

x——样品所含 μg 数；

y——样品扫描积分值（mm）；

w——样品称样量（g）；

V_x——样品点样量（ml）；

V——样品浸泡液的体积（ml）。

【实验记录】

1．绘出显色后的薄层图谱，计算胆酸及去氧胆酸斑点的 R_f 值。

2．计算丸药中胆酸及去氧胆酸的百分含量。

【思考题】

1．用磷钼酸乙醇液做显色剂的优点和不足之处？

2．除胆汁酸类化合物外，中药牛黄中还含哪些成分，可以采用什么方法测定其含量。

【相关资料】

牛黄解毒丸由牛黄、雄黄、石膏、冰片、大黄、黄芩、桔梗、甘草八味药组成。除牛黄、冰片外，雄黄水飞或粉碎成极细粉；其余石膏等五味粉碎成细粉；将牛黄冰片研细，与上述粉末配研，过筛，混匀。每 100g 粉末加炼蜜 100～110g 制成大蜜丸即得。

牛黄解毒丸中化学成分有许多，其中胆酸和去氧胆酸为牛黄（或人工牛黄）的有效成分。本次实验是用双波长薄层扫描法测定胆酸（cholic acid）及去氧胆酸（deoxycholic acid）的含量。

胆酸的分子量为 376.55。含 1 个结晶水的胆酸为块状结晶（稀醋酸），熔点 198℃，$[\alpha]_D^{20} + 37°$（C＝0.6，乙醇），pK＝6.4。

去氧胆酸的分子量为 392.56。为白色结晶（乙醇），熔点 176～178℃，$[\alpha]_D^{20} + 55°$（乙醇），pK＝6.58。

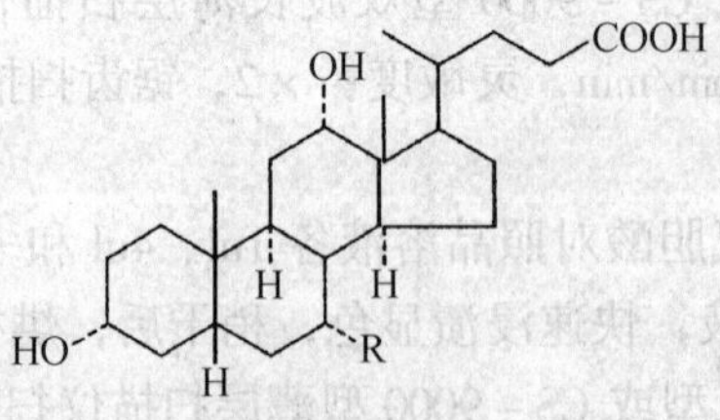

去氧胆酸 (deoxycholic)R-H

胆酸 (cholic acid)　　R-H

21 Determination of the Contents of Cholic Acid And Deoxycholic Acid in Niuhuang Jiedu Wan

Purpose

To understand the methods of analysis the quality of Traditional Chinese Patent Medicines and be familiar with the character of steroids

Principle

Cholic acid and deoxycholic acid were extracted with organic solvent, separated by TLC, colored, and then determined with dual – wavelength scanner.

Procedure

1. Preparation of reference solution

Cholic acid reference solution: weigh accurately 0.9mg of cholic acid, dissolve it with absolute ethanol in a 1ml of volumetric flask, dilute to volume and mix well.

Deoxycholic acid reference solution: weigh accurately 0.7mg of deoxycholic acid, dissolve it in absolute ethanol in a 1ml of volumetric flasks, dilute to volume and mix well.

2. Preparation of test solution

Take a quantity of the pill, oven dried, pulverized, weighed accurately, into a ground – glass test tuber, add accurately 2.5ml of a mixture of ethyl acetate – ethanol (10:1), ultrasonicdisposal for 30 minutes, allow it to stand overnight for use.

3. Conditions

Coating substance: Silica gel G – 0.8%CMC – Na,

Mobile phase: isooctane – ethyl acetate – methanol – acetic acid (7:25:0.8:1.6)

Colorant: 3.5% solution of Phosphomolybdic acid in absolute ethanol

Scanning condition: CS – 930 dual – wavelength scanner, $\lambda_R = 720$nm, $\lambda_S = 480$nm, slit: 1.25 × 1.25mm, scanning speed: 20mm/min, sensitivity: × 2, zigzag scan, reflection method.

4. Assay

Apply separately to the plate 1μl of cholic acid reference solution, 4 μl of deoxycholic acid reference solution, and a quantity of test solution, after developing to a distance of 12cm and removal of the plate, dry it, soak quickly it into 3.5% solution of phosphomolybdic acid in absolute ethanol. Heat for about 15 minutes; take it out and cool to room temperature. Measure the integral quantity of the spots with the scanner. Calculate as follows:

$$y - y_1/y_2 - y_1 = x - x_1/x_2 - x_1$$

$$x = (y - y_1)(x_2 - x_1)/(y_2 - y_1) + x_1$$

$$\% = x/w.\ V_x/V \times 100\%$$

in which, x_1 is the weight (μg) of $1\mu l$ of the reference solution;

x_2 is the weight (μg) of $4\mu l$ of the reference solution;

y_1 is the integral quantity (mm) of $1\mu l$ of the reference solution;

y_2 is the integral quantity (mm) of $4\mu l$ of the reference solution;

x is the weight (μg) of the test solution;

y is the integral quantity (mm) of the test solution;

w is the weight (g) of the pill being examined;

V_x is the volume (ml) of test solution applied to TLC

V is the volume (ml) of the scouring liquid of the pill being examined

Experiment record

1. Plot the thin – layer chromatograph after developing, and calculate the R_f of the cholic acid and deoxycholic acid spot.

2. Calculate the content of cholic acid and deoxycholic acid in the pills.

Questions

1. What are the advantages and disadvantages of using the solution of Phosphomolybdic acid in absolute ethanol as colorant?

2. what other compounds are included in cow – bezoars besides cholic acids, and how to determine them?

实验二十二　双波长分光光度法测定口腔溃疡散中靛玉红含量

【目的要求】

1．熟悉双波长分光光度法的原理及技术。

2．掌握双波长分光光度法在中成药分析中的应用。

【原理】

口腔溃疡散由青黛、硼砂、冰片组成，其中青黛的主要成分是靛蓝和靛玉红。

本实验利用靛玉红和靛蓝各自的等吸收值这一性质来达到消除干扰而直接测定的目的。

用作图法选出靛玉红和靛蓝的组合波长，在靛玉红 $\lambda_{max}=530nm$ 处作垂直于 X 轴直线交靛蓝吸收曲线于 a 点，自 a 点引一平行于 X 轴的直线和靛蓝曲线交于 b 点，此交点波长是 640nm。因靛蓝在 a、b 两点波长处吸收度相等，故靛玉红组合波长为 $\lambda_s=530nm$，$\lambda_R=640nm$，即可排除靛蓝干扰测定靛玉红含量。

$$A=A_{530nm}-A_{640nm}$$

同理：靛蓝的组合波长为 $\lambda_s=603nm$，$\lambda_R=420nm$。

【条件】

1．仪器　可见－紫外分光光度计，索氏提取器，容量瓶，吸量管。

2．样品　口腔溃疡散。

3．对照品　靛玉红、靛蓝。

4．试剂　氯仿。

【实验】

1．标准曲线的制备　精密称取靛玉红及靛蓝对照品各 10mg，分别置于 100ml 及 500ml 容量瓶中，用氯仿溶解并定容，用吸量管分别精密吸取靛玉红对照品溶液 0.1，0.2，0.4，0.6，0.8，1.0，1.2ml；靛蓝对照品溶液 0.5，1.0，2.0，3.0，4.0，5.0，6.0ml 放入 10ml 容量瓶中，加氯仿至刻度。分别在 530nm、640nm 处测定吸收度，以靛玉红的浓度 C（mg/ml）为横作标，A（$A_{530nm}-A_{640nm}$）为纵坐标绘制标准曲线，并按最小二乘法原理求得回归方程。

2．样品测定　精密称取口腔溃疡散 1g，置索氏提取器中，加氯仿 50ml，在水浴上回流提取至提取液中无红色存在（约 4～5 小时）。提取液过滤于 100ml 容量瓶中，残渣用氯仿 40ml 分三次洗涤，合并洗涤液于容量瓶中，并稀释至刻度，摇匀。在 530nm 、640nm 处测吸收度，求出 A，用回归方程算出靛玉红含量。

计算公式：靛玉红含量（%）= $C_{测} \times 100/W$（g）$\times 10^6 \times 100\%$

【实验记录】

1. 绘制靛玉红的标准曲线。
2. 计算口腔溃疡散中靛玉红的含量。

【思考题】

1. 双波长分光光度法中测定波长和参比波长是如何选择的？
2. 建立回归方程有什么意义？

【相关资料】

靛玉红（indirubin）的分子量为262.26。为红色针状结晶（丙酮－丁醇），熔点356～358℃，可升华，略溶于乙醇和醋酸，不溶于水。UV$\lambda_{Max}^{CHCl_3}$nm：242，292，362，540。

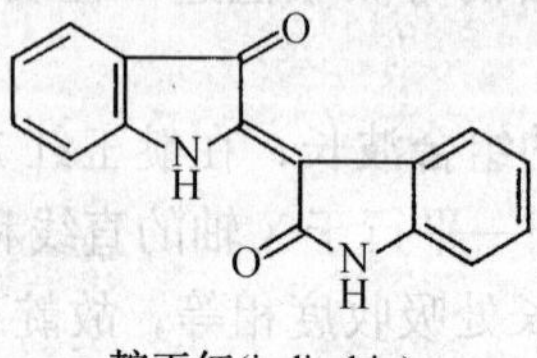

靛玉红(indirubin)

22 Determination of Indirubin in Kouqiang Kuiyang San by Dual Wavelength Spectrophotometry

Purpose

1. To be familiar with the principle and techniques of dual – wavelength spectrophotometry.

2. To grasp the application of dual – wavelength spectrophotometry in analysis of Chinese medicine.

Principle

Kouqiang Kuiyang San is made up of natural indigo, borax and borneol. And the main components of natural indigo are indigo and indirubin. To eliminate the interference of coexistence, we utilize the absorbance of indirubin and indigo to determine their content in this experiment. Based on the figures, the combination wavelengths of indirubin and indigo are selected. First, raw a vertical line at $\lambda = 530$nm (the maximum absorption wavelength of indirubin) to X – axis, this line meets the absorption curve of indigo at point a. Second, draw a line parallel from a, meeting the absorption curve of indigo at point b, the wavelength of b is 640nm. Because of the same absorbance of indigo at wavelengths a and b, we can eliminate the interference of indigo when we determine the content of indirubin. With this principle, we determine the combination wavelengths for indirubin as $\lambda_S = 530$nm and $\lambda_R = 640$nm.

$$A = A_{530\text{nm}} - A_{640\text{nm}}$$

Based on the same principle, we determine the combination wavelengths for indigo as $\lambda_S = 603$nm and $\lambda_R = 420$nm.

Requirement

1. Apparatus Visible – UV spectrophotometer, Soxhlet's extractor, volumetric flasks, pipettes.

2. Sample Kouqiang Kuiyang San.

3. CRS indigo and indirubin.

4. Reagent chloroform.

Procedure

1. Preparation of standard curve:

About 10mg, accurately weighed, of indirubin and indigo CRS are dissolved respectively in 100ml and 500ml volumetric flasks with chloroform, dilute to volume and mix well. Transfer separately 0.1, 0.2, 0.4, 0.6, 0.8, 1.0 and 1.2ml of indirubin CRS and 0.5, 1.0, 2.0, 3.0, 4.0, 5.0 and 6.0ml of indigo CRS, to 10ml volumetric flask, add chloroform to volume separately and mix well. Measure the absorbance at 530nm and 640nm, separately. Plot a standard curve, the concentration of indirubin (C, mg/ml) as abscissa, and A ($A_{530nm} - A_{640nm}$) as ordinate. Calculate the regression equation by linear leastsquares.

2. Assay

Weigh accurately 1g of Kouqiang Kuiyang San to Soxhlet's extractor, add 50ml of chloroform and reflux on a water bath until its color (red) disappears (about 4 to 5 hours). Filter the extracted solution to a 50ml volumetric flask, wash the residue with 40ml chloroform, in 3 portions. Combine the eluant to the same volumetric flask, dilute to volume and mix well. Measure the absorbance separately at 530nm and 640nm, calculate the content of indirubin with the regression equation.

Calculate as follows: indirubin (%) $= Cs \times 100/W\ (g) \times 10^6 \times 100\%$

Experiment record

1. Plot the standard curve of indirubin.
2. Calculating the content of indirubin in Kouqiang Kuiyang San.

Question

1. How to choose the mensuration wavelength and the reference wavelength in dual wavelength spectrophotometry?
2. What's the purpose of establishing the regression equation?

实验二十三　一阶导数光谱法测定香连丸中小檗碱的含量

【目的要求】

1．掌握一阶导数光谱法的原理和技术。

2．掌握一阶导数光谱法在中成药分析中的应用。

【原理】

香连丸是由黄连（吴茱萸制）及木香组成的中成药丸剂，小檗碱是其主要有效成分之一。对黄连、木香、吴茱萸、香连丸的提取液及小檗碱溶液作紫外吸收光谱，可知，黄连、香连丸及小檗碱在300～400nm之间有一吸收峰（345nm左右），而吴茱萸、木香在300～400nm之间呈一次吸收，故可用一阶导数光谱消除吴茱萸、木香对测定香连丸中小檗碱含量的干扰。再对以上各样品分别测定其一阶导数光谱，在300～400nm之间，黄连、香连丸及小檗碱的波峰在320nm，波谷在351nm，而木香、吴茱萸的一阶导数光谱在此区间内为一直线，故选取318nm、322nm、349nm、353nm作为测定波长，并按下式计算 A：

$$A = A_{320 \pm 2\text{nm}} + A_{351 \pm 2\text{nm}} = (A_{322\text{nm}} - A_{318\text{nm}}) + (A_{349\text{nm}} - A_{353\text{nm}})$$

【条件】

1．仪器　可见－紫外分光光度计，索氏提取器，层析柱，容量瓶，吸量管。

2．样品　香连丸粉碎过三号筛。

3．对照品　盐酸小檗碱。

4．试剂　中性氧化铝（层析用），盐酸－甲醇（1:100），0.05mol/L硫酸，95%乙醇。

【实验】

1．标准曲线的制备　精密称取干燥的盐酸小檗碱对照品适量，用0.05mol/L硫酸配成标准液（4、8、12、16、20μg/ml）在751－G型（或7520型、UV－2000型）分光光度计上测定 A，以 C 为横坐标，A 为纵坐标绘制标准曲线，并求出回归方程及相关系数。

2．样品测定　取香连丸粉末1g，精密称定，置索氏提取器中，用盐酸－甲醇（1:100）加热回流提取，至提取液无色为止，将提取液（适当浓缩）转移至50ml容量瓶中，用盐酸－甲醇（1:100）少量洗涤容器，洗液并入提取液中，并加至刻度。再精密吸取次此液5ml，加于处理好的氧化铝柱（内径9mm、中性氧化铝5g、湿法装柱、用95%乙醇30ml预洗），用95%乙醇25ml分次洗脱，收集洗脱液，置50ml容量瓶中，加乙醇至刻度，精密吸取2ml，置50ml容量瓶中，加0.05mol/L硫酸至刻度，摇匀，在751－G型（或7520型、UV－2000型）分光光度计上测定 A，按标准曲线计算含量。

【实验记录】

1．绘制盐酸小檗碱的一阶导数标准曲线图。

2．计算香连丸中小檗碱的百分含量。

【思考题】

1．为什么选择318、322、349、353nm作为测定波长？

2．如果其他含小檗碱的中成药，处方中的其他成分在300～400nm间为一次吸收，是否也可用此方法测定？

3．欲证明此方法的可靠性，须做什么实验？

23 Determination of Berberine in Xianglian Wan by First – Derivative Spectrum Analysis

Purpose

1. To master the principle and technology of first – order derivative spectrum.

2. To master the application first – order derivative spectrum in Chinese Traditional Patent Medicine.

Principle

Berberine is one of the principal effective constituents of Xianglian Wan, which is composed of Rhizoma Coptidis (processed with Fructus Evodiae) and Radix Aucklandiae. After acquiring the ultraviolet absorption spectrum of Rhizoma Coptidis, Radix Aucklandiae, Fructus Evodiae, extract of Xianglian Wan and berberine respectively. We found that Rhizoma Coptidis, xianglian Wan and berberine presented an absorption band within the range of 300 ~ 400nm (345nm or so), while Fructus Evodiae and Radix Aucklandiae presented first – order absorption. So disturbance arised from Fructus Evodiae and Radix Aucklandiae could be dissipated by first – order derivative spectrum when determine the content of berberine in xianglian Wan. Then we acquired the first – order derivative spectrum of the entire sample, the peak A_{320} and the valley A_{351} of xianglian Wan and berberine presented in the coordinate, while the linear correlations of Radix Aucklandiae and Fructus Evodiae were observed within the range of 300 ~ 400nm. According to the principle above, 318nm, 322nm, 349nm and 353nm are chosen as the determinative wavelength. The absorbance may be calculated as follows:

$$A = A_{320 \pm 2\text{nm}} + A_{351 \pm 2\text{nm}} = (A_{322\text{nm}} - A_{318\text{nm}}) + (A_{349\text{nm}} - A_{353\text{nm}})$$

Conditions

1. Apparatus Ultraviolet – Visible spectrophotometer, Soxhlet's extractor, Chromatography column, Volumetric flask, Pipette.

2. Sample Powder of Xianglian Wan (through No. 3 sieve)

3. Reference substance berberine hydrochloride

4. Reagents Neutral aluminum oxide (for chromatography used); Hydrochloric acid – methanol (1:100) 0.05mol/l sulfuric acid; 95% ethanol

Procedure

1. Preparation of Standard Curve

Dissolve the dried berberine hydrochloride CRS, weighed accurately, in 0.05mol/l sulfuric acid to produce solutions containing 4μg、8μg、12μg、16μg and 20μg per ml respectively as the standard solutions. After measuring the absorbance with UV – 9100 spectrophotometer, calculate the percentage content according to the standard curve.

2. Assay

Weigh accurately about 1g of the powdered Xianglian Wan to a soxhlet's extractor, heat under reflux with a mixture of hydrochloric acid – methanol (1∶100) until the colorless. Transfer the extract (concentrate the extract if necessary) to a 50ml volumetric flask, wash the container with a small quantity of hydrologic acid – methanol and combine the washings to the volumetric flask, and dilute to volume. Apply 5ml of the above solution, measured accurately, to a alumnium oxide column (9mm internal diameter, packed with 5g of neutral alumnium oxide by wet method, washed with 30ml of 95% ethanol), eluent with 25ml of 95% ethanol in portions, collect the eluent into a 50ml volumetric flask, dilute with ethanol to volume and mix well, transfer 2ml of the solution, accurately measured, to a 50ml volumetric flask, dilute with 0.05mol/l sulfuric acid to volume and mix well, measure the absorbance with 751 – G (7520 or UV – 2000) spectrophotometer. Calculate the percentage content of berberine according to the standard curve.

Experimental record

1. Plot the first – order derivative standard curve of berberine hydrochloride CRS.
2. Calculate the percentage content of berberine in Xianglian Wan.

Question

1. Why are 318nm, 322nm, 349nm and 353nm chosen as the detect wavelength?
2. Can this method be applied to determine berberine in other Chinese Traditional Patent Medicine if other constituents in the medicine present first – order absorption within the range of 300 ~ 400nm?
3. What test should be done to prove the accuracy of the method?

实验二十四　差示光谱法测定六味地黄丸中丹皮酚的含量

【目的要求】

掌握差示光谱法测定中药有效成分的原理及操作。

【原理】

六味地黄丸中丹皮酚的含量测定，中国药典用水蒸汽蒸馏，紫外分光光度法测定，本实验采用乙醇浸出提取、双波长差示光谱法测定。根据丹皮酚的差示光谱，选择 352nm 为测定波长，386nm 为参比波长，消除干扰组分对测定的影响，直接测定了样品中丹皮酚的含量。

【条件】

1．仪器　紫外分光光度计，具塞锥形瓶，容量瓶，漏斗，吸量管。

2．样品　六味地黄丸（市售）粉碎成粉末。

3．对照品　丹皮酚。

4．试剂　95%乙醇、蒸馏水、0.01mol/L NaOH 溶液。

【实验】

1．标准曲线的制备　精密称取丹皮酚 5.00mg，置 50ml 容量瓶中，加 95%乙醇溶解并定容，精密吸取 0.8，1.0，1.2，1.4，1.6ml 各二份，分别置于 10ml 容量瓶中，其中一份加水稀释至刻度作为参比溶液，另一份加碱液稀释至刻度作为样品溶液。将上述参比液和样品液分别于 352 nm 和 386 nm 波长处测定其吸收度，计算 ΔA 值。根据 ΔA 与对照品浓度 C 绘制标准曲线，求出回归方程。

2．样品测定　取成药样品粉末 0.5g，精密称定，置 25ml 具塞锥形瓶中，加乙醇 15ml，摇匀，静置过夜，过滤，滤液定容至 25ml 。精密吸取 5ml 各二份，分别置于 25ml 容量瓶中，一份加水稀释至刻度，另一份加碱液稀释至刻度。按上述“标准曲线的制备”方法测定，由标准曲线计算出样品中丹皮酚的含量。

计算公式：

样品中丹皮酚的含量（%）＝标准曲线计算值（mg）$\times 25/10/W_s \times 5/25 \times 10^3 \times 100\%$

【实验记录】

1．绘制丹皮酚的标准曲线图谱。

2．计算六味地黄丸中丹皮酚的含量。

【思考题】

1．为何能用示差光谱法直接测定六味地黄丸中丹皮酚的含量?

2．请设计用其他方法测定六味地黄丸中丹皮酚的含量。

【相关资料】

六味地黄丸由熟地黄、山茱萸（制）、牡丹皮、山药、茯苓、泽泻等六味药制成。丹皮酚（paeonol）为牡丹皮的主要活性成分。

丹皮酚的分子量为166.17。为无色针状结晶（乙醇），熔点50℃，稍溶于水，能随水蒸汽挥发，溶于乙醇、乙醚、丙酮、氯仿、苯和二硫化碳。$UV\lambda_{Max}^{MeOH}$ nm（lgε）：291（4.01），274（4.17），316（3.84）。

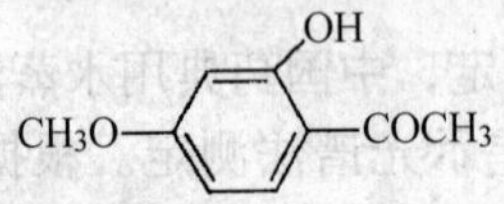

丹皮酚(paeonol)

24 Determination of Paeonol in Liuwei Dihuang Wan by Differential Spectrophotometry

Purpose

To master the theory and operation of differential spectrophotometry in determination of effective component of traditional Chinese patent medicine

Principle

The method recorded in ChP for determination of paeonol in Liuwei Dihuang Wan is vapor distillation and ultraviolet c. In this experiment, exaction with ethanol and dual-wavelength differential spectrophotometry is used. According to the differential spectrum of paeonol, 352nm is selected as determination wavelength and 386nm as reference wavelength so as to eliminate the interference and determine the content of paeonol in sample directly.

Condition

1. Apparatus spectrophotometer, stopper conical flask, volumetric flask, funnel, Pipette.

2. Sample powdered Liuwei Dihuang Wan (on sale)

3. CRS paeonol

4. Reagent 95% ethanol, distilled water, 0.01mol/l NaOH solution

Procedure

1. Preparation of standard curve and test solution:

Dissolve 5.00g of paeonol CRS, accurately weighed, with 95% ethanol in a 50ml volumetric flask and dilute to volume. Transfer accurately 0.8, 1.0, 1.2, 1.4, 1.6ml, each two shares into 10 ml volumetric flasks, separately. Dilute one share with distilled water to volume as reference solution and the other with 0.01% NaOH solution as test solution. Measure the absorbance of both reference and test solutions, separately at 352nm and 386nm. Plot the standard curve and calculate the regression equation.

2. Assay

Weigh accurately 0.5g of powered pills to a 25ml stopper conical flask, add 50ml of ethanol, mix well, allow it to stand overnight, filter, and dilute the filtrate to 25ml. Measure two quantities of 5ml of above solution to 25ml volumetric flasks, separately, dilute one share with distilled water and the other with 0.01% NaOH solution to volume, separately. Measure the absorbance in the same manner as above, and calculate the percentage content of paeonol in Liuwei Dihuang Wan according to the regression equation.

Formula:

paeonol (%) = Weight calculated according to regression equation (mg) × 25/10/Ws × 5/25 × 10^3 × 100%

Experiment record

1. Plot the standard curve of paeonol.
2. Calculate the percentage content of paeonol in Liuwei Dihuang Wan.

Question

1. Why can differential spectrophotometry be used to determine the content of paeonol in Liuwei Dihuang Wan directly?
2. Please design other methods to determine the content of paeonol in Liuwei Dihuang Wan?

实验二十五　薄层扫描法测定九分散中士的宁的含量

【目的要求】

1．熟悉薄层扫描法的原理及技术。

2．了解影响薄层扫描法结果的因素有哪些，并掌握解决的方法。

【原理】

九分散是传统中成药，由马钱子、麻黄、乳香、没药四味药粉碎混合而成。马钱子中的士的宁是主要有效成分。士的宁属生物碱类成分，可用碱性有机溶剂提取，然后用酸水萃取入酸水层，调酸水的 pH 使之成碱性后，生物碱又可被有机溶剂萃取入有机溶剂层。这样反复的碱酸萃取，就可以把非生物碱成分除去，而得到总生物碱。薄层色谱可以把士的宁与其它生物碱分离，把分离后的薄层板放在扫描仪上，可直接求得士的宁的含量。

【条件】

1．仪器　薄层扫描仪，微量注射器，具塞锥形瓶，分液漏斗。

2．试剂及药品　浓氨水，氯仿，硫酸，甲苯，丙酮，乙醇，士的宁对照品，硅胶 GF_{254}薄层板（10cm × 20cm）。

【实验】

1．对照品溶液的制备　精密称取士的宁对照品适量，用氯仿制成 0.4mg/ml 的溶液，即对照品液。

2．供试液的制备　取九分散10包，混合均匀。取混合均匀供试品 2g，精密称定，置带塞锥形瓶中，精密加氯仿 20ml 与浓氨水 1ml，轻轻摇匀，称重，于室温放置 24 小时，再称重，用氯仿补足原重，摇匀，滤过。精密吸取滤液 10ml，用硫酸（3 – 100）分次提取，至生物碱提尽，合并硫酸，置一分液漏斗中，加浓氨呈碱性，用氯仿分次提取，合并氯仿液蒸干，残渣中精确加氯仿 5ml 使溶解，即成供试液。

3．薄层的点样、展开、扫描　取供试液及对照品液点于同一硅胶 GF_{254}板上，以甲苯 – 丙酮 – 乙醇 – 浓氨水（8:6:0.5:2）的上清液为展开剂，展开，取出，晾干。定位，以 $\lambda_S = 254nm$，$\lambda_R = 325nm$，在薄层扫描仪上扫描测量积分值，计算即得样品中士的宁的含量［药典要求每包（2.5g）含量应为 4.5 ~ 5.0mg。］

【实验记录】

1．绘制薄层层析图谱，计算士的宁的 R_f 值。

2．计算九分散中士的宁的含量。

【思考题】

1．碱－酸萃取的目的在于除去杂质，是否萃取的次数越多越好？

2．$\lambda_S = 254nm$，$\lambda_R = 325nm$ 是怎样确定的？

3．薄层扫描法定量的影响因素有哪些？

【相关资料】

士的宁（strychnine）又称番木鳖碱，分子量为 334.40。为极苦的斜方棱柱结晶（乙醇），熔点 286～288℃，d_4^{20} 1.36，$[\alpha]_D^{20} - 104°$（C = 0.5，无水乙醇）。UV λ_{Max}^{EtOH} nm（ε）：255（11482）。1g 溶于 6400ml 水、150ml 乙醇、5ml 氯仿、180ml 苯和 260ml 甲醇，极微溶于乙醚和石油醚。

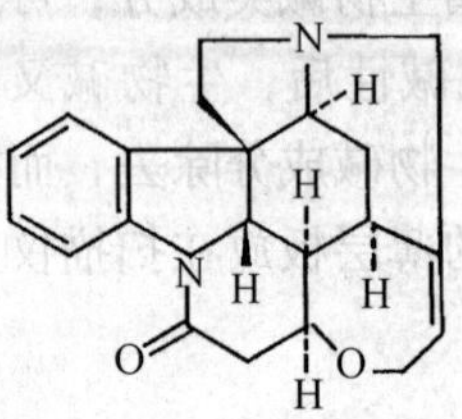

士的宁 (strychnine)

25 Determination of Strychnine in Jiufen San By TLCS

Purpose

1. To be familiar with the principle and technology of TLCS.

2. To comprehend the influential factors to the result of TLCS and to master the countermeasures.

Principle

Jiufen San is a kind of Chinese Traditional Patent medicine. It is composed of *Semen Strychni*; *Herba Ephedrae*; *Olibanum* and *Myrrha*, which are pulverized and mixed. Strychnine in Semen Strychni is the main effective ingredient. Strychnine belongs to alkaloids and it can be extracted by organic solvent, and then extracted by acid water. Adjust the pH value and make it alkaline in order that the alkaloids can be extracted again into organic solvent layer. These repeated acid and base extractions can get rid of the non – alkaloid components and get the total alkaloids. Last strychnine can be separated from other alkaloids by thin layer chromatography. Place the plate where strychnine is separated on the Thin Layer Chromatogram Scanner, and we can determine the content of strychnine directly.

Condition

Apparatus: thin layer chromatogram scanner, microsyringe, stopper conical flask, separating funnel.

Rcagents and chemicals: strong ammonia TS, chloroform, sulfuric acid, toluene, acetone, ethanol, strychnine CRS and silica gel GF_{254} thin layer chromatoplate (10cm × 20cm).

Procedure

1. preparation of reference solution

Dissolve some strychnine CRS, accurately weighed, in chloroform to produce a solution containing 0.4 mg per ml as the reference solution.

2. preparation of test solution

Secure 10 packs of Jiufen San and mix well, weigh accurately 2g to a stopper conical flask, add accurately 20 ml of chloroform and 1 ml of strong ammonia TS, shake gently and weigh. Allow it to stand at room temperature for 24 hours, weigh again, replenish the loss of chloroform, shake thoroughly and filter. Measure accurately 10ml of the succesive filtrate to be extracted with sulfuric acid solution (3 – 100) in portions until the alkaloids are extracted thoroughly. Combine the sulfuric acid solutions to another separating funnel, make alkaline with strong ammonia TS and extract with chloroform in portions. Combine the chloroform extracts, evaporate it to dryness and cool. To the residue add accurately 5ml of chloroform to provide a test solution.

3. Application, development and scanning of the TLC plate

Apply separately to the silica gel GF_{254} plate each of the two solutions, using the supernatant liquid of toluene – acetone – ethanol – strong ammonia TS (8:6:0.5:2) mixture as mobile phase. After developing and removal of the plate, dry it in air. Fix it on TLC scanner, scan and measure its integration values at following wavelength λ_S = 254mn, λ_R = 325mn. Calculate the content of strychnine of the powder [each pack (2.5g) contains 4.5 ~ 5.5 mg of strychnine, complied with the China Pharmacopeia requirements.]

Experiment record

1. Plot the thin layer chromatogram and calculate the R_f value of strychnine.
2. Calculate the percentage content of strychnine in Jiufen San.

Question

1. Whether is it the more the better since the acid – base extraction is to get rid of impurity?
2. How are λ_S = 254nm, λ_R = 325nm determined?
3. Which factors will influent the quantitative analysis by TLCS?

实验二十六　气相色谱法测定风油精中薄荷脑的含量

风油精由薄荷脑、樟脑、水杨酸甲酯等具挥发性的芳香油类组成，本实验采用气相色谱法测定风油精中薄荷脑的含量。

【目的要求】

1．熟悉气相色谱仪的原理、使用。
2．掌握已知浓度样品对照法的应用。

【原理】

根据同一物质在同一色谱柱上保留时间相同的原理，以薄荷脑对照品液为对照，确定出样品液中薄荷脑峰的位置；再采用内标法测定风油精中薄荷脑的含量。

【条件】

1．仪器　气相色谱仪，1m 不锈钢螺旋柱，5μl 微量注射器。
2．样品　风油精（市售品）。
3．对照品　薄荷脑。
4．内标物　萘。

【实验】

1．内标溶液的配制　取萘0.5g，精密称定，置 50ml 容量瓶中，加乙酸乙酯溶解（如不溶可用 60℃水浴加热溶解）。

2．对照品溶液的配制　取薄荷醇对照品0.1g，精密称定，置 10ml 容量瓶中，用内标液溶解并稀释至刻度。

3．样品溶液的配制　精密吸取风油精0.5ml，置 10ml 容量瓶中，用内标液溶解并稀释至刻度。

4．气相色谱条件　进样器温度：180℃；柱箱温度：120℃；检测器温度：140℃；载气（N_2）流速：20ml/min；氢气流速：35ml/min；空气流速：300ml/min；灵敏度：$10^8\times 1/2$；纸速：4ml/min；检测器：氢火焰离子化检测器：进样量：0.5～1μl。

5．样品测定　在同一色谱条件下，对照品液与样品液分别进样。

【实验记录】

从色谱图上测量出各组分峰高（h）及半峰宽（W/2），根据下式计算薄荷脑的含量。

$$Ci\% = (Ai/As)_{样品} / (Ai/As)_{对照品} \times m_1/m \times 100\%$$

其中：Ai：薄荷醇峰面积；As：内标峰面积；

m_1：对照品中薄荷醇的含量；m：样品重量；

A = h × W/2。

【思考题】

1. 实验中是否要严格控制进样量？为什么？
2. 若实验过程中载气流量稍有变化，对定量结果有何影响？
3. 本实验是否可改用峰高进行定量？

26 Determination of Menthol in Fengyou Jin by GC

Purpose

1. To be acquainted with the principle and operation of gas chromatogram.

2. To master the application of internal standard method in known – concentration substances.

Principle

Fengyou Jin is composed of menthol, camphor, methyl salicylate and other volatile odorous oil. In this test gas chromatography is used to determine the content of menthol in Fengyou Jin.

Based on the theory that the same substance has a definite retention time through a same column in GC, we can identify of menthol in test solution taking menthol as reference, and determine the content of menthol with the internal standard method.

Conditions

Apparatus: Gas Chromatogram, 1 ml spiral stainless steel column, 5μl micro syringe
Sample: Fengyou Jin (for sale)
Reference: Menthol
Internal standard: Naphthalene

Procedure

1. Preparation of internal standard solution

Dissolve 0.5g of naphthalene, accurately weighed, in a 50ml volumetric flask, with ethyl acetate (heat in a water bath at 60℃ if necessary)

2. Preparation of reference solution

Weigh accurately 0.1g of reference menthol, into a 10ml volumetric flask, add internal standard solution, and swirl until dissolved. Dilute with internal standard solution to volume, and mix.

3. Preparation of test solution

Transfer 0.5ml of Fengyou Jin, accurately measured, to a 10ml volumetric flask, add internal standard solution, and swirl until dissolved. Dilute with internal standard solution to volume.

4. Chromatographic system

Injector temperature: 180℃; Oven temperature: 120℃; Detector temperature: 140℃; Flow rate of Carrier gas (N_2): 20ml/min; Flow rate of Hydrogen: 35ml/min; Flow rate of air: 300ml/min; Sensitivity: $10^8 \times 1/2$; Chart speed: 4cm/min; Detector: Flame Ionization Detector; Injection volume 0.5 ~ 1μl.

Assay

Inject reference and test solution respectively under the same chromatographic system.

Experiment record

The peak height corresponding to the component (h) and the peak width of interest at half peak height (W/2) are concerned in the chromatogram. From the values obtained, calculate the content of menthol as follows:

$$Ci\% = (Ai/As)\ sam / (Ai/As)_{ref} \times m_1/m \times 100\%$$

in which,

Ai = peak area of Menthol;

As = peak area of the internal standard;

m_1 = content of Menthol in reference solution;

m = weight of sample

The peak area is defined by the expression: $A = h \cdot w/2$

Question

1. Is it necessary to control the sample size strictly? Why?
2. What effect will it have on the results of quantitative analysis if the flow volume of carrier gas changes a little?
3. Can the quantitative analysis of this test rest on the height of peak?

实验二十七　复方甘草片中吗啡的测定

【目的要求】

1. 熟悉成药中活性组分的分析检测。

2. 掌握高效液相色谱法在中成药定量分析中的应用。

【原理】

复方甘草片是祛痰镇咳药，由甘草浸膏粉、阿片粉、樟脑、八角茴香油、苯甲酸钠组成。根据吗啡为阿片中的主要生物碱，吗啡的含量是复方甘草片的主要指标，吗啡具有酸碱两性，先加入 NaOH 中和其酸性，然后加入氯化铵缓冲液，再用有机溶剂提取以得到游离的吗啡。其在 254nm 处有最大吸收，故选用紫外检测器在 254nm 波长进行测定。

【条件】

1. 仪器　高效液相色谱仪、泵、紫外检测器、化学工作站、旋涡混合器、离心机、微量进样器。

2. 试药　吗啡对照品；复方甘草片。

3. 试剂　氯化铵缓冲液（pH 9），（于 1mol/ L 氨水溶液中加入 2mol/L 盐酸调节 pH 为 9.0 ± 0.1 ）提取溶剂为氯仿 – 异丙醇（3∶1）；0.5mol/L NaOH 溶液。

4. 色谱条件与系统适用性

分析柱：十八烷基硅烷键合硅胶柱（5um × 4.6mm × 250mm）；流动相为 0.1mol/L 磷酸二氢钠 – 甲醇（5∶1）；流速 1.2ml/min ；柱温 35℃；检测波长 254nm；理论板数按吗啡计算应不低于 1000。

【实验方法】

1. 定性鉴别

（1）取本品 2 片，研细，加水约 7ml 混匀，加 10%无水碳酸钠水溶液至 pH 值约为 9，用氯仿 – 异丙醇（3∶1）提取 2 次，每次 20ml，合并提取液，用少量氨试液洗涤，再用少量水洗，然后浓缩蒸干，加甲醇 0.3ml 使溶解，作为供试品溶液；另取吗啡对照品适量，加甲醇溶解，制成每 1ml 中含 2mg 的溶液，作为对照品溶液，照薄层色谱法试验，取上述两种溶液各 10μl，分别点于同一硅胶 G 薄层板上，以醋酸乙酯 – 甲醇 – 浓氨溶液（35∶10∶5）为展开剂，展开后，晾干，喷以碘化铋钾试液，使显色，供试品应出现与吗啡对照品位置相同，色泽亦相同的斑点。

（2）取本品的细粉适量，加水使溶解，滤过，取滤液少量加稀硫酸 1 ~ 2 滴，立即析出极易溶于浓氨溶液的浅棕色沉淀。

2. 含量测定

(1) 对照品溶液的制备：取无水吗啡对照品适量，精密称定，加甲醇制成每 1ml 含 0.2mg 的溶液，作对照溶液。

(2) 样品前处理：取本品 20 片，精密称定，研细；精密称取相当于 1 片的细粉，置 10ml 具塞离心试管中，精确加 0.5mol/L NaOH 溶液 0.2ml，加氯化铵缓冲液 3ml，置旋涡混合器上混合溶解，再精密加氯仿 - 异丙醇（3∶1）的混合液 5ml，置混合器上充分混合提取 1min，离心（3000r/min）10min，将有机层全部吸出置另一具塞离心管中，加水 4ml 洗涤，置混合器上混合提取 1min，离心 10min，准确吸取有机层 2ml 于磨口小烧瓶中，70℃水浴上减压蒸干，残渣精密加甲醇 2ml 溶解，作为供试品溶液。

(3) 测定方法：取对照品溶液和供试品溶液各 10μl，分别注入液相色谱仪，记录色谱图，外标一点法以峰面积计算含量。

【实验记录】

1. 绘制定性鉴别的薄层色谱图，计算 R_f 值。

2. 计算复方甘草片中吗啡的含量。

【思考题】

1. 本实验中定性鉴别（1~2）项的结果是检查处方中的什么？

2. 实验中加入 0.5mol/L NaOH 溶液量的多少对测定结果有无影响？会出现怎样的结果？

3. 理论板数有什么意义？

【相关资料】

罂粟科植物罂粟 *Papaver somniferum* L. 果实液汁（阿片）中含有 10% 左右的吗啡（morphine）。

吗啡有强大的中枢性镇痛作用，有成瘾性。分子量为 285.33。为短斜方棱状结晶（苯甲醚）。熔点 254℃（分解），亚稳相熔点为 197℃，$[\alpha]_D^{25}$ − 132°（甲醇）。UV $\lambda_{Max}^{0.1NH_4Cl}$ nm (ε)：285（1580）。1g 溶于 5000ml 水、1100ml 沸水、210ml 乙醇、1220ml 氯仿、6500ml 乙醚。

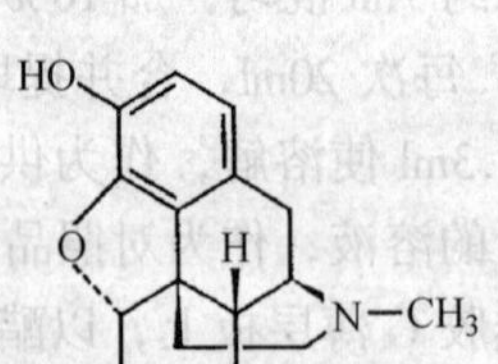

吗啡 (morphine)

27 Determination of Morphine In Fufang Gancao Pian

Purpose

1. To be familiar with analysis of active component in traditional Chinese patent medicine.

2. To grasp the application of high performance liquid chromatogram in quantitative analysis of traditional Chinese patent medicine.

Principle

Fufang Gancao Pian is a kind of antitussive expectorants. It is composed of extract of Liquorice, Opium powder, Camphor, Anise oil and sodium benzoate. Morphine is the main alkaloid of Opium powder, therefore the content of morphine is the main sign of Fufang Gancao Pian. Morphine has acid – base property so first we can add sodium hydroxide to neutralize its acidity, then add ammonium chloride buffer solution, after that extract it with organic solution to produce free morphine. Morphine has a maximum absorption at 254 nm, so we can determine it with ultra – violet detector at 254nm.

Condition

1. Apparatus high performance liquid chromatograph, pump, data processing machine, ultraviolet detector, vortex mixer, centrifuger, microsyringe.

2. Drug morphine CRS, Fufang Gancao Pian

3. Reagent ammonium chloride buffer solution (pH 9) (add 2mol/l hydrochloric acid to 1mol/l ammonia water to adjust pH value to 8.9 ~ 9.1), chloroform – isopropanol (3:1), 0.5mol/l sodium hydroxide solution

4. Chromatographic system and system suitability

Column: octadecylsilane bonded silica gel (5um × 4.6mm × 250mm); Mobile phase: 0.1mol/l sodium dihydrogen phosphate solution – methanol (5:1); Column temperature 35℃; Detector wavelength: 254nm; the number of the theoretical plates of the column is not less than 1000, calculated with reference to the peak of morphine.

Procedure

1. Identification

(1) Shake thoroughly 2 powdered tablets with 7ml of water and adjust pH to 9 with 10% anhydrous sodium carbonate solution. Extract twice with 20ml each of a mixture of chloroform – isopropanol (3:1). Wash the combined extracts with a small quantity of ammonia TS and water in sequence, evaporate the extracts to dryness, dissolve the residue in 0.3 ml of methanol as the test solution; dissolve a quantity of morphine CRS in methanol to produce a solution of 2 mg per ml as reference solution. Carry out the thin layer chromatography, using silica gel G as the coating substance and a mixture of ethyl acetate – methanol – concentrated ammonia solution (35:10:5) as the mobile phase. Apply separately to the same plate 10ul each of the solutions, after developing and removal of the plate, dry it in air, and spray with potassium iodobismuthate TS. The color and position of the principal spot in the chromatogram obtained with the test solution correspond to the principal spot obtained with the reference solution.

(2) Dissolve a quantity of powdered tablets in water and filter. To a small quantity of the filtrate add 1 ~ 2 drops of diluted sulfuric acid, a faint brown precipitate is produced immediately, which is very soluble in concentrated ammonia solution.

Assay

1. Preparation of reference solution

To a quantity of a hydrous morphine, accurately weighed, add methanol to produce a solution containing 0.2mg per ml as the reference solution.

2. Preparation of test solution

Weigh accurately 20 tablets and grind to powder. Triturate a quantity of the powder, accurately weighed, equivalent to about 1 tablet in stopper centrifuge tube. Add 0.2ml of 0.5mol/l sodium hydroxide solution and 3ml of ammonium chloride buffer solution accurately. Put it on vortex mixer to extract completely for 1 min, centrifuge (3000r/min) for 10 min, transfer the whole of organic layer to another stopper centrifuge tube, wash with 4ml of water, extract on mixer for 1 min, centrifuge for 10 min. Transfer accurately 2.0 ml of organic layer to a small flask with stopple and evaporate in vacuum to dryness on water bath at 70℃. Dissolve the residue with 2ml of methanol, accurately measured, as test solution.

3. Assay

Inject 10ul of each of the reference solution and test solution respectively into the chromatogram, record the chromatogram, calculate the content on the peak area obtained with the chromatogram by the external standard one – point method.

Experiment record

1. Plot the thin layer chromatogram for qualitative identification and calculate the R_f value.

2. Calculate the content of morphine in Fufang Gancao Pian.

Question

1. Which ingredient can be examined in item 1 ~ 2 of identification?

2. Does the quantity of 0.5mol/l sodium hydroxide solution in the experiment have effect on the result of determination and how does it effect?

3. What is the significance of the number of the theoretical plates of column?

实验二十八　如意金黄散的定性定量分析

【目的要求】

1．掌握薄层层析法检出中成药中组成药材的定性方法。

2．掌握薄层扫描法分析中成药有效成分的定量方法。

【原理】

如意金黄散是常用中成药散剂，由大黄、黄柏、姜黄、苍术、厚朴、陈皮、甘草、生南星、白芷、天花粉十味中药组成。本实验采用薄层层析法，通过对照品与该成药及组成药材进行对照，对其中的8味药进行定性检出；并用双波长薄层扫描法对其中姜黄素进行定量分析。

【条件】

1．仪器　薄层扫描仪，超声波振荡器，回流装置。

2．样品　如意金黄散（市售）及组成药材。

3．对照品　大黄酸、大黄素、芦荟大黄素、小檗碱、姜黄素、苍术酮、苍术素、厚朴酚、和厚朴酚、橙皮苷、甘草酸、异欧前胡素、氧化前胡素。

4．药品　甲醇、氯仿、乙酸乙酯、石油醚等、硅胶G层析板、硅胶GF_{254}层析板。

【实验】

1．定性分析

（1）黄柏、陈皮、姜黄、厚朴的检出：取成药1g，用甲醇20ml加热回流提取30分钟，过滤，滤液浓缩至约1ml，制成成药溶液。

另取黄柏、陈皮粉末各0.5g，分别同上制备，制成黄柏、陈皮对照药材溶液。

取姜黄、厚朴粉末各0.2g，分别用甲醇5ml温浸3分钟，制成姜黄、厚朴药材溶液。

黄柏的展层条件：吸附剂硅胶G，展开剂正丁醇－冰醋酸－水（7:1:2），对照品小檗碱，展距10cm，荧光灯下检视。

陈皮的展层条件：吸附剂硅胶G，展开剂丙酮－氯仿－95%乙醇－甲酸（7:2:1:0.05），对照品陈皮苷，展距10cm，喷1%三氯化铝甲醇溶液，荧光灯下检视。

姜黄的展层条件：吸附硅胶G，展开剂正丁醇－6%氨水－甲醇（30:3:1），对照品姜黄素，展距10cm，可见光下检视。

厚朴的展层条件：吸附剂硅胶GF_{254}，展开剂苯－甲醇（27:1），对照品厚朴酚及和厚朴酚，展距10cm，荧光灯下检视。

（2）苍术、白芷的检出：成药1g，用石油醚（30~60℃）索氏提取器回流2小时，石油醚液浓缩至0.5ml，即为成药溶液。

取苍术、白芷粉末各 0.2g，同法制备，制成对照药材溶液。

苍术的展层条件：吸附剂硅胶 G，展开剂苯－乙酸乙酯－正己烷（15∶15∶70），对照品苍术酮、苍术素，展距 10cm，显色剂 5%香草醛浓硫酸。

白芷的展层条件：吸附剂硅胶 G，展开剂石油醚（60～90℃）－乙醚（5∶2），对照品氧化前胡素、异欧前胡素，展距 10cm，荧光灯下检视。

（3）大黄的检出：取成药 0.5g，用甲醇 20ml 冷浸 1 小时，过滤，取滤液 5ml，蒸干，残渣加水 5ml，滴加盐酸 0.5ml，加热回流 30 分钟，立即冷却，水解液用乙醚 15ml 分两次萃取，乙醚液蒸干加氯仿 0.5ml，制成成药溶液。

取大黄粉末 0.1g 同法制备，制成药材溶液。

展层条件：吸附剂硅胶 GF_{254}，展开剂氯仿－乙酸乙酯（8∶2），对照品大黄酸、芦荟大黄素、大黄素、展距 10cm，荧光灯下检视。

（4）甘草的检出：取成药 1g，用水 10ml，滴加浓氨水 3 滴，超声振荡提取 20 分钟，即成成药溶液。

取甘草粉末 0.2g，同法制备，制成对照药材溶液。

展层条件：吸附剂硅胶 GF_{254}，展开剂正丁醇－3M 氨水－95%乙醇（5∶2∶1），对照品甘草酸，展距 10cm，荧光灯下检视。

2．姜黄素的含量测定

（1）层析及扫描条件：硅胶 G 薄层板，正丁醇－3M 氨水－甲醇（30∶3∶1）为展开剂，展距 8cm；薄层扫描仪线性参数 $S_x = 3$，锯齿扫描，$\lambda_s = 430$nm，$\lambda_R = 700$nm。

（2）标准曲线的制备：取姜黄素 2.00mg，精密称定，置 10ml 容量瓶中，以甲醇溶解并定容至刻度，制成对照品溶液。在同一薄层板上，分别点样 2.0，4.0，6.0，8.0，10.0μl 对照液，按上述条件展开，扫描，以积分值为纵作标，对照品点样量为横作标绘制标准曲线，并计算出回归方程及相关系数。

（3）样品测定：取成药 1g 精密称定，置 10ml 容量瓶中，加甲醇定容至刻度，超声振荡提取 2 小时，过滤，滤液即为样品液。在同一薄层板上，点样品液 10μl 及对照品溶液 4μl、8μl，按上述条件展开、扫描，按外标两点法计算出如意金黄散中姜黄素的含量。

【实验记录】

1．绘制薄层层析图谱并计算相关斑点的 R_f 值。

2．计算如意金黄散中姜黄素的含量。

【思考题】

1．如意金黄散由 10 味中药组成，现检出了其中 8 味，请设计检出其余的生南星和天花粉两味中药。

2．用外标两点法为什么要制备标准曲线及计算回归方程、相关系数？

【相关资料】

姜黄素（curcumin）为姜科植物姜黄 *Curcuma longa* L. 的主要有效成分。分子量为 368.37。为橙黄色结晶性粉末，熔点 183℃。UV λ_{Max}^{EtOH} nm（ε）：430（50119）。易溶于甲醇、

无水乙醇、丙酮、醋酸乙酯和碱溶液中，不溶于水和乙醚。

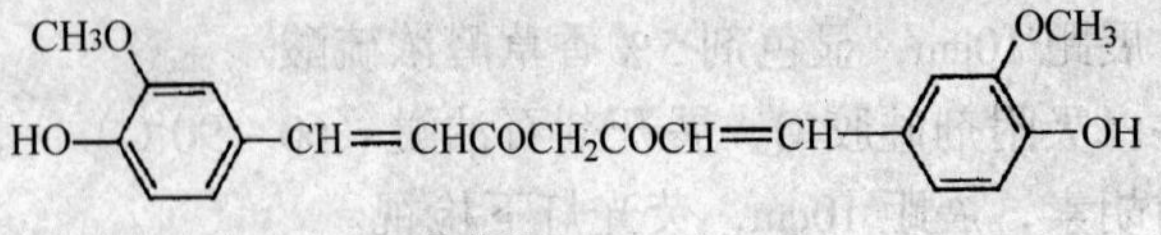

姜黄素 (curcumin)

28 The Qualitative Analysis And Quantitative Analysis Of Ruyi Jinhuang San

Purpose

1. To master the qualitative analysis of composing drugs of Chinese traditional patent medicine. by thin layer chromatogram.

2. To master the quantitative analysis of effective components in Chinese traditional patent medicine by thin layer chromatography scan

Principle

Ruyi Jinhuang San is a kind of Chinese traditional patent medicine. The powders consist of ten kinds of crude drugs. The ingredients are Radix et Rhizoma Rhei; Cortex Phellodendri; Rhizoma Curcumae Longae; Cortex Magnoliae officinalis; Pericarpium Citri Reticulatae; Radix Glycyrrhizae; Rhizoma Arisaematis; Radix Angelicae Dahuricae and Radix Trichosanthis. In this test thin layer chromatogram is used to identify eight kinds of crude drugs in comparison with reference drugs, and two – wavelength thin layer chromatogram scan is used to determine the content of curcumin.

Condition

1. Apparatus thin layer chromatogram scanner, ultrasonic surge, reflux equipment

2. Sample Ruyi Jinhuang San (on sale) and ingredient drugs.

3. Chemical reference substances rhein, aloe – emodin, emochin, berberine hydrochloride, curcumin, atractylone, atractylodin, magnolol, honokiol, hesperidin, glycyrrhizic acid, isoimperatorin, oxypeucedanin.

4. Reagents methanol, chloroform, ethyl acetate, petroleum ether, silica gel G, silica gel GF_{254}.

Assay

1. Qualitative analysis

(1) The identification of Cortex Phellodendri;

Rhizoma Curcumae Longae; Pericarpium Citri Reticulatae; Radix Glycyrrhizae: dissolve 1g of powder in 20ml of methanol, heat under reflux for 30 minutes, filter, concentrate filtrate to about 1ml to produce test solution. Prepare solutions of Cortex Phellodendri powder 0.5g and Pericarpium Citri Reticulatae powder 0.5g in the same manner as the reference drug solutions. Macerate warmly Rhizoma Curcumae Longae powder 0.2g and Radix Glycyrrhizae powder 0.2g in 5ml of methanol for 3 minutes as reference drug solutions.

Chromatographic system for Cortex Phellodendri:

Coating substance: silica gel G; mobile phase: n – butanol – glacial acetic acid – water (7:1:2); CRS: berberine hydrochloride; Developing distance: 10cm; Examining method: under fluorescent light.

Chromatographic system for Pericarpium Citri Reticulatae:

Coating substance: silica gel G; mobile phase: acetone – chloroform – 95% ethenol – formic acid (7:2:1:0.05); CRS: hesperidin; Developing distance: 10cm; Examining method: spray with 1% solution of aluminium trioxide in methanol and examineunder fluorescent light.

Chromatographic system for method of Rhizoma Curcumae Longae:

Coating substance: silica gel G; mobile phase: n – butanol – 6% ammonia TS – methanol (30:3:1) ; CRS: curcumin ; Developing distance: 10cm; Examining method: under visible light.

Chromatographic system for Radix Glycyrrhizae :

Coating substance: silica gel G; mobile phase: benzene – methanol (27:1) ; CRS: honokiol and magnolol; Developing distance: 10cm; Examining method: under fluorescent light.

(2) The identification of Rhizoma Atractylodis and Radix Angelicae Dahuricae:

Weigh 1g of the powder to soxhlet' s extractor, add petroleum ether (30 ~ 60℃) and heat under reflux for 2 hours, concentrate petroleum ether solution to 0.5ml to produce test solution.

Weigh 0.2g of Cortex Magnoliae officinalis powder and 0.2g of Radix Angelicae Dahuricae powder and prepare reference drug solutions in the same manner separately.

Chromatographic system for Cortex Magnoliae officinalis

Coating substance: silica gel G; mobile phase: benzene – ethyl acetate – n – hexane (15:15:70); CRS: atractylone and atractylodin; Developing distance: 10cm

Colorant: 5% solution of vanillin in sulfuric acid.

Chromatographic system for Radix Angelicae Dahuricae;

Coating substance: silica gel G; mobile phase: petroleum ether (60 ~ 90℃) – ethyl ether (5:2); CRS: isoimperatorin and oxypeucedanin; Developing distance: 10cm; Examining method: under fluorescent light.

(3) The identification of Radix et Rhizoma Rhei: Macerate 0.5g of powder in 20ml of methanol for 1 hour, filter, evaporate 5ml of the filtrate to dryness , dissolve the residue with 5ml of water, add 0.5ml of hydrochloric acid, heat under reflux for 30 minutes and

cool immediately. Extract with two 15ml quantities of ether, combine the combine the ether extract, evaporate it to dryness. Dissolve the residue with 0.5ml of chloroform as the test solution.

Prepare a solution of Radix et Rhizoma Rhei powder in the same manner as the reference drug solution.

Chromatographic system for Radix et Rhizoma Rhei:

Coating substance: silica gel GF_{254}; Mobile phase: chloroform – ethyl acetate (8:2); CRS: rhein, emodin and aloe – emodin ; Developing distance: 10cm; Examining method: under fluorescent light.

(4) The identification of Radix Glycyrrhizae: dissolve 1g of the powder in 10ml of water, add 3 drops of strong ammonia TS, ultrason ic disposal for 20 minutesto produce test solution.

Prepare solutions of Radix Glycyrrhizae powder 0.2 g in the same manner as the reference drug solution.

Chromatographic system for Radix Glycyrrhizae:

Coating substance: silica gel GF_{254}; mobile phase: *n* – butanol – 3M stvong ammonia TS – 95% ethanol (5:2:1); CRS: glycyrrhizic acid; Developing distance: 10cm; Examining method: under fluorescent light.

Assay of curcumin

1. Chromatographic system silica gel GF_{254} as coating substance, *n* – butanol – 26% ammonia TS – methanol (30:3:1) as mobile phase and developing distance is 10cm;

Linear parameters of thin layer chromatography scan: $S_x = 3$, zigzag scan, λ_s = 430nm, λ_n = 700nm.

2. Preparation of standard curve

Weight accurately 2.00mg curcumin to 10ml volumetric flask, dilute with methanol to the volume and mix well to to provide a referencc solution. Apply 2.0, 4.0, 6.0, 8.0, 10.0μl of reference solution to the same plate, respectively. Develop and scan the plate. Plot standard curve, with score as Y – axis and sample amount as X – axis. Then calculate regression equation and correlation coefficient.

3. Preparation of test solution and assay

Weight accurately 1g of the powder to 10ml volumetric flask, dilute with methanol to volume, ultrasonic disposal for 2 hours, filter, and filtrate as test solution. Apply 10μl of test solution and 4.0, 8.0 μl of reference solution to a same plate, develop and scan it, then calculate the content of curcumin in Ruyi Jinhuang San by external standard of two – point.

Experiment record

1. Plot the thin – layer chromatogram and calculate the R_f of main spots.

2. Calculate the percentage content of curcumin in Ruoyi Jinhuang San.

Question

1. Ruyi Jinhuang San is composed of ten kinds of crude drugs, eight of which can be identified with the above method, please design a test to identify the rest two (Rhizoma Arisaematis and Radix Trichosanthis).

2. Why should we prepare standard curve and calculate regression equation and correlation coefficient when using external standard of two – point?

第七章 附 录

附录1 常用中药质量分析方法

一、分光光度法

分光光度法是通过测定被测物质在特定波长处或一定波长范围内的光吸收度，对该物质进行定性和定量分析的方法。

常用的波长范围为：(1) 200～400nm 的紫外光区；(2) 400～760nm 的可见光区；(3) 2.5～25μm（按波数计为 4000～400cm^{-1}）的红外光区。所用仪器为紫外分光光度计、可见分光光度计（或比色计）、红外分光光度计或原子吸收分光光度计。为保证测量的精密度和准确度，所有仪器应按照国家计量检定规程或本附录规定，定期进行校正检定。

单色光辐射穿过被测物质溶液时，被该物质吸收的量与该物质的浓度和液层的厚度（光路长度）成正比，其关系如下式：

$$A = \lg \frac{1}{T} = ECL$$

式中 A 为吸收度；

T 为透光率；

E 为吸收系数，采用的表示方法是（$E_{1cm}^{1\%}$），其物理意义为当溶液浓度为 1%（g/ml），液层厚度为 1cm 时的吸收度数值；

C 为 100ml 溶液中所含被测物质的重量（按干燥品或无水物计算），g；

L 为液层厚度，cm。

物质对光的选择性吸收波长，以及相应的吸收系数是该物质的物理常数。当已知某纯物质在一定条件下的吸收系数后，可用同样条件将该供试品配成溶液，测定其吸收度，即可由上式计算出供试品中该物质的含量。在可见光区，除某些物质对光有吸收外，很多物质本身并没有吸收，但可在一定条件下加入显色试剂或经过处理使其显色后再测定，故又称比色分析。由于显色时影响呈色深浅的因素较多，且常使用单色光纯度较差的仪器，故测定时应用标准品或对照品同时操作。

二、紫外分光光度法

1．仪器的校正和检定

由于温度变化对机械部分的影响，仪器的波长经常会略有变动，因此除应定期对所用的仪器进行全面校正检定外，还应于测定前校正测定波长。常用汞灯中的较强谱线237.83nm、253.65nm、275.28nm、296.73nm、313.16nm、334.15nm、365.02nm、404.66nm、435.83nm、546.07nm、与576.96nm，或用仪器中氘灯的486.02nm与656.10nm谱线进行校正，钬玻璃在279.4nm、287.5nm、333.7nm、360.9nm、418.5nm、460.0nm、484.5nm、536.2nm与637.5nm波长处有尖锐吸收峰，也可作波长校正用，但因来源不同会有微小的差别，使用时应注意。

吸收度的准确度可用重铬酸钾的硫酸溶液检定。取在120℃干燥至恒重的基准重铬酸钾约60mg，精密称定，用0.005mol/L硫酸溶液溶解并稀释至1000ml，在规定的波长处测定并计算其吸收系数，并与规定的吸收系数比较，如下表，相对偏差在±1%以内。

表7-1　吸收系数校正表

波长/nm	235（min）	257（max）	313（min）	350（max）
吸收系数 $E_{1cm}^{1\%}$	124.5	144.0	48.62	106.6

杂散光的检查可按下表的试剂和浓度，配制成水溶液，置1cm石英吸收池中，在规定的波长处测定透光率，应符合表中的规定。

表7-2　溶剂透光率校正表

试剂	浓度%（g/ml）	测定用波长nm	透光率%
碘化钠	1.00	220	<0.8
亚硝酸钠	5.00	340	<0.8

2．对溶剂的要求

测定供试品前，应先检查所用的溶剂在供试品所用的波长附近是否符合要求，即用1cm石英吸收池盛溶剂，以空气为空白（即空白光路中不置任何物质）测定其吸收度。溶剂和吸收池的吸收度，在220～240nm范围内不得超过0.40，在241～250nm范围内不得超过0.20，在251～300nm范围内不得超过0.10，在300nm以上时不得超过0.05。

3．测定法

测定时，除另有规定外，应以配制供试品溶液的同批溶剂为空白对照，采用1cm的石英吸收池，在规定的吸收峰波长±2nm以内测试几个点的吸收度，以核对供试品的吸收峰波长位置是否正确，除另有规定外，吸收峰波长应在该品种项下规定的波长±2nm以内；否则应考虑该试样的真伪、纯度以及仪器波长的准确度，并以吸收度最大的波长作为测定波长。一般供试品溶液的吸收度读数，以在0.3～0.7之间的误差较小。仪器的狭缝波带宽度应小于供试品吸收带的半宽度，否则测得的吸收度会偏低；狭缝宽度的选择，应以减小狭缝宽度时供试品的吸收度不再增加为准，由于吸收池和溶剂本身可能有空白吸收，因此测定供试品的吸收度后应减去空白读数，再计算含量。

用作鉴别和检查项目的方法，分别按各品种项下的方法进行。鉴别项下吸收度读数的范围可根据制剂的实际含量和供试液的稀释倍数估算。

用于含量测定的方法一般有以下几种。

（1）对照品比较法

按各品种项下的方法，分别配制供试品溶液和对照品溶液，对照品溶液中所含被测成分的量应为供试品溶液中被测成分标示量的100% ± 10%，所用溶剂也应完全一致，在规定的波长测定供试品溶液和对照品溶液的吸收度后，按下式计算供试品中被测溶液的浓度：

$$C_X = \frac{A_X}{A_R} C_R$$

式中　C_X 为供试品溶液的浓度；

A_X 为供试品溶液的吸收度；

C_R 为对照品溶液的浓度；

A_R 为对照品溶液的吸收度。

（2）吸收系数法

按各品种项下的方法配制供试品溶液，在规定的波长处测定其吸收度，再以该品种在规定条件下的吸收系数计算含量。用本法测定时，应注意仪器的校正和检定。

（3）计算分光光度法

采用计算分光光度法应慎重。本法有多种，使用时均应按品种项下规定的方法进行。当吸收度处在吸收曲线的陡然上升或下降的部位测定时，波长的微小变化可能对测定结果造成显著影响，故对照品和供试品测试条件应尽可能一致。若测定时不用对照品，如维生素 A 测定，则应在测定时对仪器作仔细的校正和检定。

三、比色法

用比色法测定时，应取对照品同时操作。除另有规定外，比色法所用的空白系指用同体积的溶剂代替对照品或供试品溶液，然后依次加入等量的相应试剂，并用同样方法处理。在规定的波长处测定对照品和供试品溶液的吸收度后，按紫外分光光度法项下（1）对照品比较法的计算式计算供试品浓度。

当吸收度和浓度关系不呈线形时，应取数份梯度量的对照品溶液，用溶剂补充至同一体积，显色后测定各份溶液的吸收度，然后以吸收度与相应的浓度绘制标准曲线，再根据供试品的吸收度在标准曲线上求出其含量。

四、红外分光光度法

1．仪器及其校正，可使用傅里叶变换红外光谱仪或色散型红外分光光度计。用聚苯乙烯薄膜（厚度约为 0.05mm）校正仪器，绘制其光谱，用 $2851cm^{-1}$、$1601cm^{-1}$、$1028cm^{-1}$、$907nm^{-1}$处的吸收峰对仪器的波数进行校正。在 $2000 \sim 400cm^{-1}$区间允许相差 $\pm 4cm^{-1}$以内，在 $4000 \sim 2000cm^{-1}$区间允许相差 $\pm 8cm^{-1}$以内。

仪器的分辨率要求在 $3110 \sim 2850cm^{-1}$范围内应能清晰地分辨出 7 个峰，$2924cm^{-1}$与 $2851cm^{-1}$吸收带的分辨深度不小于 18%透光率，$1601cm^{-1}$与 $1583cm^{-1}$吸收带的分辨深度不小于 8%透光率。仪器的标称分辨率，除另有规定外，应不低于 $2cm^{-1}$。

2．试样的制备方法除另有规定外，用做鉴别时应按照药典委员会编订的《药品红外光谱集》第一卷（1995 年版）与第二卷（2000 年版）收载的各光谱图所规定的制备方法制备。具体操作技术可参见《药品红外光谱集》的说明。

3．各品种项下规定“应与对照的图谱（光谱集××图）一致”，系指《药品红外光谱集》第一卷（1995 年版）与第二卷（2000 年版）的图谱。

4．具有多晶现象的固体药品由于供测定的供试品晶型可能不同，导致绘制的光谱图与《药品红外光谱集》所收载的光谱图不一致，遇此情况时，应按该药品光谱图中备注的方法进行预处理后再绘制比较。

由于各种型号的仪器性能不同，试样制备时研磨程度的差异或吸水程度不同等原因，均会影响光谱的形状。因此，进行光谱对比时，应考虑各种因素可能造成的影响。

5．用作晶型、异构体限度检查或含量测定时，试样制备和具体测定方法均按各品种项下有关规定操作。

五、原子吸收分光光度法

由待测元素灯发出的特征谱线通过供试品蒸气时，被蒸气中待测元素的基态原子所吸收，吸收遵循一般分光光度法的吸收定律，通过测定辐射光强度减弱的程度可求出供试品中待测元素的含量。通常借比较标准品和供试品的吸收度，求得供试品中待测元素的含量。

原子吸收分光光度法所用仪器为原子吸收分光光度计，它由光源、原子化器、单色器和检测器等部件组成。光源通常用待测元素作为阴极的空心阴极灯，原子化器由雾化器及燃烧灯头组成。燃烧火焰由不同种类的气体混合物产生，常用空气－乙炔火焰。仪器某些工作条件（如波长、狭缝、光源灯电流、火焰类型、火焰状态）的变化可影响灵敏度、稳定程度和干扰情况，应按各品种项下的规定选用。

1．含量测定法

（1）第一法（标准曲线法）

在仪器推荐的浓度范围内，制备含待测元素的标准溶液至少 3 份，浓度依次递增，并分别加入供试品溶液配制中的相应试剂。除另有规定外，一般用去离子水制成水溶液。将仪器按规定启动后，先将去离子水喷入火焰，调读数为零，再将最浓的标准溶液喷入火焰，调节仪器至近满量程的读数；然后依次喷入每一标准溶液，读数。每喷完 1 份溶液后，均用去离子水喷入火焰充分冲洗灯头并调零。取每一浓度 3 次读数的平均值，与相应浓度作标准曲线。

按各品种项下的规定制备供试品溶液，使待测元素的估计浓度在标准曲线浓度范围内，将供试品溶液喷入火焰，取 3 次读数的平均值，从标准曲线上查得相应的浓度，计算元素的含量。

（2）第二法（标准加入法）

取同体积按各品种项下规定制备的供试品溶液 4 份，分别加至 4 个同体积的量瓶中，除 1 号量瓶外，其他 2、3、4 号量瓶分别再准确加入比例量的待测元素标准液，均用去离子水稀释至刻度，形成加入量从零开始递增的一系列标准液。按上述标准曲线法自“将仪器按规定启动后”操作，并依次将溶液喷入火焰，读数；将读数与相应的待测元素加入量作图，延长此直线至与含量轴的延长线相交，此交点与原点间的距离即相当于供试品溶液取用量中待测元素的含量（如下图所示）。再以此计算供试品中待测元素的含量。

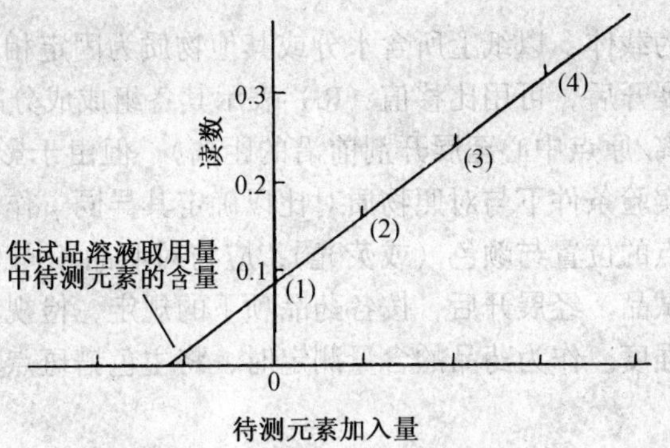

图 7-1　标准加入法测定图

2．杂质检查法

取供试品，按各品种项下的规定，制备供试品溶液；另取等量的供试品，加入限度量的待测元素溶液，制备成对照品溶液。照上述标准曲线法自“将仪器按规定启动后”操作，并将对照溶液喷入火焰，调节仪器使具合适的读数 a；在相同的操作条件下喷入供试品溶液，读数 b；b 值应小于（a-b）。

六、色谱法

色谱法（又称层析法）根据其分离原理可分为：吸附色谱、分配色谱、离子交换色谱与排阻色谱等。吸附色谱法是利用被分离物质在吸附剂上吸附能力的不同，用溶剂或气体洗脱使组分分离；常用的吸附剂有氧化铝、硅胶、聚酰胺等有吸附活性的物质。分配色谱是利用被分离物质在两相中分配系数的不同使组分分离；其中一相被涂布或键合在固体载体上，称为固定相，另一相为液体或气体，称为流动相。常用的载体有硅胶、硅藻土、硅镁型吸附剂与纤维素粉等。离子交换色谱是利用被分离物质在离子交换树脂上交换能力的不同使组分分离；常用的有不同强度的阳离子交换树脂、阴离了交换树脂，流动相为水或含有机溶剂的缓冲液。分子排阻色谱法又称凝胶色谱法，是利用被分离物质分子大小的不同导致在填料上渗透程度不同使组分分离；常用的填料有分子筛、葡聚糖凝胶、微孔聚合物、微孔硅胶或玻璃珠等，根据固定相和供试品的性质选用水或有机溶剂作为流动相。

色谱法又可根据分离方法分为：纸色谱法、薄层色谱法、柱色谱法、气相色谱法、高效液相色谱法等。所用溶剂应与供试品不起化学反应，纯度要求较高。分析时的温度，除气相色谱法或另有规定外，一般均在室温操作。分离后各成分的检出，应采用各品种项下所规定的方法。采用纸色谱法、薄层色谱法或柱色谱法分离有色物质时，可根据其色带进行区分；分离无色物质时，可在短波（254nm）或长波（365nm）紫外光灯下检视，其中纸色谱或薄层色谱也可喷以显色剂使之显色，或在薄层色谱中用加有荧光物质的薄层硅胶，采用荧光猝灭法检视。柱色谱法、气相色谱法和高效液相色谱法可用接于色谱柱出口处的各种检测器检测。柱色谱法还可分部收集流出液后用适宜方法测定。

七、纸色谱法

纸色谱法系以纸为载体，以纸上所含水分或其他物质为固定相，用展开剂进行展开的分配色谱。供试品经展开后，可用比移值（R_f）表示其各组成成分的位置（比移值 = 原点中心至斑点中心的距离/原点中心至展开剂前沿的距离），但由于影响比移值的因素较多，因而一般采用在相同实验条件下与对照物质对比以确定其异同。作为药品的鉴别时，供试品在色谱中所显主斑点的位置与颜色（或荧光），应与对照品相同。作为药品的纯度检查时，可取一定量的供试品，经展开后，按各药品项下的规定，检视其所显杂质斑点的个数或呈色（或荧光）的强度。作为药品的含量测定时，将主色谱斑点剪下洗脱后，再用适宜的方法测定。

1．仪器与材料

（1）展开室

通常为圆形或长方形玻璃缸，缸上具有磨口玻璃盖，应能密闭。用于下行法时，盖上有孔，可插入分液漏斗，用以加入展开剂。在近顶端有一用支架架起的玻璃槽作为展开剂的容器，槽内有一玻棒，用以压住色谱滤纸；槽的两侧各支一玻棒，用以支持色谱滤纸使其自然下垂，避免展开剂沿滤纸与溶剂槽之间发生虹吸现象。用于上行法时，在盖上的孔中加塞，塞中插入玻璃悬钩，以便将点样后的色谱滤纸挂在钩上；并除去溶剂槽和支架。

（2）点样器

常用具支架的微量注射器或定量毛细管，应能使点样位置正确、集中。

（3）滤纸

质地均匀平整，具有一定机械强度，不含影响展开效果的杂质；也不应与所用显色剂起作用，以致影响分离和鉴别效果，必要时可进行处理后再用。用于下行法时，取色谱滤纸按纤维长丝方向切成适当大小的纸条，离纸条上端适当的距离（使色谱纸上端能足够浸入溶剂槽内的展开剂中，并使点样基线能在溶剂槽侧的玻璃支持棒下数厘米处）用铅笔划一点样基线，必要时，可在色谱滤纸下端切成锯齿形便于展开剂滴下。用于上行法时，色谱滤纸长约 25cm，宽度则按需要而定，必要时可将色谱滤纸卷成筒形；点样基线距底边约 2.5cm。

2．操作方法

（1）下行法

将供试品溶解于适当的溶剂中制成一定浓度的溶液。用微量吸管或微量注射器吸取溶液，点于点样基线上，溶液宜分次点加，每次点样后，俟其自然干燥、低温烘干或经温热气流吹干，样点直径为 2～4mm，点间距离约为 1.5～2.0cm，样点通常应为圆形。

将点样后的色谱滤纸上端放在溶剂槽内并用玻棒压住，使色谱纸通过槽侧玻璃支持棒自然下垂，点样基线在支持棒下数厘米处。展开前，展开缸内用各品种项下规定的溶剂的蒸气使之饱和，一般可在展开缸底部放一装有规定溶剂的平皿或将浸有规定溶剂的滤纸条附着在展开缸内壁上，放置一定时间，俟溶剂挥发使缸内充满饱和蒸气。然后添加展开剂使浸没溶剂槽内的滤纸，展开剂即经毛细管作用沿滤纸移动进行展开，展开至规定的距离后，取出滤纸，标明展开剂前沿位置，俟展开剂挥散后按规定方法检出色谱斑点。

(2) 上行法

点样方法同下行法。展开缸内加入展开剂适量，放置俟展开剂蒸气饱和后，再下降悬钩，使色谱滤纸浸入展开剂约 0.5cm，展开剂即经毛细管作用沿色谱滤纸上升，除另有规定外，一般展开至约 15cm 后，取出晾干，按规定方法检视。

展开可以向一个方向进行，即单向展开；也可进行双向展开，即先向一个方向展开，取出，俟展开剂完全挥发后，将滤纸转动 90o，再用原展开剂或另一种展开剂进行展开；亦可多次展开、连续展开或径向展开等。

八、薄层色谱法

薄层色谱法，系将适宜的吸附剂或载体涂布于玻璃板、塑料或铝基片上，成一均匀薄层。待点样、展开后，与适宜的对照物按同法在同板上所得的色谱图对比，并可用薄层扫描仪进行扫描，用以进行药品的鉴别、杂质检查或含量测定的方法。

1. 仪器与材料

(1) 玻板

除另有规定外，用 10cm × 10cm、10cm × 15cm、20cm × 10cm 或 20cm × 20cm 的规格，要求光滑、平整，洗净后不附水珠，晾干。

(2) 吸附剂或载体

最常用的有硅胶 G、硅胶 GF_{254}、、硅胶 H、硅胶 HF_{254}、其次有硅藻土、硅藻土 G、氧化铝、氧化铝 G、微晶纤维素、微晶纤维素 F_{254} 等。其颗粒大小一般要求直径为 10～40μm。薄层涂布，除另有规定外，一般可分无黏合剂和含黏合剂两种；前者系将吸附剂或载体用水适量调成糊状，均匀涂布于玻璃板上，后者系在吸附剂或载体中加入一定量的黏合剂，一般常用 10%～15%的煅石膏（$CaSO_4 \cdot 2H_2O$ 在 140℃加热 4 小时），混匀后加水适量使用，或用羧甲基纤维素钠水溶液（0.2%～0.5%）适量调成糊状，均匀涂布于玻璃板上。也有含一定改性剂如荧光剂或缓冲液等的薄层。

(3) 涂布器

应能使吸附剂或载体在玻璃板上手工或自动涂成一层符合厚度要求的均匀薄层。

(4) 点样器

一般采用微升毛细管或与之相应的点样器材。

(5) 展开室

可用适合薄层板大小的专用玻璃缸，底部平底或有双槽，盖子须密闭。

2. 操作方法

(1) 薄层板的制备

除另有规定外，将吸附剂 1 份和水 3 份在研钵中向一方向研磨混合，去除表面的气泡后，倒入涂布器中，在玻板上平稳地移动涂布器进行涂布（厚度为 0.25～0.5mm），取下涂好薄层的玻板，于室温下，置水平台上晾干，在反射光及透射光下检视，表面应均匀，平整，无麻点、无气泡、无破损及污染，于 110℃烘 30 分钟，冷却后立即使用或置干燥箱中备用。

(2) 点样

除另有规定外，用点样器点样于薄层板上，一般为圆点。点样基线距底边 1.0～1.5cm，样点直径一般不大于 2mm，点间距离可视斑点扩散情况以不影响检出为宜。点样时必须注意勿损伤薄层表面。

（3）展开

将点好样品的薄层板放入展开缸的展开剂中，浸入展开剂的深度为距原点 5mm 为宜，密闭，待展开至规定距离，除另有规定外，一般为 8～15cm，取出薄层板，晾干，按正文项下的规定检测。

展开缸如需预先用展开剂预平衡，可在缸中加入适量的展开剂，必要时并在壁上贴二条与缸一样高、宽的滤纸条，一端浸入展开剂中，盖严，使展开缸平衡或按正文规定操作。

如需用薄层扫描仪对色谱进行扫描供鉴别、检查或含量测定，则可用薄层扫描法。

3．薄层扫描法

系指用一定波长的光照射在薄层板上，对薄层色谱中有吸收紫外光或可见光的斑点，或经激发后能发射出荧光的斑点进行扫描，将扫描得到的图谱及积分数据用于药品的鉴别、杂质检查或含量测定。

除另有规定外，薄层扫描方法可根据各种薄层扫描仪的结构特点及使用说明，结合具体情况，选择反射方式，采用吸收法或荧光法，用双波长或单波长扫描。测定方法有内标法及外标法。由于影响薄层扫描结果的因素很多，故薄层扫描定量测定应在保证供试品斑点的量在校正曲线的线性范围内的情况下，与对照品同板点样，展开，扫描，积分和计算。

用外标法测定时，若对照品各数据点在校正曲线上呈一通过原点的直线时，可用一点法校正，如不通过原点宜采用二点法校正，必要时用多点法校正。含量测定时，供试品溶液和对照品溶液应交叉点于同一薄层板上，供试品点样不得少于 4 个，对照品每一浓度不得少于 2 个，薄层扫描定量用的对照品纯度应符合含量测定用对照品的要求。

九、高效液相色谱法

高效液相色谱法是用高压输液泵将具有不同极性的单一溶剂或不同比例的混合溶剂、缓冲液等流动相泵入装有固定相的色谱柱，经进样阀注入供试品，由流动相带入柱内，在柱内各成分被分离后，依次进入检测器，色谱信号由记录仪或积分仪记录。

1．对仪器的一般要求

所用的仪器为高效液相色谱仪。色谱柱的填充剂和流动相的组分应按各品种项下的规定。常用的色谱柱填充剂有硅胶和化学键和硅胶，后者以十八烷基硅烷键合硅胶最为常用，辛基硅烷键合硅胶次之，氰基或氨基键合硅胶也有使用。离子交换填充剂，用于离子交换色谱；凝胶或玻璃微球等填充剂，用于分子排阻色谱。除另有规定外，柱温均为室温，检测器为紫外吸收检测器。

在用紫外吸收检测器时。所用流动相应符合紫外分光光度法项下对溶剂的要求。

正文中各品种项下规定的条件除固定相种类、流动相组分、检测器类型不得任意改变外，其余如色谱柱内径、长度、固定相牌号、载体粒度、流动相流速、混合流动相各组分的比例、柱温、进样量、检测器的灵敏度等，均可适当改变，以适应具体品种并达到系统适用性实验的要求。一般色谱图约于20分钟内记录完毕。

2. 系统适用性实验

按各品种项下要求对仪器进行适用性实验，即用规定的对照品对仪器进行试验和调整，应达到规定的要求；或规定分析状态下色谱柱的最小理论板数、分离度、重复性和拖尾因子。

(1) 色谱柱的理论板数 (n)

在选定的条件下，注入供试品溶液或各品种项下规定的内标物质溶液，记录色谱图，量出供试品主成分或内标物质峰的保留时间 t_R（以分钟或长度计，下同，但应取相同单位）和半峰高（$W_{h/2}$）宽，按 $n = 5.54\ (t_R/W_{h/2})^2$ 计算色谱柱的理论板数。如果测得理论板数低于各品种项下规定的最小理论板数，应改变色谱柱的某些条件（如柱长、载体性能、色谱柱充填的优劣等），使理论板数达到要求。

(2) 分离度

定量分析时，为便于准确测量，要求定量峰与其他峰或内标峰之间有较好的分离度。分离度（R）的计算公式为：

$$R = \frac{2\ (t_{R2} - t_{R1})}{W_1 + W_2}$$

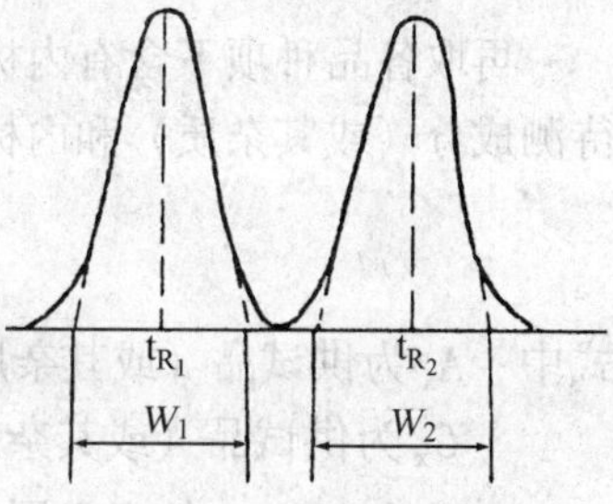

图 7-2　分离度计算示意图

式中　t_{R2}为相邻两峰中后一峰的保留时间；

t_{R1}为相邻两峰中前一峰的保留时间；

W_1 及 W_2 为此相邻两峰的峰宽（如图 7-2）。

除另有规定外，分离度应大于1.5。

(3) 重复性

取各品种项下的对照溶液，连续进样5次，除另有规定外，其峰面积测量值的相对标准偏差应不大于2.0%。也可按各品种校正因子测定项下，配置相当于80%、100%和120%的对照品溶液，加入规定量的内标溶液，配成3种不同浓度的溶液，分别进样3次，计算平均校正因子，其相对标准偏差也应不大于2.0%。

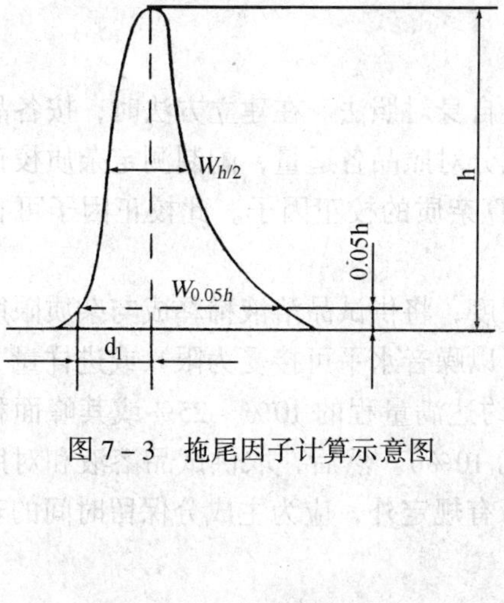

图 7-3　拖尾因子计算示意图

(4) 拖尾因子

为保证测量精度，特别当采用峰高法测量时，应检查待测峰的拖尾因子（T）是否符合各品种项下的规定，或不同浓度进样的校正因子误差是否符合要求。拖尾因子计算公式为：

$$T = \frac{W_{0.05h}}{2d_1}$$

式中　$W_{0.05h}$为0.05峰高处的峰宽；

d_1为峰极大至峰前沿之间的距离（如图 7-3）。

除另有规定外，T应在0.95～1.05之间。

3．测定法

定量测定时，可根据供试品的具体情况采用峰面积法或峰高法。测定杂质含量时，须采用峰面积法。

（1）内标法加校正因子测定供试品中某个杂质或主成分含量

按各品种项下的规定，精密称（量）取对照品和内标物质，分别配成溶液，精密量取各溶液，配成校正因子测定用的对照溶液。取一定量注入仪器，记录色谱图。测量对照品和内标物质的峰面积或峰高，按下计算校正因子：

$$校正因子（f）=\frac{A_S/C_S}{A_R/C_R}$$

式中 A_S 为内标物质的峰面积或峰高；

A_R 为对照品的峰面积或峰高；

C_S 为内标物质的浓度；

C_R 为对照品的浓度。

再取各品种项下含有内标物质的供试品溶液，注入仪器，记录色谱图，测量供试品中待测成分（或其杂质）和内标物质的峰面积或峰高，按下式计算含量：

$$含量（C_x）=f\cdot\frac{A_x}{A_S/C_S}$$

式中 A_x 为供试品（或其杂质）峰面积或峰高；

C_x 为供试品（或其杂质）的浓度。

f、A_S 和 C_S 的意义同上。

当配制校正因子测定用的对照溶液和含有内标物质的供试品溶液使用同一份内标物质溶液时，则配制内标物质溶液不必精密称（量）取。

（2）外标法测定供试品中某个杂质或主成分含量

按各品种项下的规定，精密称（量）取对照品和供试品，配制成溶液，分别精密取一定量，注入仪器，记录色谱图，测量对照品和供试品待测成分的峰面积（或峰高），按下式计算含量：

$$含量（C_X）=C_R\frac{A_X}{A_R}$$

式中各符号意义同上。

（3）加校正因子的主成分自身对照法

测定杂质含量时，可采用加校正因子的主成分自身对照法。在建立方法时，按各品种项下的规定，精密称（量）取杂质对照品和待测成分对照品各适量，配制测定杂质校正因子的溶液，进样，记录色谱图，按上述（1）法计算杂质的校正因子。此校正因子可直接载入各品种正文中，用于校正杂质的实测峰面积。

测定杂质含量时，按各品种项下规定的杂质限度，将供试品溶液稀释成与杂质限度相当的溶液作为对照溶液，进样，调节仪器灵敏度（以噪音水平可接受为限）或进样量（以柱子不过载为限），使对照溶液的主成分色谱峰高约达满量程的10%～25%或其峰面积能准确积分（面积约为通常条件下满量程峰积分值的10%）。然后，取供试品溶液和对照品溶液适量，分别进样，供试品溶液的记录时间除另有规定外，应为主成分保留时间的若干倍，测量供试品溶液色谱图上各杂质的峰面积，分别乘以相应的校正因子后与对照溶液主成分的峰面积比较，依法计算各杂质含量。

(4) 不加校正因子的主成分自身对照法

当没有杂质对照品时，可采用不加校正因子的主成分自身对照法。同上述（3）法配制对照溶液并调节仪器灵敏度后，取供试品溶液和对照溶液适量，分别进样，前者的记录时间除另有规定外，应为主成分保留时间的若干倍，测量供试品溶液色谱图上各杂质的峰面积并与对照溶液主成分的峰面积比较，计算杂质含量。

若供试品所含的部分杂质未与溶剂峰完全分离，则按规定先记录供试品溶液的色谱图Ⅰ，再记录等体积纯溶剂的色谱图Ⅱ。色谱图Ⅰ上杂质峰的总面积（包括溶剂峰），减去色谱图Ⅱ上的溶剂峰面积，即为总杂质峰的校正面积。然后依法计算。

(5) 面积归一化法

由于峰面积归一化法测定误差大，因此，本法通常只能用于粗略考察供试品中的杂质含量。除另有规定外，一般不宜用于微量杂质的检查。方法是测量各杂质峰的面积和色谱图上除溶剂峰以外的总色谱峰面积，计算各峰面积占总峰面积的百分率，即得。

由于微量注射器不易精确控制进样量，当采用外标法测定供试品中某杂质或主成分含量时，以定量环进样为好。

十、气相色谱法

气相色谱法的流动相为气体，称为载气；色谱柱分为填充柱和毛细管柱两种，填充柱内装吸附剂、高分子多孔小球或涂渍固定液的载体。毛细管柱内壁或载体经涂渍或交联固定液。注入进样口的供试品被加热气化，并被载气带入色谱柱，在柱内各成分被分离后，先后进入检测器，色谱信号用记录仪或数据处理器记录。

1. 对仪器的一般要求

所用的仪器为气相色谱仪。除另有规定外，载气为氮气；色谱柱为填充柱或毛细管柱，填充柱的材质为不锈钢或玻璃，载体用直径为0.25～0.18mm、0.18～0.15mm或0.15～0.125mm经酸洗并硅烷化处理的硅藻土或高分子多孔小球；常用玻璃或弹性石英毛细管柱的内径为0.20mm或0.32mm。进样口温度应高于柱温30～50℃；进样量一般不超过数微升；柱径越细进样量应越少。检测器为氢火焰离子化检测器，检测温度一般高于柱温，并不得低于100℃，以免水气凝结，通常为250～350℃。

正文中各品种项下规定的条件，除检测器种类、固定液品种及特殊指定的色谱柱材料不得任意改变外，其余如色谱柱内径、长度、载体牌号、粒度、固定液涂布浓度、载气流速、柱温、进样量、检测器的灵敏度等，均可适当改变，以适应具体品种并符合系统适用性试验的要求。一般色谱图约于30分钟内记录完毕。

2. 系统适用性试验

同高效液相色谱法项下规定。

3. 测定法

同高效液相色谱法项下规定。气相色谱法手工进样量不易精确控制，特别应注意留针时间和室温的影响。

十一、pH 值测定法

除另有规定外，水溶液的 pH 值应以玻璃电极为指示电极，用酸度计进行测定。酸度计应定期检定，使精密度和准确度符合要求。

1．仪器校正用的标准缓冲溶液

应使用标准缓冲物质配制，配制方法如下。

（1）草酸三氢钾标准缓冲液

精密称取在 54℃ ± 3℃干燥 4 ~ 5 小时的草酸三氢钾〔$KH_3(C_2O_4)_2 \cdot 2H_2O$〕12.61g，加水使溶解并稀释至 1000ml。

（2）邻苯二甲酸氢钾标准缓冲液

精密称取在 115℃ ± 5℃干燥 2 ~ 3 小时的邻苯二甲酸氢钾〔$KHC_8H_4O_4$〕10.12g，加水使溶解并稀释至 1000ml。

（3）磷酸盐标准缓冲液（pH6.8）

精密称取在 115℃ ± 5℃干燥 2 ~ 3 小时的无水磷酸氢二钠 3.533g 与磷酸二氢钾 3.387g，加水使溶解并稀释至 1000ml。

（4）磷酸盐标准缓冲液（pH7.4）

精密称取在 115℃ ± 5℃干燥 2 ~ 3 小时的无水磷酸氢二钠 4.303g 与磷酸二氢钾 1.179g，加水使溶解并稀释至 1000ml。

（5）硼砂标准缓冲液

精密称取硼砂〔$Na_2B_4O_7 \cdot 10H_2O$〕3.80g（注意避免风化），加水使溶解并稀释至 1000ml，置聚乙烯塑料瓶中，密塞，避免与空气中二氧化碳接触。

表 7 – 3　不同温度时标准缓冲液的 pH 值

温度（℃）	草酸三钾标准缓冲液	邻苯二甲酸氢钾标准缓冲液	磷酸盐标准缓冲液（pH6.8）	磷酸盐标准缓冲液（pH7.4）	硼砂标准缓冲液
0	0	4.01	6.98	7.52	9.46
5	5	4.00	6.95	7.49	9.39
10	10	4.00	6.92	7.47	9.33
15	15	4.00	6.90	7.44	9.28
20	20	4.00	6.88	7.43	9.23
25	25	4.00	6.86	7.41	9.18
30	30	4.01	6.85	7.40	9.14
35	35	4.02	6.84	7.39	9.10
40	40	4.03	6.84	7.38	9.07
45	45	4.04	6.83	7.38	9.04
50	50	4.06	6.83	7.38	9.02

测定 pH 值时，应严格按照仪器的使用说明书操作，并注意下列事项。

2．注意事项

(1) 测定前，按各品种项下的规定，选择二种 pH 值约相差 3 个单位的标准缓冲液，使供试液的 pH 值处于二者之间。

(2) 取与供试液 pH 值较接近的第一种标准缓冲液对仪器进行校正（定位），使仪器示值与表列数值一致。

(3) 仪器定位后，再用第二种标准缓冲液核对仪器示值，误差应不大于 ±0.02pH 单位。若大于此偏差，则应小心调节斜率，使示值与第二种标准缓冲液的表列数值相符。重复上述定位与斜率调节操作，至仪器示值与标准缓冲液的规定数值相差不大于 0.02 pH 单位。否则，须检查仪器或更换电极后，再行校正至符合要求。

(4) 每次更换标准缓冲液或供试液前，应用纯化水充分洗涤电极，然后将水吸尽，也可用所换的标准缓冲液或供试液洗涤。

(5) 在测定高 pH 值的供试品时，应注意碱误差的问题，必要时选用适当的玻璃电极测定。

(6) 对弱缓冲液（如水）的 pH 值测定，先用邻苯二甲酸氢钾标准缓冲液校正仪器后测定供试液，并重取供试液再测，直至 pH 值的读数在 1 分钟内改变不超过 ±0.05 为止；然后再用硼砂标准缓冲液校正仪器，再如上法测定；二次 pH 值的读数相差应不超过 0.1，取二次读数的平均值为其 pH 值。

(7) 配制标准缓冲液与溶解供试品的水，应是新沸过的冷蒸馏水，其 pH 值应为 5.5～7.0。

(8) 标准缓冲液一般可保存 2～3 个月，但发现有浑浊、发霉或沉淀等现象时，不能继续使用。

附录2　中药成分分析常用溶液和试剂

分析工作中所用溶液和试剂，应根据分析的实际需要，合理选用相应规格的试剂，按规定浓度和需要量，计算配制所需试剂的数量，正确配制，配好的溶液和试剂必须按规定要求妥善保存。

一、一般问题

1．化学试剂的规格

化学试剂的生产，按不同用途制成各种不同规格，供各使用单位选用，我国生产的化学试剂，部颁标准规定为三级（见表7－4）。

表7－4　化学试剂的规格

级别	名称	代号	标志颜色
一级品	保证试剂优级纯	G．R	绿色
二级品	分析试剂分析纯	A．R	红色
三级品	化学纯	C．P	蓝色

此外还生产各种特种规格的化学试剂，供特殊需要，如光谱纯试剂，色谱纯试剂，基准试剂，生物试剂等。纯度较差的有实验试剂（代号L．R），适用于一般化学试验。选用试剂的主要依据是该试剂所含杂质对分析要求有无影响，若试剂纯度不符合分析要求，应对试剂进行纯化处理。

2．溶液浓度的表示法

（见表7－5　溶液浓度的表示法）

表7－5　溶液浓度的表示法

NO.	浓度名称	符号	含　义
1	比重	*d*	一定体积溶液的重量与4℃时同体积水的重量的比值
2	体积比浓度	A∶B	A体积数液体试剂与B体积数液体试剂相混合
3	重量体积浓度	w/V	单位体积中所含溶质的重量，常用的有克/升，毫克/毫升
4	重量体积百分浓度	w/V%	100毫升溶液中含有溶质的克数
5	体积百分浓度	V/V%	100毫升溶液中含有液体溶质的毫升数
6	重量百分浓度	w/w	100克溶液中含有溶质的克数
7	体积克分子浓度（摩尔浓度）	M	1升溶液中含有溶质的克分子数（或摩尔数）
8	重量克分子浓度（重量摩尔浓度）	m	1000克溶剂中含有溶质的克分子数（或摩尔数）
9	当量浓度	N	1升溶液中含有溶质的克当量数

续表

NO.	浓度名称	符号	含　义
10	克式浓度	F	1升溶液中含有溶质的克式量数有两中表示方法：1每毫升标准溶液中含有滴定剂的克数，以 T_A 表示，A是滴定剂的化学式。
11	滴定度	T	2每毫升标准溶液相当于被测物质的克数，以 $T_{A/B}$ 表示，A是滴定剂的化学式，B是被测物质的化学式
12	滴定		1/20当量浓度
13	ppm		百万分数（即 10^{-6}）
14	ppb		亿分数（即 10^{-9}）

3．溶液、试剂配制中的基本计算

（1）用固体试剂配制溶液时的计算

配制重量百分浓度（w/w%）溶液（的计算）

$$P=\frac{w}{w+w_0}\times100\%$$

式中：P——重量百分浓度；

w——溶质的重量：

w_0——溶剂的重量。

配制（当量）浓度（N）溶液（的计算）

$$N=\frac{w}{EV}$$

式中：N——当量浓度；

w——溶质的重量；

E——溶质的当量；

V——配制溶液的体积。

配制克分子浓度（M）溶液的计算：

$$M=\frac{w}{mV}$$

式中：M——溶液的克分子浓度；

w——溶质的重量；

V——配制溶液的体积；

m——溶质的克分子量。

（2）用液体试剂配制溶液时的计算

原装液体试剂通常用重量百分浓度表示含量，并注明该浓度时的比重。配制时可称取其一定重量，也可量取其一定体积。

配制重量百分浓度（w/w%）溶液时，所需液体试剂的重量W按下式计算：

$$w_2=\frac{w_1\rho_1}{\rho_2}$$

式中　w_1——配制溶液的重量；

ρ_1——配制溶液重量百分浓度；

ρ_2——液体试剂的重量百分浓度。

w_2——所需液体试剂的重量

所需液体试剂的体积 V 可按下式计算：

$$V = \frac{w_2}{d} = \frac{w_1\rho_1}{\rho_2 d}$$

式中：d——液体试剂的比重。

配制克分子浓度（M）溶液时，所需液体试剂的重量 w 按下式计算：

$$w = \frac{MVm}{P_2}$$

式中：M——配制溶液的克分子数；

V——配制溶液的体积；

m——试剂的克分子量；

P_2——液体试剂的重量百分浓度；

所需液体试剂的体积；

$$V = w/d = \frac{MVm}{P_2 d}$$

式中：d——液体试剂的比重。

（3）由浓溶液稀释配制溶液时的计算

由浓溶液稀释配制溶液时，可采用交叉法计算应取浓溶液的体积的份数和稀溶液或溶剂应取的体积的份数，计算方法如下：

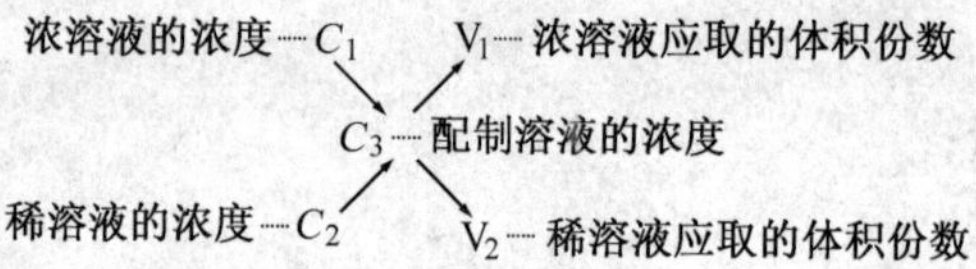

配制时，取 V_1 份浓溶液，V_2 份稀溶液（或溶剂），将其混合均匀，即得 $V_1 + V_2$ 份浓度为 C_3 的溶液。

若用溶剂（如水）稀释时，稀溶液的浓度 C_2 以 0 代人。

用交叉法计算重量百分浓度（w/w%）时，溶液的浓度 C 应分别以重量百分浓度 × 比重得到的体积代入进行计算。

此种方法是粗略的，它没有考虑两种不同浓度的混合时可能发生体积变化。

（4）调整溶液浓度的计算

在配制规定浓度的标准溶液时，若配成的溶液大于或小于所需的浓度时按下列公式计算应该补加水或浓溶液的体积。

当配成的标准溶液的浓度大于所需的浓度时，按下列公式计算补加水的体积 V_1（毫升）：

$$V_1 = \frac{N_0 - N}{N} \times V \times 1000$$

式中：V——调整前的标准溶液的体积，升；

N_0——调整前标准溶液的当量浓度或克分子浓度；

N——所需的当量浓度或克分子浓度。

当配成的标准溶液浓度小于所需的浓度时，按下列公式计算补加浓溶液的体积 V_2（毫升）：

$$V_2 = \frac{N - N_0}{N_1 - N} \times V \times 1000$$

式中：N_1——应被加浓溶液的当量浓度或克分子浓度；

N——所需的当量浓度或克分子浓度；

N_0——调整前标准溶液的当量浓度或克分子浓度；

V——调整前标准溶液的体积，升。

按照上述公式计算得出应补加的水或浓溶液数量调整溶液的浓度后，还必需按照规定重新进行标定，若不符合要求，还要重新调整，标定，直至符合规定要求为止。

4．溶液浓度的换算

（1）由重量百分浓度换算为重量体积浓度（克/升）

$$\text{重量体积浓度（克/升）} = \text{重量百分浓度} \times \text{比重} \times 10$$

（2）由重量体积浓度换算为克分子浓度（M）

$$\text{克分子浓度（M）} = \frac{\text{体积重量浓度（克/升）}}{\text{克分子量}}$$

（3）由克分子浓度换算为当量浓度（N）

$$\text{当量浓度（N）} = \frac{\text{克分子浓度（M）} \times \text{克分子量}}{\text{克当量}}$$

（4）由当量浓度换算为滴定度（T_A）

$$\text{滴定度（}T_A\text{）} = \frac{\text{当量浓度（N）} \times \text{克当量}}{1000} \text{（克/毫升）}$$

（5）由滴定度换算为重量体积浓度（克/升）

$$\text{重量体积浓度（克/升）} = \text{滴定度（克/毫升）} \times 1000$$

二、普通酸、碱溶液的配制

1．酸溶液的配制（表 7－6）

表 7－6　酸溶液的配制

名称（分子式）	比重（d）	含量（W/W%）	近似当量浓度	配制溶液的浓度 6N	2N	1N	0.5N	配制方法
				所制 1 升溶液所需的毫升数				
盐酸 HCL	1.18～1.19	36～38	12	500	167	83	42	量取所需浓酸加水稀释成 1 升
硝酸 HNO_3	1.39～1.40	65.0～68.0	15	381	128	64	32	同上
硫酸 H_2SO_4	1.83～1.84	95.0～98.0	36	167	56	28	14	量取所需浓酸在不断搅拌下缓缓加适量水，冷却后加水至 1 升
磷酸 H_3PO_4	1.69	85	45	116	36	18	9	量取所需浓酸加入适量水中，稀释至 1 升

续表

名称（分子式）	比重（d）	含量（W/W%）	近似当量浓度	配制溶液的浓度 所制1升溶液所需的毫升数 6N	2N	1N	0.5N	配制方法
冰乙酸 CH_3COOH	1.05	99.9	17	353	118	59	30	同上
高氯酸 $HClO_4$	1.68	70	12	500	167	83	42	同上
氢氟酸 HF	1.13	40	22.5	206	69	35	18	同上
氢溴酸 HBr	1.49	47.0	9	667	222	111	56	同上

2．碱溶液的配制（表7－7）

表7－7 碱溶液的配制

名称（分子式）	配制溶液的浓度 所制1升溶液所需的克数（毫升数） 6mol/L	2mol/L	1mol/L	0.5mol/L	配制方法
氢氧化钠（NaOH）	240	80	40	20	称取所需试饱和溶液浓度～0.04N剂量，溶解于适量水中，不断搅拌，注意溶解时发热，冷后用水稀释成1升
氢氧化钾（KOH）	339	113	56.5	28	同上
氨水*（NH_4OH）	400	134	77	39	量取所需浓氨水，加水配成1升
氢氧化钡［$Ba(OH)_2 \cdot 8H_2O$］	饱和溶液的浓度～0.4mol/L，配制0.1mol/L溶液所需试剂为15.78克				配成饱和溶液，或称取适量固体加水配成一定体积
氢氧化钙［Ca（OH）$_2$］	饱和溶液浓度～0.04mol/L				配成饱和溶液

* 浓氨水比重0.90～0.91，含NH3～28.0%（W/W%），近似当量浓度15N

3．缓冲液的配制

（1）枸橼酸－磷酸氢二钠缓冲液（pH 4.0）

甲液：取枸橼酸21g或无水枸橼酸19.2g，加水使溶解成1000ml，置冰箱内保存。

乙液：取磷酸氢二钠71.63g，加水使溶解成1000ml。

取上述甲液61.45ml与乙液38.55ml，混合，摇匀，即得。

（2）氨－氯化铵缓冲液（pH 8.0）

取氯化铵1.07g，加水使溶解成100ml，再加稀氨溶液（1→30）调节pH值至8.0，即得。

（3）氨－氯化铵缓冲液（pH 10.0）

取氯化铵5.4g，加水20ml溶解后，加浓氨溶液35ml，再加水稀释至100ml，即得。

（4）醋酸－醋酸钠缓冲液（pH 3.7）

取无水醋酸钠20g，加水300ml溶解后，加溴酚蓝指示液1ml及冰醋酸60～80ml，至溶液从蓝色转变为纯绿色，再加水稀释至1000ml，即得。

（5）醋酸－醋酸钠缓冲液（pH 4.5）

取醋酸钠18g，加冰醋酸9.8ml，再加水稀释至1000ml，即得。

（6）醋酸－醋酸钠缓冲液（pH 6.0）

取醋酸钠 54.6g，加 1mol/L 醋酸溶液 20ml 溶解后，加水稀释至 500ml，即得。

（7）醋酸－醋酸铵缓冲液（pH 4.5）

取醋酸铵 7.7g，加水 50ml 溶解后，加冰醋酸 6m 与适量的水使成 100ml，即得

（8）醋酸－醋酸铵缓冲液（pH 4.8）

取醋酸铵 77g，加水约 200ml 使溶解，加冰醋酸 57ml，再加水至 1000ml，即得

（9）醋酸－醋酸铵缓冲液（pH 6.0）

取醋酸铵 100g，加水 300ml 使溶解，加冰醋酸 7ml，摇匀，即得。

（10）磷酸盐缓冲液（pH 6.8）

取 0.2mol/L 磷酸二氢钾溶液 250ml，加 0.2mol/L 氢氧化钠溶液 118ml，用水稀释至 1000ml，即得。

附录3　玻璃仪器的洗涤及各种洗液的配制法

实验中所使用的玻璃仪器清洁与否，直接影响实验结果，往往由于仪器的不清洁或被污染而造成较大的实验误差，甚至会出现相反的实验结果。因此，玻璃仪器的洗涤清洁工作是非常重要的。

1．初用玻璃仪器的清洗

新购买的玻璃仪器表面常附着有游离的碱性物质，可先用肥皂水（或去污粉）洗刷再用自来水洗净，然后浸泡在1%～2%盐酸溶液中过夜（不少于4小时），再用自来水冲洗，最后用蒸馏水冲洗2～3次，在100～130℃烘箱中烤干备用。

2．用过的玻璃仪器的清洗

（1）一般玻璃仪器：如试管、烧杯、锥形瓶等（包括量筒），先用自来水洗刷至无污物，再选用大小合适的毛刷沾取去污粉（掺入肥皂粉）或浸入肥皂水内。将器皿内外（特别是内壁）细心刷洗，用自来水冲洗干净后，蒸馏水冲洗2～3次，烤干或倒置在清洁处，干后备用。凡洗净的玻璃器皿，不应在器壁上带有水珠，否则表示尚未洗干净，应再按上述方法重新洗涤。若发现内壁有难以去掉的污迹，应分别试用下述各种洗涤剂予以清除，再重新冲洗。

（2）量器：如吸量管、滴定管、量瓶等。使用后应立即浸泡于凉水中，勿使物质干涸。工作完毕后用流水冲洗，以除去附着的试剂、蛋白质等物质，晾干后浸泡在铬酸溶液中4～6小时（或过夜），再用自来水充分冲洗，最后用蒸馏水冲洗2～4次，风干备用。

（3）其他：具有传染性样品的容器，如病毒、传染病患者的血清等沾污过的容器，应先进行高压（或其他方法）消毒后再进行清洗，盛过各种毒品，特别是剧毒药品和放射性同位素物质的容器，必须经过专门处理（略），确知没有残余毒物存在方可进行清洗。

3．洗涤液的种类和配制方法

（1）铬酸洗液（重铬酸钾－硫酸洗液，有时简称为洗液）

广泛用于玻璃仪器的洗涤，常用的配制方法有下述四种：

1）取100毫升工业浓硫酸置于烧杯内，小心加热，然后小心慢慢加入5克重铬酸钾粉末，边加边搅拌，待全部溶解后冷却，贮于具玻璃塞的细口瓶内。

2）称取5克重铬酸钾粉末置于250毫升烧杯中，加水5毫升，尽量使其溶解，慢慢加入浓硫酸100毫升，随加随搅拌，冷却后贮存备用。

3）称取80克重铬酸钾，溶于1000毫升自来水中，慢慢加入工业硫酸100毫升（边加边用玻璃棒搅拌）。

4）称取200克重铬酸钾，溶于500毫升自来水中，慢慢加入工业硫酸500毫升（边加边搅拌）。

（2）浓盐酸（工业用）

可洗去水垢或某些无机盐沉淀。

（3）5%草酸溶液

用数滴硫酸酸化，可洗去高锰酸钾的痕迹。

(4) 5%～10%磷酸三钠（$Na_3PO_4 \cdot 12H_2O$）溶液

可洗去油污物。

(5) 30%硝酸溶液

洗涤 CO_2 测定仪器及微量滴管。

(6) 5%～10%乙二胺四乙酸二钠（$EDTA-Na_2$）溶液

加热煮沸可洗玻璃仪器内壁的白色沉淀物。

(7) 尿素洗涤液

为蛋白质的良好溶剂，适用于洗涤盛蛋白质制剂及血样的容器。

(8) 酒精与浓硝酸混合液

最适合于洗净滴定管，在滴定管中加入3毫升酒精，然后沿管口慢慢加入4毫升浓硝酸（比重1.4），盖住滴定管管口，利用所产生的氧化氮洗净滴定管。

(9) 有机溶剂

如丙酮、乙醇、乙醚等可用于洗脱油脂、脂溶性染料等污痕。二甲苯可洗脱油漆的污垢。

(10) 氢氧化钾的乙醇溶液和含有高锰酸钾的氢氧化钠溶液

是两种强碱性的洗涤液，对玻璃仪器的侵蚀性很强，清除容器内壁污垢，洗涤时间不宜过长，使用时应小心慎重。

上述洗涤液可多次使用，使用前必须将待洗涤之玻璃仪器先用水冲洗多次，除去肥皂去污粉或各种废液。若仪器上有凡士林或羊毛脂时，应先用软纸擦去，然后用乙醇或乙醚擦净后才能使用洗液，否则会使洗涤液迅速失效。例如：肥皂水，有机液剂（乙醇、甲醛等）及少量油污皆会使重铬酸钾－硫酸洗液变绿，减低洗涤能力。

附录4 常用溶剂性质

表中列出了最重要的有机溶剂，在数值上按 ε°增加次序排列，在测定 ε°时，Snyder 以正戊烷为参比溶剂（ε° = 0.00），然后测定标准品在不同溶剂作为流动相时的保留体积。从本质上看，此系列中溶剂的次序按照组分在固定相上吸附能力减小的次序排列，即使用第一种溶剂时，组分的 K 值最大，而使用最后一种溶剂时，由于它的洗脱能力极高，以致组分不被滞留。

表 7－8 常用溶剂性质表

溶剂名称	沸点（℃）	ε°（硅胶）	电解常数	粘度 η(20℃)	折光率（R2）	UV 截止波长(nm)	溶解度(20～25℃) 溶剂在水中(%)	水在溶剂中(%)
正戊烷	33	0.00		0.23	1.358	205		
正己烷	69	0.00	1.88	0.33	1.375	195	0.00095	0.0111
异辛烷		+0.01		0.50	1.404	197		
环己烷	81	0.03	2.02	1.00	1.427	205	0.010	0.0055
戊烯－1		+0.06		0.18	1.371	—		
二硫化碳	46	+0.11	2.64	0.37	1.626	380	0.294	<.005
四氯化碳	77	+0.14	2.24	0.97	1.466	265	0.077	0.010
二甲苯	137	+0.20	2.38	0.6～0.8	－1.5	290	0.0176	0.5402
异丙醚	68	+0.22		0.37	1.368	220		
氯异丙烷	47	+0.22		0.33	1.378	225		
甲苯	110	+0.22	2.37	0.59	1.496	285	0.1515	0.0334
苯	80	+0.25	2.29	0.65	1.501	280	0.1780	0.063
乙醚	35	+0.29	4.34	0.23	1.353	220	0.042	1.468
氯仿	61	+0.31	4.81	0.57	1.443	245	0.815	0.072
二氯甲烷	40	+0.32		0.44	1.424	233		
四氢呋喃	66	+0.35	7.58	—	1.408	220	任意	混溶
二氯乙烯		+0.38		0.79	1.445	230		
丙酮	56	+0.43	2.07	+0.32	1.359	330	溶解	度大
二氢六环	101	+0.43	2.21	1.54	1.422	220	任意	混溶
乙酸乙酯	77	+0.45	6.02	0.45	1.370	260	8.0	2.94
戊醇	138		13.9	4.1	1.410	210	2.19	7.41
二甲亚砜	189	+0.48		2.24	1.479	—		
乙腈	82	+0.50	37.5	0.37	1.344	190	任意	混溶
吡啶	115	+0.55	12.3	0.94	1.510	305		

续表

溶剂名称	沸点(℃)	ε°(硅胶)	电解常数	粘度η(20℃)	折光率(R2)	UV截止波长(nm)	溶解度(20~25℃)溶剂在水中(%)	水在溶剂中(%)
异丙醇	82	+0.63	19.92	2.3	1.38	205	任意	混溶
正丙醇	97	+0.63	20.3	2.3	1.38	205	任意	混溶
乙醇	78	+0.68	24.3	1.20	1.361	210	任意	混溶
甲醇	64	0.73	33.6	0.60	1.329	205	任意	混溶
乙酸	118	大	6.15	1.26	1.37	—	任意	混溶
水	100	大	80.4	1.00	1.333	195	任意	混溶

附录5　色谱法预试中药化学成分

色谱法常用来进一步确证定性实验呈正反应的各类化学成分。它是将上述正结果的供试液进行适当的浓缩，再按可能含有的某类化学成分的一般色谱条件进行薄层色谱或纸上色谱分离，最后进行该类化合物的显色反应，观察结果，这样可以排除一部分其他化合物的干扰，各类成分的色谱条件参阅下表。

表7-9　各类成分色谱预试条件

化合物	色谱条件		检测方法		附注
	吸附剂或载体	展开剂	显色剂	结果	
生物碱	氧化铝-CMC	苯,氯仿,乙酸乙酯,乙醇等单一溶剂;氯仿-甲醇(9:1);苯-乙醇(8:2)	改良碘化铋钾	橙红色斑点	碱性生物碱在选用纸色谱或薄层色谱时,可选用碱性展开剂或将硅胶板氨气饱和后展开。碱性弱的生物碱可选用吸附薄层色谱
	硅胶-CMC	氯仿-二乙胺(NH_4OH)(9:1);氯仿-丙酮-二乙胺(5:4:1)			
	层析滤纸	正丁醇:醋酸:水(4:1:5)(上层);乙酸乙酯:吡啶:水(2:1:2)	观察荧光	各种荧光斑点	
糖和多糖	层析滤纸	正丁醇:醋酸:水(4:1:5)(上层);乙酸乙酯:吡啶:水(2:1:2)	茴香醛 氨性硝酸银	不同颜色的斑点;棕黑色斑点	氨性硝酸银需加热至110℃始能显色主要用于检出还原糖
酚类鞣质	层析滤纸 硅胶-CMC	正丁醇:醋酸:水(4:1:5)(上层);氯仿:丙酮(9:1)	三氯化铁 三氯化铁-铁氰化钾(1:1)	蓝、绿、黑等各色斑点	
黄酮	硅胶-CMC	氯仿-甲醇-丙酮(40:25:35);乙酸乙酯-丁醇-丙酮-水(3:3:1:1)	10% Na_2CO_3水液、氨气熏、10% $AlCl_3$醇液(喷试剂前后观察荧光)	观察喷洒Na_2CO_3氨熏前后荧光的变化,多为黄色或黄绿色荧光斑点	在醋酸水系统中可区分苷或苷元,苷元多在原点,苷可展开;在正丁醇-醋酸-水系统中苷元的R_f值较苷大
	层析滤纸	15%醋酸水;正丁醇-醋酸-水(4:1:5)(上层)			
	聚酰胺	甲醇-水(8:2);乙醇-水(3:2);丙酮-水(1:1)			
蒽醌	硅胶-CMC	苯-乙酸乙酯(3:17);乙酸乙酯-甲醇-水(100:1.65:1.35);氯仿-乙醇(75:25);石油醚-丙酮-水(5:3:1)	1~2%的苛性碱醇溶液 0.5% MgAC₂甲醇液(90℃加热5分钟)	红色斑点、橙红、紫红色斑点	硅胶色谱条件适应于游离蒽醌的检出;纸色谱对苷也可以展开
香豆素萜类内酯	硅胶-CMC	甲苯-乙酸乙酯-甲酸(5:4:1);石油醚-乙酸乙酯(5:1);正丁醇-醋酸-水(4:1:5)	观察荧光	蓝绿色荧光	香豆素类苷可在硅胶板上为正丁醇-醋酸-水(4:1:5)所展开
	酸性氧化铝	石油醚-氯仿(1:1);石油醚-乙醛(1:1)	重氮化试剂	红紫色斑点	
	层析滤纸	正丁醇-醋酸-水(4:1:5)	观察荧光	蓝绿色荧光	

续表

化合物	色谱条件		检测方法		附注
	吸附剂或载体	展开剂	显色剂	结果	
强心苷	滑石粉－石膏(7:3)(甲酰胺为固定相)	氯仿－丙酮－乙酸乙酯(8:2:0.5:2.5),甲酰胺饱和	碱性3,5－二硝基苯甲酸;	红色、紫色斑点(110℃烘5分钟)	此处列出的条件中滑石粉板适合于含糖分子较多的强心苷分离。对于苷元或糖分子较少的强心苷的分离可用另两种条件,或一般的吸附色谱条件(同甾体)
	硅胶－CMC	二氯甲烷－甲醇－甲酰胺(80:19:1);氯仿－甲醇－乙酸(85:13:2);乙酸乙酯－吡啶－水(5:1:4)	氯胺T－三氯乙酸试剂	浅蓝色背景呈橙红色斑点(烘5分钟)	
	层析滤纸(甲酰胺为固定相)	苯;甲苯－氯仿－甲酰胺(6:4饱和)	碱性苦味酸试剂	橙红色斑点(110℃烘5分钟)	
氨基酸	硅胶－CMC	正丁醇－醋酸－水(4:1:5)	茚三酮	紫色斑点	
	层析滤纸	正丁醇－醋酸－水(4:1:5);水饱和的酚		少数为黄色斑点	
有机酸	硅胶－CMC	氯仿－丙酮－甲酰胺－醋酸(7:2:1.5:0.5)	溴酚兰(在喷后110℃加热数分钟)	黄色斑点	
	层析滤纸	正丁醇－醋酸－水(4:1:5)			
甾体三萜皂苷	硅胶－CMC	分配薄层:环已烷－乙酸乙酯(1:1);苯－丙酮(1:1);氯仿－丙酮(95:5).吸附薄层:氯仿－甲醇－水(下层65:35:10);水饱和正丁醇	5%磷钼酸乙醇液	蓝色至蓝紫色斑点	此处列出的层析条件适用于甾体、三萜及皂苷元的分离.皂苷的层析可参考强心苷的条件.检出试剂对甾体的灵敏度高于三萜
	层析滤纸	苯－乙酸乙酯(1:1);苯－丙酮(6:4)	20%三氯化锑氯仿液	红、棕红或绿色斑点	
挥发油	硅胶－CMC	石油醚(或苯)－乙酸乙酯(8:2)	香草醛－硫酸	斑点颜色各异	石油醚适于挥发油中萜类化合物的分离,而石油醚－乙酸乙酯混合液适于挥发油中含氧化合物的分离

附录6　常用色谱显色剂及使用

一、通用显色剂

1．碘蒸气（Iodine）

将薄层板放入底部有少许结晶碘片的密闭容器（可在广口瓶内于水浴上进行），碘则迅速升华，碘蒸气充满整个空间，能使许多化合物在淡黄的背景上产生棕色斑点。

2．硫酸（Sulphuric acid）

（1）50%硫酸的甲醇溶液（将等体积的浓硫酸与甲醇于冷却的条件下小心混合）。

（2）5%浓硫酸的乙醇溶液。

（3）15%浓硫酸的正丁醇溶液。

（4）5%浓硫酸的醋酐溶液。

（5）50%浓硫酸的醋酸溶液。

薄层板用上述试剂之一喷雾，在空气中干燥15分钟，然后于110℃加热直到展现的颜色或荧光达到最大强度为止。对于含CMC－Na粘合剂的薄层板不宜用此类检定剂，因加热时可使背景发黑而干扰观察。

注：胆甾醇、维生素A及其酯以及许多异戊间二烯类脂化合物，用2．（1）项下试剂喷雾后加热，易出现特殊颜色，胆甾醇和其酯类由红色、红紫色最后转变为棕色，维生素A和其酯类最初呈蓝色，许多化合物接着碳化，产生黑色斑点。

3．高锰酸钾－硫酸（Permanganate Potassium－sulphuric acid）

0.5g高锰酸钾溶于15ml浓硫酸中，喷雾，在粉红色背景上显示蓝色斑点，注意配置时应小量慢慢混合，因为七氧化二锰是爆炸物。

4．铬酸（Chromic acid－Sulphuric acid）

将5g重铬酸钾溶于100ml 40%的硫酸中即得。喷后薄层板需加热到150℃，该试剂特别适用于易碳化的有机物（尤其是类脂物）。

5．碱性高锰酸钾（Permanganate potassium，basic）

1%高锰酸钾溶液与0.5%碳酸钠溶液等体积混合，喷雾，还原性物质在淡红色背景下显蓝色。

6．碘溶液（Iodine）

0.5%碘的氯仿溶液，对很多化合物显黄棕色。

7．碘－碘化钾（Iodine－potassium iodine）

0.2g碘、0.4g碘化钾溶于100ml水中，许多化合物可以与其显黄棕色。

8．磷钼酸试剂（Phosphomolybdic acid）

5%磷钼酸的醇溶液，喷后于120℃烘烤，还原性物质显蓝色，再用氨气熏，则背景变成红色。

9．磷钨酸试剂（Phosphetungstic acid）

20%磷钨酸的乙醇溶液，喷后于120℃烘烤，还原性物质显蓝色。

10．铁氰化钾－三氯化铁（Ferricyanide Ferrichloride）

1%铁氰化钾与2%三氯化铁等量混合喷雾，还原性物质显蓝色，若再喷2mol/L盐酸溶液，则颜色加深。

11．荧光检定剂

(1) 0.2% 2′，7－二氯荧光素乙醇溶液。

(2) 0.01%荧光素乙醇溶液。

(3) 0.1%桑色素乙醇溶液。

(4) 0.05% 罗丹明B乙醇溶液。

喷以上任一溶液，不同的物质可能在荧光背景上显黑色或其它颜色斑点。

(5) 荧光素（钠）溶液：50毫克荧光素钠（又称荧光黄钠）溶于100毫升50%甲醇中，喷后于紫外光下观察，为芳香和杂环化合物的通用检定剂。

二、生物碱及含氮化合物

1．碘化铋钾试剂（Dragendorffs）

溶液Ⅰ：0.85g次硝酸铋溶于10ml冰醋酸与40ml水中。

溶液Ⅱ：8g碘化钾溶于20ml水中。

贮备液：溶液Ⅰ与溶液Ⅱ等体积混合，可于棕色瓶中保存较长时间，一般贮备液可作沉淀剂用。

喷雾剂：1ml贮备液与2ml乙酸、10ml水混合而得。生物碱可与之显桔红色斑点。

2．改良碘化铋钾－Ⅰ（据Bregoff－Delwiche）

贮备液：将8g碱式硝酸铋溶于20～23ml 25%硝酸中，将此液边搅拌边缓慢的加入到由20g碘化钾1ml 6mol/L盐酸和5ml水组成的混悬液中，再加水至深色沉淀中，直到变成桔红色溶液为止。本溶液体积约为95ml，滤去不溶性残渣后，加水稀释至100ml，贮备于深色容器中，于冰箱中可保存数周。

喷雾剂：下列溶液依次混合即可。20ml水，6ml mol/L盐酸，2ml贮备液，6ml 6mol/L氢氧化钠液。若氢氧化铋振摇后不溶解，可加数滴6mol/L盐酸。该喷雾剂于冰箱中可保存10日左右，用于含季铵氮的化合物。

3．改良碘化铋钾－Ⅱ（据Munier）

溶液Ⅰ：将1.7g碱式硝酸铋和20g酒石酸溶解于80ml水中。

溶液Ⅱ：16g碘化钾溶于40ml水中。

贮备液：溶液Ⅰ与Ⅱ等体积混合即得。此液在冰箱中可保存数月。

喷雾剂：将5ml贮备液加到含有10g酒石酸的50ml水溶液中即得。用于含氮有机化合物，贮备液本身可供检测维生素B_1用。

4．改良碘化铋钾－Ⅲ（据Munier&Macheboenf）

溶液Ⅰ：将0.8g碱式硝酸铋溶于10ml醋酸和40ml水中。

溶液Ⅱ：将8g碘化钾溶于20ml水中。

贮备液：溶液Ⅰ与Ⅱ等体积混合即得（在深色玻璃容器内可保存相当长时间）。

喷雾剂：1ml 贮备液和 2ml 醋酸及 10ml 水于临用前混合即得。用于含氮有机化合物。

5. 改良碘化铋钾－Ⅳ（据 Thies Ruther）

贮备液：将 25ml 醋酸、2.6g 碱式碳酸铋和 7g 碘化钠的混合液煮沸数分钟，约 12 小时后，将大量沉淀用垂熔玻璃漏斗过滤。取 20ml 澄清的红棕色滤液同 80ml 乙酸乙酯混合，再加入 0.5ml 水贮于棕色玻璃器中。

喷雾剂：由 10ml 贮备液、100ml 醋酸和 240ml 乙酸乙酯配成混合液，生物碱和其他许多不含氮的化合物，在用 5～10ml 喷雾剂喷后，可出现橙色斑点，若再喷 0.05～0.1mol/L 硫酸可显著增加检出的灵敏度，在灰色背景上呈现亮红色－桔红色斑点，可用予试验确定酸的最佳浓度和喷雾量。

6. 碘化汞钾试剂（Mayer's）

13.55g 氯化汞和 49.8g 碘化钾各溶于 20ml 水中，混合后稀释至 1000ml，再加入 1/10 体积的 17%盐酸即可用于喷雾。

注：该试剂可用作生物碱沉淀剂。

7. 碘铂酸钾（Iodoplatinate potassium）

（1）将 3ml 10%六氯铂酸溶液同 97ml 水混合，再加 100ml 6%碘化钾水溶液，此试剂应于临用前鲜配。

（2）将 5ml 5%六氯铂酸（H_2PtCl_6）和 45ml 10%碘化钾水溶液混合，加水稀释至 100ml 即可，临用前鲜配。

（3）5%六氯铂酸、10%碘化钾及水以 1:9:20 混合（稳定几个月），再加入 1%体积浓盐酸后喷雾，多数碱性药物开始显蓝－紫斑，最后变为棕黄色，仅含伯铵或仲铵功能团的药物显蓝白斑。

8. 酸性碘－碘化钾（Wagner's）

将 1g 碘和 10g 碘化钾于 5ml 水中加热溶解，再加 2ml 醋酸，用水稀释至 100ml 即可。

9. 铁氰化钾－氯化铁（Kie'ffes's）

将 100ml 0.1%$FeCl_3$ 溶液与 10ml 1%铁氰化钾溶液混合即可。喷后水洗 2～3 分钟，在紫外光下，游离生物碱和苯酚显灰到蓝色斑点。

10. 铁氰化钾－亚铁氰化钾（Ferricyanide－ferrocyanide）

将 57mg 铁氰化钾和 7.8mg 亚铁氰化钾溶于 100ml 蒸馏水中即可，用于检定吗啡。

11. 高氯酸－氯化铁（Perchloricacid－ferricchioride）

将 100ml 5%高氯酸水溶液、2ml 0.05M 氢氧化铁溶液混合即可用于喷雾。检定吲哚衍生物，但靛红和 2－羟基吲哚衍生物不发生反应。

12. 硅钨酸试剂（Bertrand's）

将 1g 硅钨酸溶于 20ml 水中，加 10%盐酸使呈酸性即得，用作生物碱的沉淀剂。

13. 磷钨酸试剂（Scheibler'）

喷雾剂：为 5%～10%磷钨酸的乙醇溶液，喷后于 120℃加热。

沉淀剂：磷钼酸钠 20g 溶于硝酸中，加水使成 10%。

14. 磷钼酸试剂（Sonnen schein's）

配制方法同二.13。

15．硫酸铁铵（Ferric ammonium suphate）

将1g硫酸铁铵溶于100ml磷酸（75%或85%）中，在热（100℃）的薄层板上喷以本试剂，用以检定长春碱。

16．硫酸高铈－硫酸（Ceric sulphate－ sulphuric acid，sonnen schein改良试剂）

喷雾剂：1g高铈悬浮于4ml水中，加1g三氯乙酸煮沸，逐渐滴加浓硫酸直到混浊消失。喷雾后于110℃加热几分钟，直到色斑出现，除阿朴吗啡、番木鳖碱、秋水仙碱、罂粟碱和毒扁豆碱均能与本试剂起反应外，也能用来检测有机碘化合物。

17．硫酸高铈铵（Cercsulphate，ammonium）

为1%硫酸高铈铵的浓磷酸（85%）溶液。用于检测长春碱及萝芙木生物碱等。Lepi－aimalicnie呈桔黄色，Tetraphyuicine呈桃红色，Veosillmine呈蓝紫或绛紫色，有的生物碱呈翠绿色、蓝黑色等。

18．硫酸铈－三氯乙酸（Ceriumsulfate－trihloro acetic acid）

0.1g硫酸铈溶于4ml含1g三氯乙酸的水中煮沸，逐渐滴加浓硫酸至溶液澄清，喷洒后加热至110℃，可检定吗啡、二甲马钱子碱、秋水仙碱、罂粟碱和扁豆碱，也可检定有机碘化合物和生育酚。

19．硫氰酸钴［Cobalt（Ⅱ）thiocyanate］

将3g硫氰酸铵和1g氯化钴溶于20ml水中即可。喷后生物碱类在白色到粉红色背景上可出现蓝色斑点，颜色可于2小时后退去，但是若用水喷之或将薄层板置于湿气饱和的空气中，则颜色又重现，用于生物碱及伯、仲、叔胺类的检识。

20．对－二甲氨基苯甲醛－硫酸（*p*－Dimethyl cminobenzaidehyde－sulphuric acid）

（1）将125mg对－二甲氨基苯甲醛溶于65ml硫酸和35ml水的混合液中，放冷，加入0.05ml 5%三氯化铁水溶液，此试液，可保存一周，用于检测麦角生物碱。

（2）0.5%对－二甲氨基苯甲醛乙醇溶液与浓硫酸以5∶1混合即可，喷后有时需于80℃加热几分钟，生物碱显红或橙色斑，麦角生物碱显蓝色斑。

（3）0.5%对－二甲氨基苯甲醛的环已烷溶液，喷后生物碱显红或橙色斑，麦角生物碱显蓝色斑。

21．对－二甲氨基苯甲醛－盐酸（Van urk′s）

将1g对－二甲氨基苯甲醛溶于50ml 36%盐酸中，再加50ml乙醇即可，喷雾前薄层板必须于50℃左右加热，以除去展开剂中一些挥发性成分，然后充分喷雾，直至出现透明为止，置于王水蒸气中，于日光下观察，可见各种颜色。

22．对－二甲基苯甲醛－盐酸（Ehrlich′s）

（1）1g本品溶于25ml 35%的盐酸和75ml甲醇的混合液中即可，用于胺类的检测。

（2）1g本品溶于100ml 95%乙醇即可，喷雾后的薄层板置于用氯化氢蒸气饱和的器皿中放3～5分钟，或者用25%盐酸喷雾，有时需要加热。

23．肉桂醛－盐酸（Cinnamaldehyde－hydrochloric acid）

5ml肉桂醛以乙醇稀释至100ml，再加入5ml 36%盐酸，用时鲜配，喷后将薄层板暴露于氯化氢中，可产生红色斑点，用于检测吲哚衍生物。

24．铬变酸（Chromotropic acid）

溶液Ⅰ：为10%的1，8－二烃萘－3，6二磺酸钠（即铬变酸钠）的水溶液。

溶液Ⅱ：为浓硫酸与水（5:3）的混合液，放冷至室温。

喷雾剂：使用前将溶液 A 和 B 以 1:1（V/V）混合，喷后于 105℃加热 30 分钟。

25．葡萄糖－磷酸（Glucose－phosphoric acid）

将 2g 葡萄糖溶于 10ml 浓磷酸（85%）和 40ml 水的混合液中，再加入 30ml 乙醇和 30ml 正丁醇即可，喷后于 115℃加热 10 分钟，用于检测芳胺类。

26．溴化氰－对氨基苯甲酸（Konig's）

取 2g 对氨基苯甲酸溶于 75ml 0.75mol/L 盐酸中，用 95% 乙醇稀释至 100ml 即可，将薄层板放于密闭容器中用溴化氰溶液熏 1 小时，可检定吡啶环的生物碱、菸酸等。

注：溴化氰的制备，在冰冷却的饱和溴水中，加足够 10% NaCN 溶液至溴的颜色褪去为止，注意溴化氰有毒。

27．磺胺酸－α－萘胺（Sulphanilic acid－o－naphthylamine）

溶液Ⅰ：10%磺胺醋酸（30%）溶液。

溶液Ⅱ：0.1%α－萘胺醋酸（30%）溶液。

喷雾剂及使用：临用前将Ⅰ和Ⅱ等体积混合，薄层板用短波紫外光照射几分钟后再喷该喷雾剂，脂肪族亚硝胺可产生红－紫色斑，芳香族亚硝酸则呈绿－蓝色。

28．硝酸钙（Calciumnitrate）

5%硝酸钙的乙酸溶液，喷后于紫外光下照射，二苯胺显绿色斑点。

29．四苯硼酸钠（Tetraphenyl borate sodium）

喷雾剂Ⅰ：为 1%四苯硼酸钠水饱和的丁酮溶液。

喷雾剂Ⅱ：为 0.015%非瑟酮或栎精（槲皮素 quercetin）的甲醇溶液。

方法：以Ⅰ喷后，将薄层板于空气中干燥，然后再喷以喷雾剂Ⅱ，再于空气中干燥，可得橙－红色斑点，在长波紫外光下可发生荧光。

30．氯铵 T（Chloramine T）

喷雾剂Ⅰ：10%氯铵 T 水溶液。

喷雾剂Ⅱ：1N 盐酸。

方法：薄层板先用Ⅰ喷，略干燥后，再以Ⅱ喷之，加热到 96～98℃直到氯的气味消失，再将此薄层板暴露于含有 25%氢氧化铵的容器中（大约 5 分钟），最后再加热至粉红色达最大强度，用于检测咖啡因。

31．二苯胺－氯化钯（Diphenylamine－palladium chloride）

1.5%二苯胺醇溶液同 0.1%氯化钯的 0.2%氯化钠溶液相混合（5:1，V/V）后喷雾经短波紫外光照射后，亚硝胺类可呈现紫色斑点。

32．茜素（Alizarin）

以 0.1%茜素的乙醇溶液喷后，在淡黄色背景上脂肪胺和氨基醇显紫色。

33．溴甲酚绿（蓝）（Bromocresol green（blue））

以 0.05%溴甲酚绿的乙醇溶液喷雾后，许多生物碱立即或在 30 分钟内显不同的暗淡绿色或蓝色斑点，若无反应可用氨水熏，除氨后，蓝色背景褪去，某些化合物显蓝色斑点，碱性溶剂喷后，背景可能变黑。

34．碘化钾镉试剂（Marme's）

先将 4g 碘化钾溶于 12ml 水中，煮沸后加入 2g CdI_2，然后与 12ml 饱和碘化钾溶液混合，用于检测生物碱。

35．奥伯迈尔试剂（Oberemayer's）

将4g三氯化铁溶于1ml盐酸（比重1.19）中即可，用于检测生物碱。

36．硫代钼酸试剂（Frochde's）

为10%钼酸或钼酸钠的浓硫酸溶液，用于检测生物碱和葡萄糖。

三、糖类

1．苯胺－邻苯二甲酸（Aniline－phthalate）

将0.93g苯胺和1.66g邻苯二甲酸溶解在100ml水饱和的正丁醇中即得。喷雾后于105℃加热10分钟。不同种类的糖会出现不同颜色的斑点，戊醛糖显红色，己醛、甲基戊糖醛、糖醛酸显褐色，己酮糖显淡褐色，在紫外灯光下观察荧光更清楚，该试剂受杂质干扰影响较小，对还原糖的检出灵敏度高。

2．对－茴香胺－邻苯二甲酸（*p*－Anisidine phthalate）

为0.1M对茴香胺和邻苯二甲酸的95%乙醇溶液。喷雾后于100℃加热10分钟，己糖显绿色，6－去氧己糖显黄绿色，戊糖显红紫色，糖醛酸显棕色。

3．苯胺－磷酸（Aniline－phosphoric acid）

将2mol/L以水饱和的苯胺正丁醇溶液，加1mol/L磷酸正丁醇溶液（1∶2，V/V）即得。喷雾后于105℃加热10分钟。

4．苯胺－二苯胺－磷酸（Aniline－diphenylamine－phosphoric acid）

将4g二苯胺、4ml苯胺和20ml 85%磷酸溶解于200ml丙酮中即可，喷雾后于85℃加热10分钟，此试剂对还原糖产生各种颜色，1，4－己醛糖、低聚糖变成蓝色。

5．联苯胺试剂（Benylidine）

将0.5g联苯胺溶于20ml冰醋酸和80ml无水醇中，喷到纸上于110℃左右加热，糖出现褐色斑点。

6．联苯胺－三氯醋酸（Benylidine－trichloroacetic acid）

将0.5g联苯胺溶于10ml醋酸中，再加10ml 40%三氯醋酸水溶液，然后以乙醇稀释至100ml，喷后暴露于日光中15分钟，糖类可呈灰棕－深红棕色斑点，加热至110℃则变成暗黑色斑点。

7．对硝基苯胺－过碘酸（*p*－Nitoaniline－periodic acid）

溶液Ⅰ：饱和的偏高碘酸溶液1份加水2份稀释。

溶液Ⅱ：1%对硝基苯胺乙醇溶液4份与1份盐酸混合。

方法：先喷溶液Ⅰ，放置10分钟，再喷溶液Ⅱ，去氧糖显黄色，紫外光下显强荧光，若再喷5%氢氧化钠甲醇溶液，则颜色转绿。

8．偏高碘酸钠－对硝基苯胺（Metaperiodate sodium－*p*－nitroaniline）

喷雾剂Ⅰ：将偏高碘酸钠饱和的水溶液用其二倍体积的水稀释之。

喷雾剂Ⅱ：将1%对－硝基苯胺的乙醇溶液同36%的盐酸混合（二者容量比为4∶1）

方法：先用Ⅰ喷之，放置10分钟再喷Ⅱ，脱氧糖和烯糖可产生黄色斑，在长波紫外光照射下可见强烈荧光，若再喷以5%氢氧化钠甲醇液，则颜色将变成绿色。

9．1，3－二羟基萘酚－磷酸（1，3－Dihydroxyhaphthol－phos phoric acid）

0.2% 1，3－二羟基萘酚乙醇溶液 100ml 与 85%磷酸 100ml 混匀后使用，喷后 105℃烤 5～10 分钟，酮糖显红色，醛糖显淡蓝色。

10．3，5－二氨基苯甲酸－磷酸（3，5－Diaminobenzoic acid－phosphoric acid，Quinaidine 反应）

取 3，5－二氨基苯甲酸溶于 80%磷酸中，并用 60ml 水稀释之即可，层析板喷雾后于 100℃加热 15 分钟，在长波紫外光下，斑点显黄色～绿色荧光，日光下呈棕色，可检出 2μg 以上的量，用于检测 α－脱氧糖。

11．邻氨基联苯－磷酸（*o*－Aminobiphenyl－phosphoric acid，据 lewio－smith 改良）

将 0.3g 邻氨基联苯和 5ml 85%磷酸溶解于 95ml 乙醇中，喷雾后于 110℃加热 15～20 分钟，糖类可产生棕色斑点。

12．双甲酮－磷酸（Dimeoude－phosphoric acid）

将 0.3g 双甲酮（5，5－二甲基环己烷－1，3－二酮）溶于 90ml 乙醇中，加 10ml 85%磷酸即得（新配的效果较好）。喷后于 110℃加热 15～20 分钟，日光中在白色背景上可见黄色斑点，紫外光下呈蓝色。用于检测酮糖。

13．萘骈间苯二酚－硫酸（Naphthoresorciol－sulphuric acid）

溶液Ⅰ：0.2%萘骈间苯二酚的乙醇溶液。

溶液Ⅱ：20%硫酸。

使用前，将Ⅰ与Ⅱ等体积混合之，喷后 100～105℃加热 5～10 分钟，用于糖类检测。

14．α－萘酚－硫酸（α－Naphthol－sulphuric acid）

为 10.5ml 15%α－萘酚溶液、65ml 浓硫酸、40.5ml 乙醇以及 4ml 水的混合溶液。喷后于 100℃加热 3～6 分钟。

15．咔唑－硫酸（Carbayole－sulphuric acid）

将 0.5g 咔唑溶解于 95ml 乙醇中，再加 5ml 浓硫酸即可（临用前鲜配）。喷后于 120℃加热 10 分钟，糖类在蓝色背景上产生斑点。

16．酚－硫酸（Phenol－sulphuric acid）

酚 3g 及浓硫酸 5ml 溶于 95ml 乙醇中，喷后于 110℃烤 10～15 分钟，糖显棕色。

17．茴香醛－硫酸试剂（anisaldehyde－sulphuric acid）

浓硫酸 1ml 加到含茴香醛 0.5ml 的 50ml 乙醇溶液中（临用前鲜配）即可，喷后 100～105℃加热，各种糖显不同颜色。

18．百里酚－硫酸（Thymol－sulphuric acid）

将 5ml 浓硫酸小心地加入含有 0.5g 百里酚的 95ml 乙醇中，喷后于 120℃加热 15～20 分钟，可得粉红、暗红色斑点。继续加热则变成浅紫色。

19．高锰酸钾试剂（Permangnate potassium）

为 0.1%高锰酸钾的 2%硫酸钠水溶液，喷到展开后的层析板上，糖类在紫红色背景上出现黄色斑点。

20．硝酸银氢氧化钠（Silver nitrate－sodium hydroxide）

喷雾剂Ⅰ：将 1ml 饱和的硝酸银溶液用丙酮稀释到 200ml，然后再加 5～10ml 的水，直到沉淀溶解为止。

喷雾剂Ⅱ：为0.5mol/L氢氧化钠的水－甲醇液（20g氢氧化钠溶解于最小量的水中，再用甲醇稀释至1000ml）。

方法：分别用喷雾剂Ⅰ、Ⅱ喷雾，最后在100℃加热1~2分钟即可，用于检测糖、聚乙醇。

21．硝酸银氢氧化铵－甲醇钠（Silver nitrate－ammonium hydroxide－sodium methoxied）

溶液Ⅰ：0.3%硝酸银甲醇液。

溶液Ⅱ：氨气饱和的甲醇液。

溶液Ⅲ：7%金属钠的甲醇溶液。

喷雾剂：使用前将20mlⅠ液、40mlⅡ液、8mlⅢ液混合即得。喷后于110℃加热1分钟。

22．邻氨基苯酚（*o*－Amino－phenol）

取0.15g 2，4－二氨基苯酚或2－氨基间苯位酚溶于200ml乙醇中，再加入50%磷酸10ml混合，喷到纸上，不同的还原糖出现不同色斑。

23．萘骈间苯二酚－三氯乙酸（Naphthoresorcinol－trichloroacetic acid）

0.2%萘骈间苯二酚的乙醇溶液与20%三氯乙酸的水溶液于临用前等体积混合。喷后置于干燥箱中100~105℃加热5~10分钟（用于酮糖），或在潮湿空气中于70~80℃水浴上加热10~15分钟（用于糖醛酸）。

注：可力丁或吡啶的存在可干扰颜色反应，可用间苯二酚，苔黑酚、间苯三酚或α－萘酚代替萘骈间苯二酚，三氯乙酸溶液可用其1/10体积的磷酸代之。

24．1，3－二萘酚（1，3－Dihydroxynaphthol）

0.2%1，3－二萘酚的乙醇溶液与3%三氯乙酸溶液等体积混合即可。喷雾后于100℃加热数分钟，对酮糖或低聚糖显红色，如在70℃用水蒸气熏，则戊糖和糖醛酸呈天蓝色。

25．硝普钠－偏高碘酸钠（Nitroprusside sodium－metaperiolate sodium）

喷雾剂Ⅰ：为2.5%的偏高碘酸钠水溶液。

喷雾剂Ⅱ：由7%的硝普钠水溶液，水饱和的呱嗪乙醇液以1:30:20体积之比所组成。

方法：先用Ⅰ喷之于室温干燥10分钟，再以喷雾剂Ⅱ喷之，5~10分钟内蓝色斑点可达最大强度。用于检测脱氧糖。

26．对－二甲氨基苯甲醛－乙酰丙酮（Morgan－Elosn's）

喷雾剂Ⅰ：将5ml 50%氢氧化钾水溶液和20ml乙醇混合后，取此混合液0.5ml与10ml正丁醇－乙酰丙酮（50:0.5）溶液，于临用前均匀混合，二液均需鲜配。

喷雾剂Ⅱ：1g对－二甲氨基苯甲醛溶于30ml乙醇中，加入30ml 36%盐酸，需要时用180ml正丁醇稀释。

方法：先用Ⅰ喷之，于105℃加热5分钟后，再喷Ⅱ，90℃干燥5分钟，氨基糖可产生红色斑。

27．4－氨基马尿酸（4－Aminohippuic acid）

为0.3g 4－氨基马尿酸的乙醇溶液，喷后于140℃加热8分钟，置长紫外光下还原糖可见荧光斑点。

28．蒽酮（Anthrone）

将 0.38g 蒽酮溶解于 10ml 醛酸和 20ml 乙醇中，再加 3ml 85%磷酸和 1ml 水即可（此溶液在冰箱中可保存数周）。喷后 110℃加热 5～6 分钟后，酮糖和含酮糖的低聚糖出现黄色斑点。

29．尿酸－盐酸（Urea－hydrochloric acid）

5g 尿素溶于 20ml 2mol/L 盐酸中，再加 100ml 乙醇即得，喷后薄层板于 100℃加热直至出现最佳颜色。酮糖和含酮糖的低聚糖转为成蓝色。

30．Ehrlich 试剂

溶液Ⅰ：50ml 丁醇与 0.5ml 乙酸丙酮的混合液。

溶液Ⅱ：5ml 50%氢氧化钠与 20ml 乙醇的混合液。

溶液Ⅲ：1g 对二甲胺苯甲醛溶于 10ml 浓盐酸，再加入 18ml 丁醇。

喷雾剂及用法：取 0.5ml Ⅰ液和 10ml Ⅱ液混合喷于滤纸上，于 105℃加热 5 分钟，再喷溶液Ⅲ，于 90℃保持 5 分钟，有氨基糖存在时出现紫红色斑点，其他还原糖显色后迅速褪去。

31．四唑试剂（Triphenyl－tetrayolivum chloride，TTC）

2%四唑水溶液和 1mol/L 的氢氧化钠溶液等体积混合，喷到展开后的层析纸上，于 40℃用水蒸气熏，水洗除过量的 TTC，还原糖呈红色斑点。

32．费林试剂（Fehling's）

溶液Ⅰ：硫酸铜溶液，溶解 34.66g 硫酸铜于水中，并稀释至 500ml。

溶液Ⅱ：碱性酒石酸盐溶液，溶解 173g 酒石酸钾和 50g 氢氧化钠于水中，再稀释至冷时为 500ml，临用时，两液等体积混合。用于检测还原糖。

33．佩维溶液（Pavy's）

在 120ml 费林试剂中加入 300ml 氨水（比重 0.88）用水稀释至 1L 即可。用于检测葡萄糖。

34．醋酸酮试剂（巴福特试剂，Barfoed's）

溶解 66g 醋酸铜和 10ml 冰醋酸于水中，稀释至 1L 即可。用于检测还原单糖。

四、酚类化合物

1．重氮化试剂（Diazetised reagent）

重氮盐的制备：取 50g 对氨基苯磺酸溶于 250ml 10%的氢氧化钠溶液中，一面冷却一面滴加 10%的亚硝钠溶液 200ml。另外在 80ml 浓盐酸中加入 40ml 水并用冰水冷却后滴加到上述溶液中，即生成重氮盐沉淀，过滤，用冰水、乙醇、乙醚依次洗涤沉淀物，风干即得纯重氮盐。

喷雾剂：取 0.1g 纯重氮盐溶于 20ml 10%氢氧化钠中，即可喷雾，滤纸上酚类化合物呈现红色斑点。

2．重氮化氨基苯磺酸试剂（Diazotiseld－aminobenzene sulfonia acid）

对氨基苯磺酸 0.9g，加热溶于 9ml 12mol/L 盐酸中，用水稀释到 100ml，取此溶液 10ml 用水冷却，加入冰冷的 4.5%亚硝酸钠溶液 10ml，0℃放 15 分钟（0℃可保存 3 天），用前加等体积1%碳酸钠溶液即可，喷后香豆精显黄、橙、红棕、紫等颜色，也用于酚类、芳香胺及能偶合的杂环化合物的检验。

3．重氮化对硝基苯胺试剂（Diazotised－nitroaniline）

取对硝基苯胺0.7g溶于12mol/L盐酸9ml，用水稀释到100ml，将此溶液4ml逐滴加入到冰冷的1%亚硝酸钠溶液5ml中，再用冰冷的水稀释至100ml即可（临用时鲜配），喷后香豆精显黄、橙、红、棕、紫等颜色，也用于酚类显色。

4．重氮化联苯胺（Diazotised benzidine）

联苯胺贮备液：5g联苯胺和14ml 36%盐酸混合，加水稀释至1000ml。

亚硝酸盐溶液：为10%亚硝酸钠的水溶液，临用前鲜配。

喷雾剂：在0℃条件下，将20ml联苯胺溶液和20ml亚硝酸钠溶液混合，且不断搅拌（本试剂仅能保存2～3小时），喷后不同酚的颜色可迅速出现或在几小时后才出现。

5．重氮化磺胺酸（Pauly's）

4.5g磺酸溶于45ml温热的12mol/L盐酸中，并用水稀释至500ml，取此稀释液于冰中冷却，加入10ml 4.5%亚硝酸钠冷溶液，本试剂于0℃保持15分钟，本喷雾剂临用前应加等体积10%磺酸钠水溶液，用于检测酚类、胺类及能偶合的杂环化合物。

6．间苯三酚－浓硫酸试剂（Phloroglucinol－sulphuric acid）

为2%间苯三酚乙醇溶液与浓硫酸的等体积混合液，用于检测原儿茶醛。

7．三氯化铁试剂（Ferric chloride）

1%～5%三氯化铁的0.5mol/L盐酸的水或乙醇溶液，酚类呈蓝色或绿色，本试剂还可用作试管与点滴反应。

8．铁氰化钾－氯化铁（Ferricyanide－ferric chloride）

将1%铁氰化钾水溶液同2%氯化铁水溶液于使用前等体积混合即可。喷后再喷以2mol/L盐酸，色泽可以增强，用于检测酚类、胺类、硫代硫盐酸和异硫氰酸盐，还可用于阿魏酸的定量测定。

9．三氯化铝试剂（Aluminum chloride）

为1%三氯化铝乙醇液或5%三氯化铝水溶液，用于检测黄酮，试管检识与喷雾均可。

10．三氯化锑试剂（Antimony（Ⅲ）chloride）

为10%三氯化锑的氯仿溶液，喷雾后，黄酮可在长波紫外光下产生黄色炎光斑点。

11．牢坚蓝B盐（重氮化试剂）［Fast blue Bsalt（Diazonium reagent）］

喷雾剂Ⅰ：为新鲜制备的0.5%牢坚蓝B盐的水溶液。

喷雾剂Ⅱ：为0.1mol/L氢氧化钠液。

方法：分别以喷雾剂Ⅰ、Ⅱ喷之，用于检测酚类及可偶合之胺类。鹤草酚可用此试剂检测。

12．钒酸铵－茴香胺（Ananoninm Vanadutc V－*p*－methoxyaniline）

溶液Ⅰ：饱和的钒酸铵溶液。

溶液Ⅱ：0.5g茴香胺溶于2ml磷酸中，用乙醇稀释至100ml，过滤。

方法：先喷溶液Ⅰ，在潮湿板上再喷Ⅱ，80℃干燥，酚类在粉红背景上显特征色斑。

13．钒酸铵试剂［Ammonium Vanadate（V）］

先往滤纸上喷钒酸铵的饱和水溶液，再喷0.5mol/L硫酸。

14. 4－氨基匹林铁氰化钾（4－Amitnoantnyiprine potassivum ferrcyianide，Emerson 反应）

喷雾剂Ⅰ：为2% 4－氨基匹林乙醇溶液。

喷雾剂Ⅱ：为8%铁氰化钾水溶液。

方法：分别用喷雾剂Ⅰ、Ⅱ喷后，将层析谱放入含有25%氢氧化铵的密闭容器中显示红橙～淡红斑点，用于检测酚类、香豆精。

15. 碱性醋酸铅（Lad acetate，basic）

为25%碱性醋酸铅的水溶液，喷后在长波紫外光下观察荧光，用于检测黄酮类化合物。

16. 二苯硼酸－β－氨基乙酯（Didhenylboric acid－β－aminoethyiester，Neu's 试剂，又称 Naturstoff A 试剂）

为二苯硼酸－β－氨基乙酯的1%甲醇溶液，层析谱用约10ml该试剂喷雾，在长波紫外光下观察可见荧光，用于检测α和rhv吡喃酮（烃基黄酮醇）。

17. 硫酸铜柠檬酸钠（Cupic dulphatecitrate sodium，Benedict's 试剂）

1.73g 硫酸铜（$CuSO_4.5H_2O$），1.73g 柠檬酸钠和10g 无水碳酸钠溶于水中，加水至100ml 即可，用于检测黄酮、邻二羟基香豆素。

注：有邻二羟基基团的化合物，在长波紫外光下的荧光可被喷雾剂所减弱或完全熄灭，而不具此基团的这类化合物是不改变的，甚至可增强（在此情况下，通常发生荧光颜色的变化）。

18. 米龙试剂（Milleon's）

为5g 汞溶解于10g 硝酸中，加10ml 水，在白色背景上可出现黄－橙色斑点。若于100～110℃加热，颜色可发生很大变化，用于检测酚类、酚醚及苷。

19. 福林西卡尔顿试剂（Follin cciocalteu's）

喷雾剂Ⅰ：20%碳酸钠水溶液。

喷雾剂Ⅱ：10g 钨酸钠和2.5g 钼酸钠溶于70ml 水中，加5ml 85%磷酸及10ml 36%盐酸，此混合液回流10小时，然后加入15g 硫酸锂，5ml 水以及1滴溴液，将此溶液再加热回流15分钟以上，放冷，添加水至100ml（应无绿色），即可贮存，使用前用三倍量体积的水稀释之。

方法：分别以喷雾剂Ⅰ、Ⅱ喷之，用于检测酚类。

20. 硝酸银（Silver nitrate）

在20ml 丙酮中加入1ml 饱和硝酸银水溶液，边加边搅拌，然后逐滴加水直到硝酸银沉淀刚好溶解为止，可得淡粉红～深绿色斑点，用于检测酚类。

五、醌类化合物

1. 醋酸镁试剂（Magnesim acetate）

0.5%醋酸镁的甲醇溶液喷后于90℃加热5分钟醌类化合物即可显色，该反应灵敏，邻位酚羟基蒽醌呈紫～蓝紫色；对位二酚羟基蒽醌呈紫红～紫色；每个苯环上各有一个α－羟基或有间位羟基者，呈橙红～红色；母核只有一个α或一个β－酚羟基者，或者有两

个 β - 酚羟基但不在同环上，呈黄橙色至橙色。

2．3%氢氧化钠或碳酸钠溶液（Borntrager’s 反应）

以此试剂喷雾或进行试管反应均可。

3．无色亚甲蓝试剂（Leuco - methylencblue）

将含有 0.25g 锌粉的 1ml 醋酸混悬液加入 5ml 的 0.02% 的亚甲蓝丙酮溶液中即可，用于检测醌类（一般、结合）和生育醌。

4．氢氧化钾试剂（Potassium hydroxide）

为 5% 氢氧化钾甲醇溶液，层析谱干燥后可在日光和长波紫外光下检识，用于检测香豆精、蒽醌及其苷。

5．磷钼酸试剂（Phosphomotybdic acid）

见一 .8，灯盏细辛苷（Erigeroside）呈深蓝色。

6．对 - 亚硝基二甲苯胺试剂（*p* - Nitroso - *N*，*N* - dimethyl aniline）

为 0.1% 对 - 亚硝基二甲苯胺的吡啶溶液，可与羟基蒽醌类化合物，尤其是 9，12 未取代的 1，8 - 二羟基蒽酮生成紫红、绿、蓝以及灰、亮红、紫等不同颜色，随分子结构不同而异，不仅可用于蒽酮类化合物定性，而且还可用于微量定量。

7．哌啶试剂（Piperidine）

为 50% 哌啶的苯溶液。

8．乙酸铝试剂（Aluminum acetate）

为 0.5% 乙酸铝溶液。

9．碳酸锂试剂（Lithium carbonate）

为饱和的碳酸锂溶液。

10．硼砂试剂（Sodium tetraborate）

为饱和的硼砂溶液。

11．牢坚蓝 B 盐试剂（Fast blue B salt）

为 0.5% 牢坚蓝 B 盐溶液。

六、萜类化合物

1．碘蒸气（Indine）

见一 .1，可检测香茶菜、冬凌草中的二萜 Oridonin 等及烃基马桑毒素等多种有机化合物。

2．磷钼酸试剂（Phosphomolybdic acid）

为 10% 磷钼酸的乙醇溶液，用于检测马桑毒素（Oriamyrtin）等。

3．香草醛 - 硫酸试剂（Vanillin - sulphuric acid）

1% 香草醛的浓硫酸溶液或 1% 香草醛的 50% 磷酸溶液，喷后加热至显色，于日光和紫外光下观察，用于检测萜烯类。

4．氯酚红试剂（Chlorophenol red）

为 2% 氯酚红的醇溶液，用于检测倍半萜内酯 brilanin 等。

5．苯酚－溴（Phenol－bromine）

为50％苯酚的四氯化碳溶液，喷后置于溴蒸气中，用于检定萜烯类化合物。

6．无水氯化铁试剂（Ferric chloride，anhydrous）

为饱和的无水氯化铁甲醇溶液，用于检定萜烯类。

7．对－二甲氨基苯甲醛－磷酸（*p*－Dimethyl aminobenzaldehyde－phosphoric acid）

1g对－二甲氨基苯甲醛溶解于5g浓磷酸和50ml冰醋酸中，用水稀释至100ml，贮于棕色瓶中，喷后100℃加热几分钟，奥类显深蓝色斑。

8．偏钒酸胺－硫酸试剂（Ammonium metavnadate－sulphuric acid）

4g偏钒酸胺溶于100ml 50％硫酸中，喷后自然光下观察，有时需加热，芫花二萜显土红色，烤后变为蓝～黑色。对于含有CMC－Na的薄层板不能烤。

9．香草醛－高氯酸试剂（Vaillin－erchloric acid）

5ml 10％香草醛的冰醋酸溶液与1ml高氯酸临用时混合，喷后加热烘烤至显色，用于检测倍半萜莪术醇（Carcumol）等。

10．高定试剂（Godin's）

喷雾剂：1％香草醛乙醇溶液和3％高氯酸水溶液临用时等量混合即可。

用法：喷后室温挥干溶剂，80～90℃烤分钟后即显出斑点。

七、挥发油

1．硫酸（Sulphuric acid）

13％硫酸喷后110℃加热至显色，不适用于带有CMC－Na的薄层板。

2．碘蒸气（Iodine），见一.1。

3．香草醛－硫酸（Vanillin－sulphuric acid）

（1）1％香草醛的浓硫酸溶液。

（2）0.5％香草醛的硫酸－乙醇（4:1）溶液。

（3）5％香草醛的浓硫酸溶液。

喷后于120℃加热或红外灯烘烤，直到取得最大程度的色斑为止，可出现各种颜色，反应灵敏。

4．香草醛－盐酸（Vanillin－chloric acid）

为5％香草醛的浓盐酸溶液，喷后于120℃加热，挥发油中各成分可呈现各种颜色。

5．茴香醛－浓硫酸试剂（Anisaldehyde－Sulphuric acid）

（1）浓硫酸1ml加入50ml冰乙酸中，加茴香醛0.5ml，必须临用时新配。

（2）茴香醛－浓硫酸－乙醇（1:1:18）配成喷雾剂，以上二试剂之一喷雾，喷后于105℃烘烤，可使挥发油中各成分显不同颜色。

6．荧光素－溴试剂（Fluorescein－bromine）

溶液Ⅰ：0.1％荧光素的乙醇溶液。

溶液Ⅱ：5％溴的四氯化碳溶液。

方法：薄层板喷溶液Ⅰ后，放入盛溶液Ⅱ的槽中，溴将荧光素转变成粉红色的曙红（cosin），它在长波紫外光下不显荧光，如果薄层上有乙烯基化合物，则溴与它作用而不与荧光素作用，在长波紫外光下观察时，此处仍显荧光素的黄色荧光。

7．异羟污酸铁试剂

溶液Ⅰ：5%盐酸羟胺溶于12ml水中，再用乙醇稀释到50ml，储于冷处。

溶液Ⅱ：10g氢氧化钠溶于少量水中，再用乙醇稀释到100ml。

溶液Ⅲ：溶液Ⅰ和溶液Ⅱ以1:2混合，滤出氯化钾沉淀，所得滤液必须放冰箱中，可稳定两周。

溶液Ⅳ：10g三氯化铁溶于20ml 36%盐酸中，与200ml乙醚振摇，得均匀的溶液，密塞储存可长久使用。

用法：先喷溶液Ⅲ，于室温稍干燥后，再喷溶液Ⅳ，喷后斑点显淡红色，可能是挥发油中的酯和内酯。

8．二苯三硝基苯肼（Diphenylpicrylhydrazine）

0.06g二苯三硝基苯肼溶于100ml氯仿中，喷后于110℃加热5～10分钟，在紫色背景上可形成黄色色斑。

9．2%高锰酸钾溶液

2%高锰酸钾溶液，喷后如呈现黄色斑点，表明挥发油中含有不饱和化合物。

10．2，4－二硝基苯肼（2，4－Pinitrophenylhydrazine）

（1）0.4% 2，4－二硝基苯肼的2mol/L盐酸溶液。

（2）将1g 2 ,4－二硝基苯肼溶于1000ml乙醇中，加入10ml 36%盐酸即得。

以二试剂之一喷雾，饱和酮类与2，4－二硝基苯肼可立即产生蓝色，饱和醛则作用较慢并转变成草绿色，不饱和羟基化合物的色泽只是慢慢的改变或根本不发生变化，用于特定挥发油中羟基化合物。

11．邻联二茴香胺试剂（*o*－Dianisidine's）

0.3%邻联二茴香胺的冰醋酸溶液，喷后如呈现黄色斑点，表明样品中含有醛。

八、甾体化合物

1．醋酐－浓硫酸（Acetic anhydride－sulphuric acid，Liebermann－Burchard试剂）

在冷却条件下，小心地将5ml醋酐同5ml浓硫酸混合，同样在冷却情况下，将此混合物谨慎地加入50ml无水乙醇中，临用前鲜配，喷后100℃干燥10分钟，置长波紫外光下观察，用于检测甾醇、三萜皂苷及甾醇类。

2．肉桂醛－醋酐－硫酸（Cinnamaldehyde－acetic anhydride－sulphuric acid）

喷雾剂Ⅰ：1%肉桂醛的乙醇溶液。

喷雾剂Ⅱ：醋酐与浓硫酸的12:1（V/V）混合液，临用前鲜配。

薄层板以喷雾剂Ⅰ喷后，于90℃干燥5分钟，再喷Ⅱ，于室温放置1～2分钟后，移放于干燥箱中，再于90℃加热至斑点出现为止，用于检测甾体皂苷。

3．硫酸高铈－硫酸（Ceric sulphate－sulphuric acid）

为硫酸高铈的65%硫酸饱和溶液，喷后于120℃加热15分钟，用于检测茄属甾体生物碱和甾体皂苷。

注：不能用于氧化铝薄层板。

4．茴香醛－浓硫酸试剂（Anisaldehyde－sulphuric acid）

见七 .5。喷后于 100～105℃加热，直至色斑呈最大强度为止。粉红色斑暴露于水蒸汽中时色泽褪去。地衣成分、酚类、萜类、糖类和甾体化合物可根据分别呈紫、蓝、红、灰和绿色斑来检测。

改良喷雾剂：为新配的 0.5%茴香酮、9ml 乙醇、0.5ml 浓硫酸和 0.1ml 醋酸混合液，可用于检测含糖物质，喷后于 90～100℃加热 5～10 分钟。

5．阿兰试验（Allen 试验）

以浓硫酸－乙醇－水（40:9:1）之混合液喷雾，喷后 1，6－脱氢甾族化合物及其醋酸酯显紫、红紫、玫瑰红或黄色斑点。

6．甘醇酸（又称羟基乙酸、乙醇酸，Glycollic acid）

50%乙醇酸水溶液，喷后于 80℃加热 45 分钟，于 254nm 紫外光下观察，能检出 α、β－不饱和甾酮和缩酮。

7．氯磺酸－醋酸（Chlorosulphonic acid－acetic acid）

5ml 氯磺酸在冷却条件下，溶于 10ml 醋酸中，喷后于 130℃加热 5～10 分钟，在长波紫外光下可见到荧光，用于检测三萜与甾体化合物。

8．三氯醋酸（Trichloroacetic acid）

（1）25%三氯醋酸的氯仿溶液。

（2）1%三氯醋酸的氯仿溶液（检查维生素 B）

（3）3.3g 三氯醋酸溶于 10ml 氯仿中，再加 1～2 滴 30%过氧化氢（H_2O_2）即可。

以上三试剂喷雾后，于 120℃加热 5～10 分钟，色斑在日光和长波紫外光下可检出，用于检测甾体、洋地黄毒苷、藜芦生物碱。

9．三氟乙酸（Trifluorcacetic acid）

1%三氟乙酸的氯仿溶液，喷后于 120℃加热 5 分钟，用于检测甾体化合物。

10．三氯化铋〔Bismush（Ⅲ）chloride〕

33%三氯化铋的乙醇溶液，喷后于 110℃加热，直到在紫外光下出现最适宜的荧光为止。用于检测甾醇类。

11．三氯化锑（Carr－Price 试剂）

将 25g 三氯化锑溶解于 75g 氯仿中即可，而一般采用的是氯化锑饱和的氯仿或四氯化碳溶液。喷后于 100℃加热 10 分钟，在长波紫外光下观察，用于检测甾体皂苷、甾体糖、维生素 A、维生素 D、类胡萝卜素及萜类衍生物。

12．氯－氯化锑〔Chlorine－antimony（Ⅱ）chloride〕

三氯化锑（$SbCl_3$）的氯仿－醋酐（8:2）饱和溶液。薄板在氯气中熏 20 分钟，喷上检定剂。90℃加热 2～4 分钟，于紫外光下观察，甾体化合物显荧光色斑。

13．三氯化锑－醋酸〔Antimony（Ⅲ）chloride－acetic acid〕

将 20g 三氯化锑溶解于 20ml 醋酸和 60ml 氯仿的混合液中，喷后于 100℃加热 5 分钟，在紫外光下观察，用于检测甾体、二萜类化合物，后者出现红黄～蓝紫的色斑。

14．五氯化锑〔Antimony（Ⅴ）chloride〕

25%五氯化锑的氯仿或四氯化碳溶液，用前鲜配，喷后于 120℃加热，直到色斑出现，在长波紫外光下检之，用于检测甾体皂苷、萜类、油脂、树脂、维生素 A、D、E。

15．氯化锌（Zine chloride）

30%氯化锌的甲醇溶液，溶后过滤即得，喷后将薄层板于105℃加热1小时，然后立即用一玻璃板覆盖，以防止湿气对其影响，色斑在长波紫外光下可见荧光，用于检测甾体和甾体皂苷。

16．氯化锡（Stannic chloride）

将10g氯化锡加入160ml氯仿－醋酸1:1混合液中，喷后层析谱于100℃加热5～10分钟，随后在日光和长波紫外光下检之。

17．高氯酸（Perchloric acid）

20%高氯酸水溶液。用于甾体。喷后于150℃加热约10分钟，直至形成最显著色斑，在长波紫外光下可观察到荧光。

18．磷酸试剂（Phosphoric acid）

（1）浓磷酸（85%）与水的1:1（V/V）混合液。

（2）15%浓磷酸的甲醇溶液。

以上二者之一充分喷雾薄层板，直至透明，然后于120℃下加热约15～30分钟，个别需改变加热时间，以使出现最显著的颜色或荧光，用于检测甾醇、甾体化合物。

19．甲醛－磷酸（Formaldehyde－phosphoric acid）

在室温下，将0.03g甲醛溶于100ml 85%磷酸中，边溶解边振摇，该溶液可保存数周。用于检测甾体生物碱、甾体皂苷。

20．香草醛－磷酸（Vanillin－phosphoric acid）

1g香草醛溶于100m l50%磷酸水溶液中即得，喷后于120℃加热10～20分钟，用于检测甾体。

21．对甲苯磺酸（*p*－Toluene sulphonic acid）

为20%对甲苯磺酸氯仿液。喷后100℃加热数分钟，在长波紫外光下可见黄色荧光斑点，用于检测甾体、黄酮、儿茶酸。

22．多聚甲醛－磷酸（Paraformaldehyde－phosphoric acid）

将0.03g多聚甲醛与100ml 85%磷酸在室温下振摇直至溶解，该试剂可保存数周。用于检测茄属甾体生物碱、甾体皂苷。

23．1，2－萘醌－4－磺酸－高氯酸（1，2－Naphthoquinone－4－sulphonic acid－perchloric acid）

将0.1g 1，2－萘醌－4－磺酸溶于100ml的下述混合液（20ml乙醇、10ml 60%高氯酸、1ml 40%甲醛和9ml水）中即得。喷后将薄层板于70～80℃加热，观察颜色的演变，斑点先转变为粉红色，继续加热，再变为蓝色，用于检测甾醇类。

24．间二硝基苯试剂（*m*－Dinitrobenzene）

2%间二硝基苯的乙醇溶液与2.5mol/L的氢氧化钾的甲醇溶液等体积混合即得。喷后于80℃加热1～2分钟，17－甾酮类可产生紫色斑点。

25．苯二胺－邻苯二甲酸（Phenyleo nediamine－*o*－phthalic acid）

0.9%苯二胺和1.6%邻苯二甲酸的水饱和的正丁醇溶液，临用前配制。喷后于100～110℃加热，甾体显黄或棕色斑点。

26．氢氧化钠（Sodium hydroxide）

10%氢氧化钠溶液，喷后于80℃干燥10分钟，于紫外光下观察，Δ^4-3-酮甾族化合物显黄色荧光。

九、氨基酸

1．茚三酮试剂（Ninhydrin）

（1）茚三酮0.3g溶于正丁醇100ml中，加冰醋酸3ml。

（2）茚三酮0.2g溶于乙醇100ml中。

用上述试剂之一喷雾，喷后于110℃加热至显出颜色，为了使茚三酮的显色稳定，可采用下法：用茚三酮试剂显色后，用硝酸铜试剂（饱和硝酸铜溶液1ml与10%硝酸溶液0.2 ml及96%乙醇100ml混合）喷，斑点由蓝紫色转为红色。

（3）茚三酮浸泡显色法，把配成0.25%的茚三酮丙酮溶液（99%以上的无水丙酮）放在瓷盘内，把展开后的滤纸浸到丙酮溶液中，取出后风干，于90℃加热显色，此法干燥迅速，显色快，颜色均匀鲜艳。

2．茚三酮－硝酸铜试剂（Ninhydrin－cupricnitrate）

溶液Ⅰ：将10ml醋酸和2ml可力丁（Collitin）加到含0.1g茚三酮的50ml无水乙醇中。

溶液Ⅱ：0.5g硝酸铜溶于50ml无水乙醇中。

喷雾剂：使用前，将溶液Ⅰ和Ⅱ以50:3之比例混合，喷后将薄层板放置在一块热板上直到颜色展现为止。在透过光线之后，可见到色泽逐渐增强，有些氨基酸首先出现色斑，根据不同氨基酸形成色斑的速度不同，利用铅笔及时标记就可以检测互相重迭的成分，许多氨基酸呈现特殊颜色。

3．茚三酮－乙酸镉（Ninhydrin－cadmium acetate）

1g茚三酮、2.5 g乙酸铬〔$Cd(Ac)_2$〕和10ml冰醋酸溶于490ml甲醇中，喷后烘箱中于120℃加热，用于检定氨基酸。

4．茚三酮－可力丁试剂（Ninhydrin－colliodine）

0.2~0.3g茚三酮溶于95 ml水饱和的异丙醇或丁醇溶液中，加5 ml可力丁（2，4，6－三甲基吡啶），喷后80~90℃加热30~60分钟，氨基酸显蓝色斑。

5．去氢抗坏血酸（Dehydroascorbic acid）

0.1g去氢抗坏血酸溶于5ml 60℃水中，用丁醇稀释至100ml，喷雾后100℃加热5分钟，羟脯氨酸显淡紫蓝斑（25ug）；其他氨基酸显粉红到红斑（1~3μg）。

6．重氮化试剂（Diazotised reagent）

把对氨基苯甲酸的盐酸（2%~3%）饱和溶液和5%亚硝酸钠溶液等体积混合后喷雾，再立即喷1mol/L氢氧化钠溶液，当酪氨酸、组氨酸存在时呈红橙色。

7．重氮化对氨基苯磺酸试剂（Pauly试剂）

对氨基苯磺酸4.5g加热溶于12mol/L盐酸溶液45ml中，用水稀释至500ml，取稀释液10ml于冰浴中冷却后加入冷却的4.5%亚硝酸钠水溶液10ml，此试剂于0℃保留15分钟（低温时可稳定1~3天）。喷前加等体积的7%碳酸钠水溶液。

8．氯气－邻联甲苯胺试剂（Calorine－o－tolidine）

邻苯甲苯胺 160ml 溶于 30ml 乙酸中，再用 500ml 水稀释，然后再加碘化钾 1g 即可。将展开后之薄层放在氯气中，若氯气是从前筒中得到的，放置 5～10 分钟，若是由高锰酸钾溶液及 10%盐酸（1:1）的混合物制得的，则需放置 15～20 分钟，然后将薄层置空气中 5 分钟以除去过量的氯气，再喷试剂，用于检测氨基酸。

9．N－羟基酞花酰胺

为 0.5% N－羟基酞花酰胺的 95%乙醇溶液。喷后于空气中干燥，再于 140℃加热 5 分钟，则氨基酸呈蓝、绿、紫色斑点。

10．苔黑酚（5－甲基苯二酚）试剂（Orcin）

层析谱喷 0.1%苔黑酚的 0.002mol/L 硫酸溶液，于 110～120℃加热干燥 30 分钟，在红紫色背景上出现白色斑点，对氨基酸的定量分析最适宜。

11．钯试剂（Palladium reagent）

取 4 ml 0.02mol/L 的氯化钯的 0.1mol/L 盐酸溶液、0.25ml 的 1mol/L 碘化钾、0.4ml 2mol/L 盐酸与 76ml 丙酮混合使用。胱氨酸及其衍生物存在时则在浓黄色背景上出现白色斑点。

12．铂试剂（Platinium reagent）

取 4ml 0.02mol/L 的氯铂金酸、0.25ml 的 1mol/L 碘化钾、0.4ml 的 2mol/L 盐酸和 76ml 丙酮，使用前混合，把层析后滤纸浸在铂试剂溶液中，风干，如存在还原性硫化物时，如胱氨基、蛋氨酸类等，在桃红色背景上出现黄色斑点，若用盐酸蒸汽熏之，则背景颜色加深，斑点更明显。

13．坂口反应

先喷 5%氢氧化钠溶液，再喷 0.1% α－萘酚醇溶液，数分钟后再喷 5%次亚溴酸钠溶液，精氨酸存在显红色。

14．桂皮醛试剂（Cinnamaldehyde）

1%桂皮醛的甲醇溶液，喷到滤纸上待甲醇挥发后，再用盐酸蒸汽熏，色氨酸暗褐红斑点，脯氨酸、羟脯氨酸呈淡褐紫色，羟基色氨酸呈黄色。

15．对－二甲氨基苯甲醛－盐酸试剂（Ehrlich's）

把 2g 对－二甲氨基苯甲醛溶于 100ml 20%盐酸中，以此溶液喷滤纸后，于 60℃加热干燥，当色氨酸及其衍生物存在时出现紫色斑点。

16．8－羟基喹啉－次溴酸钠试剂（Sakajuchi's）

试剂 Ⅰ：0.1% 8－羟基喹啉丙酮溶液。

试剂Ⅱ：0.2ml 溴溶于 100ml 0.5mol/L 氢氧化钠溶液中。

方法：先喷试剂Ⅰ，干燥后再喷试剂 Ⅱ，精氨酸显橙至红色斑点。

17．吲哚醌试剂（Isatin）

（1）1%吲哚醌的乙醇或丙酮溶液加入 10ml 冰醋酸。

（2）含 4%醋酸和 0.2%吲哚醌的丙酮溶液喷后于 100～110℃加热 10 分钟。

18．高碘酸钠－Nessler's 试剂（Sodium metaperiodate－Nessler's）

试剂Ⅰ：1%高碘酸钠水溶液。

试剂Ⅱ：Nessler's 试剂：碘化汞 5g 用少量水调成糊状，加入碘化钾 5g，然后将氢氧化钠20g溶于80ml冰中，加到上述混合物中，用水调节体积成100ml，此时糊状物立即成为溶液，将此溶液放置数天，使之沉淀，倾出上层液即得。分别以试剂Ⅰ、Ⅱ喷之。用于检测含羟基的丝氨酸、苏氨酸。

19．靛红试剂（Indigocarmine）

为0.3%靛红的正丁醇溶液（含4%醋酸），喷后滤纸上，于100℃加热10分钟，脯氨酸及羟基脯氨酸存在时，呈现天蓝色斑点。

20．靛红－醋酸锌（Isatin－zine acetate）

将1g靛红和1.5 g醋酸锌溶于100ml 80℃的95%异丙醇中，冷却后加入1 ml醋酸，贮于冰箱中。喷后一般于80～85℃加热30分钟即可。但较好的办法是将层析谱于室温下放置20小时，用于检测氨基酸。

21．1，2－萘醌－4－磺酸钠试剂（1，2－Naphthopinone－4－sulpnonic acidsodium，Folin's）

将0.2g 1，2－萘醌－4－磺酸钠溶于100ml 5%的碳酸钠中即可。此试剂应鲜配，喷后将层析谱于室温干燥，各种氨基酸即可显出不同颜色。

十、强心苷

1．3，5－二硝基苯甲酸（3，5－Dinitrobenzonic acid，Kedde's）

喷雾剂Ⅰ：将1 g3，5－二硝基苯甲酸溶于50ml 甲醇和50ml 2mol/L氢氧化钾混合液中。

喷雾剂Ⅱ：2%3，5－二硝基苯甲酸甲醇溶液。

喷雾剂Ⅲ：5.7%氢氧化钾醇液，薄层板先用Ⅱ轻轻喷之，再喷过量的Ⅲ，可得蓝～紫色斑点。

注：喷雾剂 Ⅰ应单独使用。

2．碱性苦味酸试剂（Baljet's）

9ml 1%苦味酸乙醇溶液与1ml 10%氢氧化钠混匀即可，临用鲜配。

3．亚硝酰铁氰化钠（硝普钠）－氢氧化钠试剂（Legal's）

1g亚硝酰铁氰化钠溶于100ml 2mol/L氢氧化钠－乙醇（1∶1）溶液，可作显色剂用，若作一般试管检识用，则需先加0.3%亚硝酰铁氰化钠溶液，再加10%氢氧化钠溶液即可。

4．间二硝基苯试剂（Raymond's）

喷雾剂Ⅰ：10%间二硝基苯的苯的溶液。

喷雾剂Ⅱ：6 g氢氧化钠溶于25ml水中，再加45ml甲醇。

方法：先喷Ⅰ，于60℃干燥后，再喷Ⅱ，强心苷显紫斑后变蓝并褪去，对于甲酰胺浸过的薄层板，喷雾前当于60℃烘干。

5．氯胺T－三氯醋酸（Chlormine T－trichloroacetic acid）

溶液Ⅰ：为新鲜制备的3%氯氨T水溶液。

溶液Ⅱ：为25%三氯醋酸的乙醇液（可保存几天）

方法：临用前把10ml Ⅰ液与40ml Ⅱ液混合，喷后于110℃加热7分钟，对于洋地黄苷在长波紫外光下可观察到蓝或黄色荧光。

6．2，4，6－三硝基苯甲酸（2，4，6－Trinitrobenzoic acid）

喷雾剂Ⅰ：为0.1% 2，4，6－三硝基苯甲酸的水－二甲基甲酰胺水溶液。

喷雾剂Ⅱ：为5%碳酸钠水溶液。

喷雾剂Ⅲ：为5%磷酸二氢钠溶液。

方法：薄层板分别以喷雾剂Ⅰ、Ⅱ喷后，在90~100℃加热4~5分钟，放冷，最后喷以Ⅲ，强心苷呈橙~红色斑点。

7．硫酸－次氯酸盐（Sulphuric acid－hypochloride）

10ml 2mol/L硫酸和3 ml次氯酸钠溶液（10%有效氯）的混合液，喷后于125℃加热10~15分钟，A~E组的洋地黄苷类在长波紫外光下，可显示出各种不同的荧光。

8．磷酸－溴（Phosphoric acid－bromine）

喷雾剂Ⅰ：为10%磷酸水溶液。

喷雾剂Ⅱ：将2ml饱和的溴化钾水溶液和2ml饱和溴酸钾水溶液及2ml 25%盐酸混合即可。

方法：用喷雾剂Ⅰ喷后，于120℃加热12分钟，洋地黄苷B、D和E在长波紫外光下产生兰色荧光。薄层板于120℃再加热，然后以Ⅱ轻喷之，在紫外光下洋地黄苷A和C分别显示呈色和灰绿~灰兰色。

9．2，4，2′，4′－四硝基联苯（2，4，2′，4′－Tetranitrobiphenyl）

喷雾剂Ⅰ：为本品的饱和苯溶液。

喷雾剂Ⅱ：为10%氢氧化钾的甲醇－水（1:1）溶液。

方法：先以 Ⅰ 喷之，室温干燥后，再喷Ⅱ，强心苷类呈兰色。

十一、有机酸类

1．溴酚蓝试剂（Bromphenol blue）

（1）0.1g溴酚蓝溶解在5ml乙醇中，再与3ml 0.05mol/L氢氧化钠和20ml水混合。

（2）0.04%溴酚蓝乙醇溶液，用0.1mol/L氢氧化钠调至微碱性即可。

2．溴甲酚绿（蓝）指示剂〔Bromocresol green（blue）indicator〕

溴甲酚绿0.04g溶于乙醇100ml，加0.1mol/L氢氧化钠溶液至兰色刚出现，喷后在兰色背景上显黄色，如果展开剂中含乙酸，则在喷雾前将薄层在120℃烘烤除去。

3．溴甲酚紫（红）指示剂〔Bromocresol purple（red）〕

溴甲酚紫0.04 g溶于50%乙醇500ml中，用0.1mol/L氢氧化钠溶液调至pH 10.0，喷前薄层在100℃烤10分钟，冷至室温后喷显色剂，有机酸存在时，则在兰色背景上显黄色。

4．百里酚酞碱溶液（Thymolphthalein）

百里酚酞50mg溶于2%氢氧化钠溶液100ml，喷后在灰或兰色背景上显白色斑点。

5．过氧化氢（Hydrogen peroxide）

用0.3%过氧化氢水溶液喷后用长波紫外光照射至产生最强兰色荧光为止。用于检测芳香酸。

6．葡萄糖－苯胺试剂（Schweppe's）

10%葡萄糖水溶液与10%苯胺的乙醇液各20ml混合后用正丁醇稀释至100ml，喷后于125℃加热5～10分钟，有机酸的存在可于白色背景下显深棕色斑点。

7．碘化物－淀粉试剂（Iodide－starch）

8%碘化钾溶液，2%碘酸钾溶液及1%淀粉溶液等量混合，用前鲜配，喷后在白色或浅兰色背景上显深兰色灵敏度为2μg。

8．二氯靛酚试剂（Dichloroiudophenyl）

2，6－二氯靛酚0.1g溶于95%乙醇100ml。喷后加热片刻，在天蓝色背景上显粉红色，如加热时间延长，则酮酸转变为白色，而其他羧酸不变，故可识别酮酸。

9．联苯胺－亚硝酸钠试剂（Benzidine－sodium nitirte）

溶液Ⅰ：联苯胺2.5g溶于浓盐酸7ml及水500ml。

溶液Ⅱ：10%亚硝酸钠溶液。

方法：临用前将Ⅰ与Ⅱ以3:2混合，喷后于紫外灯下254nm观察荧光，用于检测有机酸类。

10．2，6－二氯苯酚－靛酚钠盐（2，6－Dichlorophenol－indophenol sodium）

为0.1% 2，6－二氯苯酚－靛酚钠盐的乙醇溶液。喷后稍加热后，在兰色背景上可呈现红色斑点，用于检测有机酸酮酸。

11．吖啶试剂（Acridine）

为0.05%吖啶的乙醇溶液，用于检测苹果酸等。

十二、其他类化合物

1．硫酸肼（Hydrazinium sulphate）

取硫酸肼饱和的水溶液90ml同10ml 4mol/L盐酸溶液混合，将湿层析谱分别在暴置于氨蒸气前后于长波紫外灯下检视之，用于检测胡椒醛、香草醛及乙基香草醛。

2．偏高碘酸钠－联苯胺（Metaperiodate sodium－benzidine）

喷雾剂Ⅰ：为0.1%偏高碘酸钠的水溶液。

喷雾剂Ⅱ：将1.8g联苯胺溶于50ml 0.2mol/L盐酸。

先喷Ⅰ，5分钟后再喷Ⅱ，含1，2－二醇基（糖、多元醇）的化合物在蓝色背景可出现白色斑点。

3．四乙基铅（Iead tetraacetate）

以1%四乙基铅的苯溶液喷雾，喷后于110℃加热5分钟，1，2－二醇基化合物在棕色背景下呈白色斑点。

4．乙二胺（Fthyl enediamine）

将乙二胺与等体积的水或稀氢氧化钠混合即得。喷后于50～60℃加热20分钟，与短波或长波紫外灯下检查，用于检测儿茶酚胺类化合物。

5．氯化铜试剂（Cupricy chloride）

以0.5%氯化铜的水溶液喷雾。β－肟络合物在喷后立即呈绿色，α－肟络合物则于喷雾后在110℃ 加热10分钟后才生成棕绿色的斑点。

6．甲醛－硫酸（Formaldehyde－sulphuric acid）

将0.2ml 37%甲醛溶液溶于10ml浓硫酸中，展开后之薄层板立即用喷雾剂喷之，用于检测多环芳香族化合物，不同的芳香族化合物可产生不同的颜色。也可用于生物碱的测定。

7．铁氰化钾（Patassium ferricyanide）

溶液Ⅰ：1%铁氰化钾水溶液。

溶液Ⅱ：15%氢氧化钠溶液。

喷雾剂：取1.5ml溶液Ⅰ，以20ml水稀释之，加10ml溶液Ⅱ即得。喷后于长波紫外灯下观察，用于检测维生素B（硫胺反应）。

8．硝普钠－氢氧化钠（Sodium nitroprusside－sodium hydroxide.Legal试验）

配制见十.3，对于甲基铜，活性亚甲基的化合物呈红紫色斑点。

9．羟胺－氯化铁（Hydroxylamine－ferricchloride）

溶液Ⅰ：将20g氯化羟基胺（盐酸羟胺）溶于50ml水中，加乙醇稀释至200ml，存放于冷处。

溶液Ⅱ：将50g氢氧化钾溶于最少量的水中，用乙醇稀释至500ml。

喷雾剂Ⅰ：将溶液Ⅰ与Ⅱ以1:2之比混合，并把氢氧化钾沉淀滤去，所的最终溶液应保存于冰箱中，此液约可稳定2周。

喷雾剂Ⅱ：将10g氯化铁（$FeCl\cdot 6H_2O$）细粉溶于20ml 36%盐酸中，此液用20ml乙醚共同振摇直至成均匀溶液为止，此溶液在密闭容器中可保存较长时间。

方法：层析谱先以喷雾剂Ⅰ喷之，在室温稍干燥后，再以Ⅱ喷之。

10．硝酸银－高锰酸钾（Silvernitrate－permanganate potassium）

溶液Ⅰ：临用前将0.1mol/L硝酸银，2mol/L氢氧化铵和2mol/L氢氧化钠以1:1:2之比混合即得。

溶液Ⅱ：将0.5g高锰酸钾和1g碳酸钠溶于100ml中即得。

喷雾剂：将等体积的Ⅰ、Ⅱ混合，因本试剂不稳定，应于临用前鲜配，喷后还原性物质在蓝～绿色背景上可出现淡黄色斑点。

11．硝酸银－氢氧化铵（Tollen's或zaffaroni's）

0.1mol/L硝酸银与5mol/L氢氧化铵于临用前按1:5混合即得。（注意久置会生成重氮化银爆炸物）。喷后于105℃加热5～10分钟，至暗黑色变至最深为止，用于检测还原性化合物。

12．磷钼酸试剂

喷后于120℃加热直至形成最佳色斑为止，用于检测还原性合物、类脂、甾醇及甾体化合物。

13．硫酸－硝酸铈铁（Sulphuric acid－ceric ammonium nitrate）

为含1%硝酸铈铵的50%硫酸溶液，喷后于105℃烘10分钟至显色，用于检测鬼臼毒素类化合物等。

14．4－羟基苯甲醛－硫酸（4－Hydroxyben zaldehyde－sulphuric acid，Komarowsku's）

溶液Ⅰ：50%硫酸。

溶液Ⅱ：2% 4－羟基苯甲醛的甲醇溶液。

喷雾剂：使用前将溶液Ⅰ 5ml与溶液Ⅱ 50ml充分混合，喷后于105℃加热3～4分钟或于60℃加热10分钟，皂苷元、皮质甾体（α位未取代的3－甾酮类化合物）应产生黄～粉红色斑点。

15．斯托克试剂（Stake's）

溶解30g硫酸亚铁（$FeSO_4$）和20g酒石酸于水中，稀释至1L，在临用前加浓氨水直至沉淀刚出现又重新溶解为止。

16．碘化钾－碘化汞（Brucske's）

溶解50g碘化钾于500ml水中，再以碘化汞使之饱和（约需120g）。用前稀释即可。

17．埃斯巴赫试剂（Esbach's）

为10%苦味酸和柠檬酸的水溶液。